You Might Be Able
to Get There
from Here

You Might Be Able to Get There from Here

Reconsidering Borges and the Postmodern

Mark Frisch

Madison • Teaneck
Fairleigh Dickinson University Press

Associated University Presses
2010 Eastpark Boulevard
Cranbury, NJ 08512

The paper used in this publication meets the requirements of the American National Standard for Permanence of Paper for Printed Library Materials Z39.48-1984.

Library of Congress Cataloging-in-Publication Data

Frisch, Mark F., 1950–
    You might be able to get there from here : reconsidering Borges and the postmodern / Mark Frisch.
        p. cm.
    Includes bibliographical references and index.
    ISBN 0-8386-4044-3 (alk. paper)
    1. Borges, Jorge Luis, 1899—Criticism and interpretation.   2. Postmodernism (Literature)   I. Title.

PQ7797.B635Z7163   2004
868'.6209—dc22   2004008044

PRINTED IN THE UNITED STATES OF AMERICA

To Beth

Contents

Acknowledgments

I WANT TO GIVE SPECIAL THANKS TO THE STUDENTS IN MY CLASSES ON THE postmodern and on Borges at Duquesne University and at La Universidad Nacional de Córdoba, who allowed me to test some of these ideas and whose valuable insights provided me much to consider. I am grateful to the Fulbright Foundation for the grant to Argentina, which helped advance this project. In granting me a leave of absence to take advantage of the Fulbright opportunity, a Presidential Scholarship Award, and a sabbatical leave to work on various parts of this manuscript, Duquesne University helped make the completion of this project possible. I want to thank the journal, *Confluencia*, for permission to use major portions of my article on Borges's impact on Robert Coover's novel, *The Universal Baseball Association, Inc., J. Henry Waugh, Prop.* I am grateful to la Fundación Internacional Jorge Luis Borges and to la Sra. Kodama for permission to cite Borges's texts in Spanish. My thanks also to Stanley Kurtz, Donald Petesch, Mimi Yang, and Margaret Mary Vojtko whose careful readings, comments, and suggestions helped immeasurably. I am deeply indebted to Beth, Ben, and David. Without their love, support, patience, and understanding, this study would not have been possible.

A Note on the Texts Cited

MOST OF MY CITATIONS TO BORGES'S WORKS COME FROM THE *OBRAS COM-pletas*, published by Emecé Editores. They have been published at various times. I have referred to the texts as follows:

"1974"————*Obras Completas de Jorge Luis Borges 1923–72*————This edition was first published as two volumes. I worked with the 1974 edition that was republished in 1987 as one volume. I am grateful to la Fundación Internacional Jorge Luis Borges and to la Sra. Kodama for permission to cite Borges's texts in Spanish. References here are to *Obras Completas de Jorge Luis Borges 1923–72*. Emecé Editores. Reprinted 1987.

"1989a"————*Obras Completas de Jorge Luis Borges 1975–85*———— This is the third volume of his complete works, published in 1989.

"1996"————*Obras Completas de Jorge Luis Borges IV 1975–1988*———— —This is the fourth volume, published in 1996.

I have cited various translations of Borges's individual works throughout my book. The most frequently cited translations are to "1962" and "1998". All references in the text to translations of Borges's works as "1962" are to: *(Various excerpts) By Jorge Luis Borges, Translated by James E. Irby, from* LABYRINTHS, *copyright © 1962, 1964 by New Directions Publishing Corporation. Used by permission of New Directions Publishing Corporation.*

All references to translations of Borges's works as "1998" are from: *Collected Fictions* by Jorge Luis Borges, translated by Andrew Hurley, copyright © 1998 by María Kodama; translation copyright © 1998 by Penguin Putnam Inc. Used by permission of Viking Penguin, a division of Penguin Group (USA) Inc. for the U.S.; by permission of Penguin General for the United Kingdom and the Commonwealth; for Canada, the reference is *Collected Fictions* by Jorge Luis Borges, translated by Andrew Hurley, copyright © 1999 by María Kodama; translation copyright © 1999 by Penguin Putnam Inc. Reprinted by permission of Penguin Group (Canada). Where I occasionally cited *Selected Poems,* I used that work for both the Spanish and English versions of the poem. Where no translation of a Spanish text is listed, the translation is my own.

You Might Be Able
to Get There
from Here

1

Introduction: "El Aleph" (The Aleph) and "La casa de Asterión" (The House of Asterion): Between Monism and Chaos

WRITERS, CRITICS, AND SCHOLARS HAVE REGULARLY MENTIONED JORGE Luis Borges as a precursor or as one of the first of the postmoderns. The association has become fairly automatic. Yet, at this point in the discussion of the postmodern, that relationship raises more questions than it resolves. What is the nature and what are the parameters of postmodern culture, and how does that relate to the vision and the ideas that Borges projects in his writing? Current postmodernist discussion often focuses on the dissolution of the concept of the self. What approach does Borges take toward the subject and subjectivity? Many have linked feminism and postmodernity. How does Borges portray women and love in his writing? What actual connection exists between Borges and feminism? With Jean François Lyotard's definition of postmodernity as a loss of faith in the "Great Narratives," the battle lines over the historical and political implications of the postmodern quickly formed. Those with monistic, utopian visions found their visions threatened by the postmodern turn. What do Borges's attitudes toward history have to do with postmodern studies? To what extent do Borges's writings and ideas have political implications? What are those implications for Latin America, whose writers Borges has influenced?

An attempt at answering these questions not only provides some different perspectives on both Borges and the postmodern debate, but also calls attention to an aspect of Borges's vision that poststructuralist and postmodern critics have largely overlooked or ignored. The critical readings of Borges have often focused on his challenge to the "One." His metaphor of the universe as an indecipherable, pluralistic labyrinth and his philosophical support for that vision found widespread acceptance among critics, writers, and scholars.

15

They have read his writings as a literary and cultural challenge to the monistic vision of modernism, and have regularly referred to his repeated rejection of singular, totalizing visions. Over and over again, his stories and other prose and poetic pieces question, parody, and ironically undermine a number of the totalizing qualities of the modernist vision. We may think we have finally found the exit from the labyrinth only to discover that we have entered yet another.

However, because of Borges's role as a precursor or an early postmodernist, these same critics have often overlooked the way in which he not only challenges the "One" but also affirms the "Many." He depends on the concept of a singular, totalizing vision, while acknowledging that we shall never attain such an understanding. His agnosticism does not become monistic in its negation. Neither is it an affirmation of chaos. Ultimately, the dichotomy between the "One" and the "Many" merge into irresolution in this labyrinth that expresses man's and woman's limitations. His vision continues to express and affirm certain values and urges us to define positive knowledge. Borges is a skeptical pluralist, but he avoids an absolute relativism. For Borges, the idea of the labyrinth does not automatically imply pessimism, chaos, and despair, but may suggest hope and affirmation. If the universe is a labyrinth, it has a center. For Borges, that suggests a coherent cosmos, although an inexplicable one. While such a pluralistic, labyrinthine universe may be indecipherable, certain journeys within the labyrinth or between labyrinths may still be possible. That is, we still might be able to get there from here, depending on where and how far we are attempting to go.

Reading Borges with an eye to the current debate over postmodernity and postmodern issues provides insights into aspects of his writings that have not been fully explored. It also helps introduce and clarify some of the defining themes and contentions of postmodernity. It provides the more thoroughly versed student of the postmodern with a perspective on that movement as seen from one of its early founders or precursors, and it highlights how that cultural discussion is caught in a similar debate between the "One" and the "Many," between a radical relativism and an expression of the limits of pluralism, between viewing the universe as ordered but inexplicable and viewing it as chaotic, between affirming the possibility of positive knowledge and accepting a rather nihilistic attitude. In so doing, it underscores essential similarities and definitive differences between some present-day proponents of the postmodern turn and one of its founders.

"EL ALEPH": BORGES'S METAPHOR FOR MODERNIST
AND POSTMODERNIST SENSIBILITIES

Two well-known Borges stories, "El Aleph" (The Aleph) and "La casa de Asterión" (The House of Asterion), raise a number of issues around which the postmodern discussion turns. Two critical symbols, the Aleph and the labyrinth, help define his pluralistic vision. His skeptical, agnostic intellectual position challenges totalities and argues for multiple perspectives but at the same time suggests that a delicate balance exists between monism and pluralism. "El Aleph" defines certain postmodern and modern sensibilities; at the same time, it raises a number of issues crucial to the postmodern debate, such as the nature of the self, of love, and of history. They illustrate how Borges defines a pluralistic vision that challenges and subverts some of the perceptions and values of aesthetic modernism, and yet how he avoids a radical relativism that argues for chaos rather than a cosmos.

In "El Aleph," the main character and narrator, called Borges, in mourning the loss of the woman he loved, Beatriz Viterbo, pays a yearly visit to her house on her birthday. He establishes a relationship with her cousin, Carlos Argentino Daneri, who informs him of the existence in the basement of an "Aleph," a mystical sphere that encloses the universe. In confronting the possible existence of such a totality—of a sphere that encompasses and orders the chaos of the universe, Borges plays off the monist and the pluralist, the modernist and the postmodernist visions, as well as "Borges" and Daneri. In the portrayal of the cousin and in depicting the main character's rejection of both Daneri's aesthetics and the singularity of his vision, the Argentine author questions and subverts the modernist vision and values and offers a pluralistic alternative. At the same time, Borges emphasizes the interdependence of monism and pluralism, and, thus ascribes certain limits to that pluralism. This story provides insights into Borges's attitude toward pluralism and underscores that one of the early postmodernists envisioned a pluralism, but a pluralism that emphasized man's/woman's limits in understanding the totality of the universe.

This story also has implications for other qualities and issues of the postmodern condition, such as love and the self. Borges's love for Beatriz represents a transcendent love that provides order and meaning to life and suggests such an order within the universe. The narrator ultimately abandons such a love. Furthermore, Borges, the author, suggests that the self is a fiction by inserting himself as a fictional character into the story.

Borges uses intertextual references to Dante's *Divine Comedy* in "El Aleph" to play off the One and the Many, monism and pluralism. Dante references run throughout the story (Thiem 1988, 97–121). The woman who has died and whom Borges, the narrator, longs for, is named Beatriz, like Dante's Beatrice. Beatriz's cousin, Daneri, suggests Dante Alighieri. In "Sobre el 'Vathek' de William Beckford," Borges refers to the *Divine Comedy* as "el libro más justificable y firme de todas las literaturas" [The most justifiable and solid book of all literature] (1974, 731). In an interview, he states:

> Had I to name a single work as being at the top of all literature, I think I should choose *Divina Commedia* by Dante. And yet I am not a Catholic. I cannot believe in theology. I cannot believe in the idea of punishment or of reward. Those things are alien to me. But the poem in itself is perfect. (Borges 1982a, 93)

Thus, the image of the Aleph in Borges' story suggests the unifying, totalizing vision of Dante.

Borges associates Daneri and this all-encompassing, monistic vision with the defining aesthetic vision and the prevalent values of his time, what we refer to today as aesthetic modernism and modernity. His faith in the future and in progress captures this modernistic quality.[1] Julio Ortega refers to him as the Dante of our times, voracious and grotesque (Ortega 1984, 12). Daneri writes an earthly comedy entitled *La Tierra*, (*The Earth*). He affirms reason and science. He is described as "autoritario" (authoritarian). He defends modern man, technical innovation, and modern culture. His Aleph symbolizes a totalizing, monistic vision of a seemingly chaotic universe. In 1941, after a few glasses of brandy, Daneri bursts into "una vindicación del hombre moderno" [an *apologia* for modern man]:

> Lo evoco—dijo con una animación algo inexplicable en su gabinete de estudio, como si dijéramos en la torre albarrana de una ciudad, provisto de teléfonos, de telégrafos, de fonógrafos, de operatos de radiotelefonía, de cinematógrafos, de linternas mágicas, de glosarios, de horarios, de prontuarios, de boletines . . .
>
> Observó que para un hombre así facultado el acto de viajar era inútil; nuestro siglo XX había transformado la fábula de Mahoma y de la montaña; las montañas, ahora, convergían sobre el moderno Mahoma. (1974, 618)

["I picture him," he said with an animation that was rather unaccountable, "in his study, as though in the watchtower of a city, surrounded by telephones, telegraphs, phonographs, the latest in radiotelephone and motion picture and magic lantern equipment, and glossaries, and calendars and timetables and bulletins . . ."

He observed that for a man so equipped, the act of traveling was supererogatory; this twentieth century of ours had upended the fable of Muhammad and the the mountain—mountains nowadays did in fact come to the modern Muhammad.] (1998, 275–76)

Daneri's comments show a fascination with and a certain faith in technology, the fruits of science. As these lines suggest, he implicitly expresses a belief in the notion of inevitable progress that characterized the modernist vision.

Daneri's poetry also expresses certain tendencies of aesthetic modernism. It is monistic in approach. The narrator, Borges, states that Daneri proposes to versify the entire planet. Borges finds that poetry very tedious and dull. When Daneri later asks Borges to contact an acquaintance about writing a prologue, Daneri defines what he sees as two undeniable merits of his own work, "la perfección formal y el rigor científico," (1974, 622), [Its formal perfection and its scientific rigor] (1998, 279), two qualities associated with the vision and values of aesthetic modernism. As becomes clear later in the story, Daneri's inspiration for his all-encompassing poetry is the vision of "the Aleph" that he has had. This mystical, monistic, totalizing object encompasses all of experience in a nutshell. Like many modernist writers, Daneri sees his art as discovering and extracting a perfect, unifying, totalizing vision and value from the multiplicity of experience. For him, language corresponds to things. Borges pokes fun at him for trying to duplicate the world through language (Ortega 1994, 184).

Somewhat ironically, another tendency of modernity undermines Daneri's project, the pattern of privileging scientific and technological knowledge and development at the expense of the aesthetic and the literary. The forward-looking project of Zunino and Zungri represents that pattern. Daneri suggests that Borges and he meet to have a drink at the salon-bar of Zunino and Zungri, his landlords, who have the foresight ("progresismo") to open this bar on the corner. When Borges arrives, he finds it "inexorablemente moderno, era apenas un poco menos atroz que mis previsiones" (1974, 621). [The relentlessly modern "salon-bar" was only slightly less horrendous than I had expected] (1998, 278). The fact that Zunino and Zungri are Daneri's landlords and that they share a faith in progress and technological and economic development bonds the three of them symbolically and links them to certain aspects of the modernist vision: the faith in progress, in the future, and in technological and economic development. It is ironic that this threatens Daneri's own modernist aesthetic project, his totalizing poem, *La Tierra*, as Zunino and Zungri want to destroy his house and the Aleph that inspired his poem. Borges has touched an important contradiction within modernity: the manner in which the social and cultural vision of modernity, with its faith in progress, in economic development, in technology, and in science, subverts and perhaps marginalizes the aesthetic and spiritual vision.

The timing of events in this story corresponds with some central historical events that mark a shift from modern to postmodern culture. Beatriz Viterbo died in 1929, the year of the stock market crash in the United States and the beginning of the Great Depression. Borges's encounter with the Aleph occurs in 1941, during World War II. From our present vantage point, we realize that the Great Depression, the atrocities of Hitler and Stalin, and World War II seriously undermined the faith in utopian visions upon which modernity was founded.[2] These utopian pillars include Capitalism, Marxism, Christianity, and faith in Science, Reason, and Progress. The events of these years created a disillusionment with these utopian visions and led to the demise of aesthetic modernism. This crisis of faith in our pillars of knowledge gave rise to the postmodern pluralism. Borges seems to sense that. In *The Divine Comedy,* Beatrice is the highest emblem of a way of knowledge. In Borges, we are made aware right at the beginning of the death of Beatriz. We are abandoned to a world marked by the emptying of that emblem. The world is artificial, without set guidelines (Ortega 1984, 11–12).

Borges offers a contrasting aesthetic and vision to that of Daneri. In part, he counterpoints the Dante and *Divine Comedy* references to certain images that suggest Edgar Allan Poe and to stories such as "The Fall of the House of Usher." Like Poe's story, "El Aleph" is set in an old house in which the family is crumbling, and in which a curious relationship exists between two siblings. In the Borges story they are not technically brother and sister, but rather "primos hermanos" (first cousins). (Borges may be playing on the use of the word "hermanos" [brothers and sisters] in the term "first cousins.") While Dante ascends to paradise to find Beatrice and his unifying vision, Borges descends to the cellar, as in the Poe short story, to find the Aleph and Beatriz. The Beatriz that Borges discovers is not the ideal, divine image that Dante projected, but rather a very material, human image of a woman with shortcomings who wrote obscene letters to her cousin. The mood and tone of this story with a dream/nightmare aura surrounding the old house and the Aleph also suggest Poe. The world of Poe is a world of mystery, of indeterminacy, of seeming chaos, of pluralism, of the falling away of established tradition, like the world of "El Aleph." As in "The Fall of the House of Usher," this house is also destroyed in the end, and with it, the Aleph.

The Argentine author also highlights the differences between Daneri and his narrator, Borges, in a telling way through their reactions to the experience of the Aleph. Daneri says to Borges as he is about to enter the basement: "Claro está que si no lo ves, tu incapacidad no invalida mi testimonio" (1974, 624). [Of course, . . . if you don't see it, that doesn't invalidate anything I've told you . . .] (1998, 282). His comments are those of the monist, certain of his vision and his truth, and rejecting a priori the skeptical denials of others. In contrast, the narrator, Borges, responds as a skeptical pluralist might. In describing the procedures he went through in order to see the Aleph, he leaves a doubt in the reader's mind about whether the vision was illusory or real. He must first imbibe "pseudo coñac," which he describes as "un narcótico." He must count off nineteen steps and lie down on the floor with a pillow. And he closes his eyes and opens them before seeing the Aleph. The "pseudo coñac" and the closing and opening of his eyes raise the question as to whether this vision was a dream, a drug-induced illusion, or whether he actually witnessed it. When Daneri asks Borges whether he saw it, he neither confirms nor denies it, but instead, refuses to discuss it. While he explains that this is out of spite or "venganza," it is not clear exactly what that spite is. In the end, memory loss sets in, and Borges begins to wonder what it was he saw. Most significantly, in the postscript, ever the pluralist and the skeptic, the narrator suggests that his vision was not the authentic Aleph, but "un falso Aleph" (1974, 627) [a *false* Aleph] (1998, 285). He goes on to describe sightings of other Alephs that may be more authentic. This contrasts sharply with Daneri's attitude (the Aleph exists and I saw it, even if you can't see it). In doing so, he contrasts monistic truth with pluralistic skepticism.

Also in the postscript, Borges further delineates the origin and nature of the Aleph. He states that the term "Aleph" comes from the Kabbalah, the compilation of Jewish mystical thinking and writing. Also, for the Kabbalists, this first letter of the Hebrew alphabet signifies the "En Soph," the unlimited and pure godhead. In the way the letter is written, the Aleph is also said to take the shape of a man pointing toward both heaven and earth, implying that the world below is a mirror image of the world above (Lévy 1976, 154).

Jaime Alazraki (1988a), Edna Aizenberg (1984), and Salomón Lévy (1976), have shown that the symbol of the Aleph and the Kabbalistic references are not limited to this story alone, but in many ways permeate Borges's writings as a whole. That is not to say that Borges is a religious Kabbalist, but rather that he finds symbols such as the Aleph useful aesthetically. This image of the Aleph suggests the incredible multiplicity of our world(s), while simultaneously highlighting a unity that is beyond human grasp and comprehension. The emphasis on the world below as a mirror image of the world above also corresponds with Borges's idealism that tends to distrust material and sensory perceptions.

Although Borges is not a mystic, there may be some biographical foundation to the experience of the Aleph. While Borges stated on more than one occasion that he is not a mystic, he admits, nevertheless, that twice, he had mystical experiences:

> In my life I only had two mystical experiences and I can't tell them because what happened is not to be put into words, since words, after all, stand for a shared experience. And if you have not had the experience you can't share it—as if you were to talk about the taste of coffee and had never tried coffee. Twice in my life I had a feeling, a feeling rather agreeable than otherwise. It was astonishing, astounding. I was overwhelmed, taken aback. I had the feeling of living not in time but outside time. I don't know how long that feeling lasted, since I was outside time. . . . I wrote poems about it, but they are normal poems and do not tell the experience. I cannot tell it to you, since I cannot retell it to myself, but I had that experience, and I had it twice over, and maybe it will be granted me to have it one more time before I die. (Borges 1982a, 11)

This comment suggests the balance that Borges strikes between the One and the Many, that they coexist in some form in his personal as well as his literary world, and that he did not intend solely to negate the one.

The issue of the self comes into play in this story as well. For Borges, the self is also a fictional construct that we create to make our world more tenable. Understanding the maze of the self does not differ from understanding the labyrinth of the universe. We may pretend to grasp aspects of it but will never understand it in its totality. Borges highlights this fictional nature by calling his main character by his own name, "Borges." He universalizes his concept of the self by suggesting that we contain the best and worst that woman and man are capable of. Similarly there is a sense in which Borges and Daneri are linked, as Daneri is said to work at a small library on the edge of Buenos Aires, just as Borges, the author, did (Thiem 1988, 118).

This sense of the self has implications for love and gender relations as well, and we see some of that represented here. At the beginning of the story, Borges manifests an idealized love for an unattainable object, the dead Beatriz. It is a transcendent love that provides order and meaning to life and suggests such an order in the universe. Yet, his encounter with the Aleph leads him to realize that Daneri and Beatriz have had a sexual relationship. That shatters any illusions about her, and has implications for the nature of love as a means of fulfilling the self and providing purpose and meaning to existence. In regard to gender issues, Borges, in effect, removes the woman from the pedestal.

Similarly, he emphasizes the shortcomings of language in representing the Aleph. While Daneri's totalizing, monstrous poem seeks to represent the whole world, Borges realizes his own limitations in representing such a vision:

> Arribo, ahora al inefable centro de mi relato; empieza, aquí, mi desesperación de escritor. Todo lenguaje es un alfabeto de símbolos cuyo ejercicio presupone un pasado que los interlocutores comparten; ¿cómo trasmitir a los otros el infinito Aleph, que mi temerosa memoria apenas abarca? (1974, 624)

> [I come now to the ineffable center of my tale; it is here that a writer's hopelessness begins. Every language is an alphabet of symbols the employment of which assumes a past shared by its interlocutors. How can one transmit to others the infinite Aleph, which my timorous memory can scarcely contain?] (1998, 282)

Again, the emphasis is on man's / woman's limits in grasping such a totality.

Like a couple with contrasting, contentious qualities who, nonetheless, find themselves fulfilled and complemented by the companion's opposites and achieve an amiable, if not always peaceful, equilibrium, so too monism and pluralism strike a balance and live together in Borges. The image of the Aleph captures that relationship. While not totally denying singular, totalistic visions, Borges is well aware of his own and all of our limitations in enclosing and encompassing them. Thus, the skeptical narrator's wonderment at his encounter with the Aleph, the mystical vision, is followed by an appropriate ambiguity and skepticism as to its particular authenticity. Borges, the narrator, implicitly suggests that such a monistic Aleph might actually exist. However, he argues that we are limited in grasping such a totality, and denies that the one he saw was the authentic one, implying that there are different Alephs, or different worlds in which all points in time and space merge. The subjective aspects of the Aleph that Borges sees, such as the letter that Beatriz wrote to Daneri, also imply that any totalizing vision will be always subjective.

The Argentine writer is well aware that we need the One in order to affirm the Many. He realizes the necessary balance, interdependence, and dialogue that exists between monism and pluralism. He realizes that authentic pluralism takes monism quite seriously. Pluralism calls on monism to present its strongest case in order to test its own theories about why such efforts to unify and reduce all reality will fail. He effectively captures that dynamic in "El Aleph."

THE LABYRINTH, "LA CASA DE ASTERIÓN," AND PLURALITY

While "El Aleph" helps distinguish Borges's writings, vision, and view of the world from those writers usually grouped as "modernists," his use of the labyrinth as a symbol defines an important line of debate among writers, critics, and scholars of the postmodern. Critics have rightly pointed to the labyrinth as a dominant symbol in Borges's fiction. Again and again Borges employs the image to suggest that there are limits to our knowledge and understanding, and that differences and alternative points of view may be limitless. Some have found such attitudes disheartening and despairing. Borges challenges that pessimistic association with the labyrinth. An examination of the short story, "La casa de Asterión" (The House of Asterion), from Borges's collection of stories *El Aleph* (1949), and a look at some of his comments on the subject illustrate why he sees the labyrinth as a symbol of hope rather than despair.

In the story "La casa de Asterión" (The House of Asterion),

Borges gives the Minotaur a voice. The story is based on the myth of the Minotaur and the labyrinth from Ovid's *Metamorphoses* and from Apollodorus's *Bibliotheca*. Embarrassed by the birth of the half-bull and half-man Minotaur to his adulterous wife, Minos commissions Daedalus to construct the labyrinth to house the Minotaur. Regularly, Athenian youths are sacrificed to him. In his imprisonment in a labyrinth, the Minotaur becomes the creator of a labyrinth and the hunter. Eventually, Theseus decides to rid the world of the monster. Using the thread that his lover, Ariadne, gives him, he enters the labyrinth, slays the Minotaur and succeeds in exiting.

As the beast at the center of the labyrinth, this creature represents the unitary center that those seek who attempt singularly to define and understand the universe or the self. Fundamentally, this half-man half-bull comprehends neither himself nor his circumstances. His labyrinthine house that imprisons him symbolizes the world and his ultimate failure and frustration in comprehending it. He rejects that he is the labyrinth's prisoner. "¿Repetiré que no hay una puerta cerrada, añadiré que no hay una cerradura?" (1974, 569) [Must I repeat that this house has no doors? Need I add that there are no locks and no keys?] (1981, 195) Its size, structure, and complexity mirror the labyrinthine universe:

Todas las partes de la casa están muchas veces, cualquier lugar es otro lugar. No hay un aljibe, un patio, un abrevadero, un pesebre; son catorce [son infinitos] los pesebres, abrevaderos, patios, aljibes. La casa es del tamaño del mundo, mejor dicho, es el mundo. (1974, 570)

[Each part of the house occurs many times; any particular place is another place. There is not one wellhead, one courtyard, one drinking trough, or one manger; there are fourteen [an infinite number of] mangers, drinking troughs, courtyards, wellheads. The house is as big as the world—or rather, it *is* the world.] (1998, 221)

As the Minotaur fails to grasp the nature of his labyrinth, so he misunderstands his actions and interactions. He always comes up short. He deceives, deludes, and misrepresents his world so that ultimately it costs him his life. He dismisses accusations of pride, misanthropy, and madness, and asserts that his house remains open to anyone who wishes to enter. However, his slaughter of those who do enter belies those claims. He asserts he is not imprisoned, nor the keeper of a prison, as people can come and go as they please. Yet, he seems to be both. He plays at being hunted, but is himself a hunter. He feigns sleeping and realizes from the changing light that at times he actually does sleep, suggesting a blur between waking and sleep, between "reality" and fiction. He runs happily after the nine men who enter every nine years "para que yo les libere de todo mal" (1974, 570). [So that I can free them from all evil] (1998, 221). He is not aware of his role in their deaths, his hand in evil. He asserts his uniqueness: "El hecho es que soy único" (1974, 569). [The fact is, I am unique] (1998, 220). Yet, in his solitude and isolation, he dreams that another Asterión will come to visit him. Because he has a queen for a mother, he feels superior to the masses. He considers himself to have godlike powers. "Quizá yo he creado las estrellas y el sol y la enorme casa, pero ya no me acuerdo" (1974, 670). [Perhaps I have created the stars and the sun and this huge house, and no longer remember it] (1998, 221). As a half-bull and half-man, however, he is a monster. He misinterprets Teseo's (Theseus's) purpose and role. He views him as a redeemer and offers almost no resistance as the last lines of the story suggests: "¿Lo creerás, Ariadna?" -dijo Teseo-. "El minotauro apenas se defendió" (1974, 570). [Can you believe it, Ariadne? said Theseus. The Minotaur scarcely defended itself.] (1998, 221). In short, the actions and thoughts of the Minotaur underscore that, often, we are deluded in the understanding of ourselves and of our relationship to the world. We are both the frightened and the frightening center of this labyrinth with the power of life and death. We are also Teseo doing battle with and attempting to subdue the Minotaur within us by entering the labyrinth. The story highlights a common Borges theme: the impossibility of understanding ourselves and thus the world.

While the notion of the universe as a labyrinth is a prominent and dominant image in Borges's thinking and writing, it does not necessarily suggest the desperation and chaos that many associate with it. In an interview with Roberto Alifano, Borges speaks of the labyrinth as a "magical" symbol. Alifano then asks whether he considers the image of losing ourselves in a labyrinth as a pessimistic view for the future of mankind. Borges's response provides telling insight into the dynamic at work within his writings and has implications for contemporary postmodern discourse:

B.: No, yo creo que no; creo que en la idea de laberinto hay también una idea de esperanza, o de la salvación, ya que supiéramos con certeza que el mundo es un laberinto, nos sentiríamos seguros. Pero no, posiblemente no sea un laberinto. En el laberinto hay un centro; ese centro terrible es el minotauro. Sin embargo, no sabemos si el Universo tiene un centro; tal vez no lo tenga. Por consiguiente, es probable que el mundo no sea un laberinto sino simplemente un caos y en ese caso sí estamos perdidos. (Borges 1984a, 204)

[B: No, I don't. I believe that in the idea of the labyrinth there is also hope, or salvation; if we were positively sure that the universe is a labyrinth, we would feel secure. But it may not be a labyrinth. In the labyrinth there is a center: that terrible center is the Minotaur. However, we don't know if the universe has a center; perhaps it doesn't. Consequently, it is probable that the universe is not a labyrinth but simply chaos, and if that is so, we are indeed lost.] (Borges 1984b, 24)

When Alifano asks if Borges thinks that the world may not be chaotic, but rather a cosmos and that there may be a secret center to the world, Borges replies that to think of a cosmos is to think of a labyrinth, either demonic or divine. He asserts that if the world has a center, then life is coherent, and we believe we somehow are saved. He suggests that there are facts that lead us to think that the Universe has a coherent form:

B.: Bueno, pensemos en la rotación de los astros, en las estaciones del año, en el atardecer, en la caída de las hojas en el otoño, en las edades del hombre . . . Todo eso nos hace pensar que hay un laberinto, que hay un orden, que hay un secreto centro del mundo, como usted propuso, que hay un gran arquitecto que lo concibió. Pero también nos hace pensar que no hay una razón, que no se puede aplicar una lógica, que el Universo no es explicable—en todo caso no es explicable para nosotros, los hombres—y ésa es ya una idea terrible. (Borges 1984a, 204–5)

[B. Think, for example, of the rotation of the planets, the seasons of the year, the different stages in our lives. All that leads us to believe there is a labyrinth, that there is an order, that there is a secret center of the universe, as you have suggested, that there is a great architect who conceived it. But it also leads us think that it may be irrational, that logic cannot be applied to it, that the universe is unexplainable to us, to mankind—and that in itself is a terrifying idea.] (Borges 1984b, 24)

Borges highlights here the meaning and the significance of the labyrinth, the powerful, dominant image that permeates his work. Ever the skeptic intellectually, he admits that the world may not be labyrinthine, but rather chaotic, and that we cannot know for certain.

However, the symbol of the labyrinth serves as the foreground or background for many of his best writings, as critics have frequently asserted. These comments and his repeated use of that symbol suggest his predilection toward a sense of order, but an inexplicable and possibly frightening one. That image suggests an ordered universe, but one whose understanding is beyond our reach.

This dynamic between the One and the Many permeates Borges's works. His view throughout is not simply to negate the One. He seems quite sensitive to the interdependence of the One and the Many. His best-known stories from *Ficciones* and *El Aleph,* as well as those in other collections, his poetry and his prose in books such as *Otras inquisiciones (Other Inquisitions)* suggest this symbiotic relationship. Most of his main characters do not deny the existence of the One, but rather question whether man/woman can ever grasp its totality with our limited human resources. His concepts of subjectivity and the self, of love, of history and universal history, express a similar interdependence between pluralistic and totalizing visions as well. They have implications for gender issues, historical, and political questions as well, as chapters 5, 6, and 7 illustrate. Borges captures this dynamic relationship between the One and the Many when he states in "El idioma analítico de John Wilkins" (The Analytic Language of John Wilkins):

> Notoriamente no hay clasificación del universo que no sea arbitraria y conjetural. La razón es muy simple: no sabemos qué cosa es el universo . . .
>
> La imposibilidad de penetrar el esquema divino del universo no puede, sin embargo, disuadirnos de planear esquemas humanos, aunque nos conste que éstos son provisorios. (1974, 708)

> [Obviously there is no classification of the universe that is not arbitrary and conjectural. The reason is very simple: we do not know what the universe is. . . .
>
> But the impossibility of penetrating the divine scheme of the universe cannot dissuade us from outlining human schemes, even though we are aware that they are provisional.] (1981, 142–43)

Postmodern critic, Matei Calinescu, has a related notion in mind when he states in discussing the relationship between the One and the Many:

> Incidentally, the near certainty that the effort to unify multiplicity will fail and will eventually be confronted by irreducible "facts" or "fictions"

or "worlds" does not mean that such effort should not be undertaken. On the contrary, monistic or reductionist assumptions should be constantly tested and retested against an irreducibility that in the process of being assailed from all sides, is as open to change, revision, and enrichment as are the hypotheses that challenge it. (Calinescu 1991, 163)

2
A Latin American Postmodernism?
A Borges Perspective

THERE HAVE BEEN MANY BOOKS AND ARTICLES WRITTEN IN THE LAST several years relating to postmodernity in Latin America, and to a lesser extent, to Borges and the postmodern. As Carlos Alonso states in regard to postmodern discourse: "the force and unanimity with which the topic has monopolized recent cultural deliberations in Latin America is truly a remarkable circumstance" (Alonso 1994, 253). Alonso explains that in the United States and Europe, the debate has been over the specifics of the postmodern, while Latin American critics and scholars assume a fairly homogeneous definition and have been debating the desirability of embracing the postmodern. He underscores the urgency that surrounds this debate based on the assumption that the outcome will have "profound consequences for Latin America's future" (1994, 253). One of the issues and dilemmas is that the literary expressions seem to have first sprouted and blossomed in third world countries, and in Latin America in particular, while some of the theoreticians have argued that it is the late capitalism of the industrialized countries that has generated the cultural transformations, a stage of capitalism that many of those countries have not experienced.

One of the central issues of the debate in Latin America is whether critics and writers should embrace the postmodern. Carlos Alonso points out that twentieth-century Latin American writers who embraced modernity were forced to take leave of the demands of modernism. While the material trappings did not accompany the discourse in Latin America, the writers' hope was that their societies would become fully modern. Writers found themselves in a contradictory dilemma. Their texts both argued for modernity and signaled their distance from modernity (Alonso 1994, 258–59).

This situation explains, in part, why Latin American writers such as Borges, García Márquez, Cortázar, Fuentes, and others have been on the cutting edge in defining a "post" modern expression and vision. Looking in from a marginalized, outsider position, they sought a literary and philosophical space that would include them and their cultures and countries. They defined and refined an expression that allowed them that inclusion. Critics who embrace, to different degrees, the postmodern in Latin America tend to divide into two groups. While both perspectives agree that modernism failed to fulfill its hopes and promises, they differ in their vision of the postmodern. One places Latin American writers on the cutting edge in defining the movement and views Borges as a principal player either in marking the end of modernism or the beginning of the postmodern. The second views postmodernism and other cultural, political, or social movements as responses to economic conditions. They view Latin American countries and writers as latecomers, because their economic and social situations have lagged behind the more economically "developed" countries. In this view, Borges's writings are largely irrelevant to a discussion, or if relevant, they are so because Borges was writing for a European rather than a Latin American audience. For these critics, the Cuban revolution and the fervor that surrounded it in the early stages assume greater importance in engendering the "Boom" literature. Borges's political beliefs and worldview often run counter to the Marxist vision that engendered the Cuban revolution in its early stages. These critics often look askance at postmodern critiques of culture that are applied to Latin America. They argue that they are more relevant to the United States, Europe, and industrialized countries, and suggest that superimposing them on Latin America constitutes cultural imperialism. They look for qualities that distinguish Latin America from other parts of the West, and assume that postmodernism arrived later there than in other countries.

LATIN AMERICA AND THE POSTMODERN— BORGES AS PERIPHERAL

An overview of some of the principal works concerning Latin America, postmodernity, and Borges helps outline the parameters of this discourse. In regard to the latter group, Santiago Colás has written a thoughtful work entitled *Postmodernity in Latin America: The Argentine Paradigm* (1994). Colás juxtaposes Linda Hutcheon's approach and definition to Fredric Jameson's and strongly favors the Jameson perspective. He rejects Hutcheon's discussion of Latin American literature as representative of a Euro-North American, Old World postmodernism that critics have tried to impose on Latin America. He criticizes her for excluding a social and political reading of texts from her discussion. Picking up on Jameson's charge to historicize postmodernism and attempt to preserve the concept of utopia, Colás analyzes four Argentine works in particular, Julio Cortázar's *Rayuela*, Manuel Puig's *El beso de la mujer araña*, Ricardo Piglia's *Respiración artificial*, and Tomás Eloy Martínez's *La novela de Perón* with special emphasis on the social and historical situation and the treatment of utopia. He views the former two works as expressions of modernity or modernity in crisis, and the latter two as expressions of the postmodern. Thus, the postmodern is a post-"Boom" literary expression that is oppositional in nature to the "Boom" but more respective of the uncertainty of the result and the ambiguity of the historical process. He argues that other Latin American countries follow a similar pattern. Colás's study is quite interesting but contains some significant omissions. Colás is locked into a kind of determinism in his reading. He uses a monistic, Marxist model to interpret and analyze cultural movements that suggest that those very models are in crisis and have fallen out of favor. He appears to deny that postmodernism had it roots in Latin America. He implies that Latin America came lately, and that the postmodern is a movement that will be short-lived. Very early in the work, and very briefly, he dismisses Borges as part of the Euro-North American postmodernism. He criticizes him for working in the vacuum of the "universal library," for not confronting social and political issues. Colás ignores Borges's essential role as one of the first of the postmodernists, or at least as a precursor who laid important philosophical foundations. He fails to realize that what we now call "postmodernism" is part and parcel of Borges's vision and has received one of its fullest expressions in Latin America.

In *The Postmodernism Debate in Latin America*, John Beverly and José Oviedo (1993) have brought together a group of essays that engage many of the important issues of the postmodern, especially as they relate to social and political change. These writers, a number of whom have social science backgrounds and left-leaning political affinities, highlight the promise and the problems of the postmodern turn. Most agree that Latin America is a diverse region, and that modernity, at best, has had uneven success in achieving its ideals in the

Americas. A number of critics have resisted postmodern orientations because they fear that it represents a European-North American agenda trying to impose itself once again on Central and South America. However, some have challenged that perspective.

In his essay, "Eurocentrism and Modernity (Introduction to the Frankfurt Lectures)," Enrique Dussel outlines convincingly how modernity began in 1492 when Europe "affirms itself as the 'center' of a World History that it inaugurates" (Dussel 1993, 65). He argues that the reconquest and colonization of Andalusia and the Iberian Peninsula was a model for the conquest of the Americas, and illustrates how Hegel and others assumed a condescending and racist attitude toward Latin America and Africa. At the same time, while in Germany and in talking to a German audience, Dussel discusses poignantly how in 1870:

> A poor carpenter, a socialist and a Lutheran from the town of Schweinfurt am Main only a few kilometers from here, arrived in Buenos Aires looking for work, freedom from persecution, and peace. His name was Johannes Kaspar Dussel. He was welcomed in Argentina, given opportunities to make good, and he raised a family and died in those lands. He was my great grandfather. Today, when so many foreigners come to Germany looking for the same things, by contrast they are repudiated, expelled, treated . . . like Turks! Germany has forgotten the hospitality that was extended to its poor by other countries in the nineteenth century. (Dussel 1993, 66–67)

Consciously or unconsciously, Dussel has touched on a central difference between the modern and the postmodern, and between the Old World and the New World: a pluralistic acceptance of difference.

Amaryll Chanady echoes a similar sentiment when she writes:

> Difference, in other words, is constitutive of Latin America, right from its post-Colombian beginnings, and even though no society is a homogeneous whole, in spite of strategies of nation building and homogenization, difference in the "New World" has been extensively symbolized, constantly thematized and frequently held up as one of the foundations of an "authentic" Latin American identity. (Chanady 1994, xxi)

From the Statue of Liberty in New York to el obelisco in Buenos Aires, the countries of the New World were founded on this principle. From the moment of its discovery, the Europeans have projected onto the New World their hopes, dreams, wishes, prejudices, and fears. This definition of the land as a tolerant, open, accepting place, where one can start anew and forget the mistakes of the past, is one of the more positive inheritances that came from both within and without and that often contrasted with the attitudes of the hegemonic European countries from which the settlers came. As has often been cited, the attitudes of the Native Americans who welcomed Columbus and his men as gods contrasted sharply with the responses of some Europeans toward the indigenous cultures in places when they arrived. The degree of acceptance has certainly not been perfect either north or south of the Río Grande, as the present day inequalities along racial and ethnic lines attest. Latin American countries have probably been more successful than the United States in accepting African Americans and Native Americans, as the large mestizo populations in some countries suggest. In part, this is why postmodernism could and did first flourish in Latin America.

George Yúdice, in his article "Postmodernity and Transnational Capitalism in Latin America," describes some of the problems and the opportunities that postmodernity offers the leftist critics. He takes issue with Octavio Paz, but also with Fredric Jameson, at times. He finds that Paz's poetics leave little room for "accommodating the democratic social demands of diverse social movements" and asserts, "rethinking democracy outside of the terms set by the grand récit of modernity is an enterprise many Latin American social movements see as necessary" (Yúdice 1992, 7). He affirms the heterogeneity of postmodern expressions in Latin America without denying the role of the Americas in defining the postmodern. He also challenges Jameson's suggestion that Latin American cultural practices are "national allegories." Rather, he argues that "the rearticulation of Latin America's cultural heterogeneity . . . provides one of the most significant ways for furthering democratization" (Yúdice 1992, 23).

The Real Thing: Testimonial Discourse and Latin America, Georg Gugelberger, editor, lays out the debate surrounding testimonial literature (Gugelberger 1996). The work includes a collection of essays by John Beverly, George Yúdice, Santiago Colás, Fredric Jameson, and others. Testimonials blur the line between journalism and literature, between fiction, politics, and anthropology, and between subject and object and self and other. It has taken people who were marginalized and provided them with a voice. While some have questioned whether the genre is appropriate for literary discourse, I believe that it is. Postmodern culture has problematized the divisions between these discourses. Borges suggests that all philosophical systems and all discourses are subjective and fictional. It seems to me that he would have no difficulty making a similar comment on "el testimonio." We may discuss it in different ways than we do other genres, but we certainly can bring the same literary techniques to bear on that work.

Critical Theory, Cultural Politics, and Latin American Narrative, edited by Steven M. Bell, Albert H. LeMay, and Leonard Orr (1993), is a collection of pertinent essays presented at the First Biennial Conference of the Latin American Consortium by writers and critics such as Luisa Valenzuela, Roberto González Echevarría, Fredric Jameson, John Beverly, and Ricardo Gutiérrez Mouat. Many of them touch on issues relating to Latin American postmodernity.

In "Utopía y posmodernidad en América Latina: ser o no ser . . . ," María Eugenia Piola provides a cogent and interesting discussion of the relation of utopia to modernism and postmodernism (Piola 1999). She explains the role and importance of utopian visions, and she wonders whether the present crisis of culture reflects a crisis of modernism, an end of modernism and of utopian visions, or a hybrid synthesis of modernism with something new. She underscores the force and power of utopian visions and suggests that their demise would be a severe loss. While she does not say which way she thinks the culture is tilting, she affirms the importance of utopian visions. Borges's vision may qualify as that hybrid.

A LATIN AMERICAN POSTMODERNISM—
BORGES AS MORE CENTRAL

Postmodernism as I am defining it involves a shift within the culture toward philosophical pluralism. In discussing modernism, one talks of ideas, of literary, artistic, musical expressions, and of philosophical visions that cut across various countries and cultures in distinct ways and at different times, and that lasted at least one hundred years. Some take the discussion back to the Enlightenment, and others even as far back as the Renaissance so as to see the origin and development of modernity. Similarly, I foresee this philosophical shift continuing into the extended future. Granted, this may be prescriptive, as well as descriptive. Nevertheless, I find it hard to imagine a shift back to monistic models of truth coupled with utopian visions. Pluralism and diversity will almost certainly influence thought in most intellectual and cultural spheres for the foreseeable future.

One may accuse the pluralistic vision that I am defining of being utopian in nature (a Tlön Uqbar?). There are utopian qualities to it. I hope that postmodernity will be more just and humane than modernity proved to be. However, it is definitely not a given of universal history. I recognize that there are huge pitfalls that may not make such an outcome possible. Borges would not totally reject utopian visions. Instead, he would say that they are fictions that we create to make our world more livable. The important thing, he would assert, is to realize that they are fictions, and that they will be replaced by other fictions.

Borges played a pivotal role in redefining this cultural shift and in providing the metaphors and the language to describe it. It has and will find expression in different countries at different times and in distinct ways. Some may rebel against this shift and seek to subvert it. Utopian visions such as those offered by contemporary Marxist social and political history in Latin America may be a legitimate expression of the postmodern, and Colás represents it effectively. In some ways, Catholic utopian visions may have a longer reach among the general population in Latin America than the Marxist ones, although both certainly are prominent. While postmodernity can embody both of these, it is not limited to either.

Julio Ortega offers one of the most thorough and convincing presentations of the centrality of Borges to postmodern thought and to the development of postmodern literature. While a number of his articles and books contain references to Borges and his role, his *Arte de innovar* (*Art of Innovating*) is an impressive, inclusive survey of the modern and postmodern literature of the West and of Latin America, and Borges's place within it (Ortega 1994). He demonstrates that innovation has been central to Hispanic and Latin American literature since Cervantes, while underscoring the indispensable role of Borges in the modern scene. He calls Borges's short story, "El Aleph," perhaps the most influential of the Latin American narratives in the world. ["Tal vez sea el cuento más influyente de la literatura latinoamericana en el mundo"] (Ortega 1994, 182). He asserts that if Carlos Argentino is a caricature of the modernist writer, "el otro, 'Borges', es el primer escritor postmoderno." [The other, "Borges", is the first postmodern writer] (Ortega 1994, 184).

According to Ortega, Borges suggests a break with the modern tradition, and a turning back to the tradition that preceded modernism, but now is lost. He calls for a return to the poetic promise that inhabits language (1994, 185).

Ortega finds that Borges exhibits the qualities that define the postmodern for Fredric Jameson, the transformation of reality in images and the fragmentation in a series of presents. Were Borges a modernist writer, he says, he would have tried to write another Quijote, another Comedia instead of "Pierre Menard" or "El Aleph" (Ortega 1994, 426). Just as Borges was among the first postmodernists, so too those who followed his lead defined a Latin American postmodernism that was on the cutting edge of Western postmodernism. He makes clear that innovation and the penchant for the new have been part and parcel of Hispanic and Latin American literature since Cervantes, or before, and argues that Latin American literature has been an innovative participant in both modernist and postmodernist literature. In referring to James Joyce's statement that World War II was fought to stop the reading of *Finnegan's Wake*, Ortega subtly and humorously suggests an importance and a role for art and culture that are independent of the economic, political, or social conditions. Rather than just being determined by those conditions, art can also be determining. In regard to Borges's Latin American qualities, he states, "Although the majority of the critics have preferred to call Borges's writings European, their Latin American character has been accentuated with the passing of years as an unmistakably heterodox, relativistic, and parodic intonation" (Ortega 1994, 440).

It is impossible to discuss the issues of postmodernity in Latin America without crediting the work of Octavio Paz. Paz's critique of Latin American and Western Poetry in *Los hijos del limo* (Paz 1981), (*Children of the Mire*) (Paz 1974), which he summarized and reiterated later in the article "El Romanticismo y la poesía contemporánea" (Romanticism and Contemporary Poetry) (1987), laid the foundation for much of the later criticism and theory of the postmodern.[1] His discussion of time in particular was widely accepted. Ihab Hassan, Matei Calinescu, and others who laid much of the early groundwork of postmodern thought drew upon his writings in their discussions.

Alfonso de Toro has written several articles on the postmodern and Latin America and has emphasized the centrality of Borges to this discussion. In "Postmodernidad y Latinoamérica (con un modelo para la narrativa postmoderna)" (Postmodernity and Latin America [With a Model for the Postmodern Narrative]), he asserts that postmodernity began with Borges's publication of *Ficciones* (Toro 1991). He does not see a problem with also asserting at the same time that postmodernity first begins in the United States in the '60s. He makes a useful list of the characteristics of Borgesian postmodern discourse with the implication that they define many of the parameters of postmodern literary discourse.

Toro's article, "The Epistemological Foundations of the Contemporary Condition: Latin America In Dialogue With Postmodernity and Postcoloniality," draws on Foucault, Deleuze, Guattari, and Baudillard in defining postmodernity (Toro 1997). He asserts that the cultural production does not correspond to the economic, social, or political. Latin America has produced great poetry and literature in the last one hundred years, but it has lagged in politics, economics, science, and technology. He suggests a link between the postcolonial and the postmodern, and again argues for Borges as an important early participant.

Daniel Chamberlain highlights the differences among the various perspectives on Latin American postmodernism in his article "Latin American Narrative: Perspectives and the Postmodern Context" (Chamberlain 1997). He summarizes Colás's attack on Linda Hutcheon and other North American and European theorists and underscores his reference to "the stagnant standoff between assimilationist espousal and nativist rejection of European and North American theories" (Colás 1994, 12). In this thoughtful article he attempts to mediate the divide between Colás, Fokkema, Hutcheon and others through an emphasis on the centrality of perception.

Nancy M. Kason presents a cogent argument for Borges's role in the development of postmodernity in *Borges y la posmodernidad: un juego con espejos desplazantes* (*Borges and Postmodernity: A Play of Shifting Mirrors*) (Kason 1994). She discusses how Borges's work was essential for the development of the fantastic. She defines the postmodern period as limited in time, and as a period that has already passed and inclined toward a radical pluralism.

The work, *Borges and His Successors: The Borgesian Impact on Literature and the Arts,* edited by Edna Aizenberg, discusses the diverse impact of Borges on Latin American writers such as Salvador Elizondo and Severo Sarduy, on contemporary criticism and poststructuralist thought, including Foucault, De Man, and others, and contains translations of lectures by Borges on *The Book of Job* and on Baruch Spinoza (Aizenberg 1990). It is a useful early overview on the reach of Borges, but does not attempt in any systematic way to deal with or outline the relationship between postmodernism and Borges.

Other writers have also confronted the issue of Borges's relation to postmodernity. A number of writers find that Borges leads the way toward postmodern literature and discourse but never quite sheds himself of the trapping of modernism; thus, he never arrives in that Promised Land. Raymond Leslie Williams, in *The Postmodern Novel in Latin America: Politics, Culture, and the Crisis of Truth*, presents a survey of postmodern fiction (Williams 1995). His discussion is detailed, useful, and interesting, although I find his definition of the postmodern restrictive. Repeatedly, Borges is mentioned as one of the, or the major influence. Yet, Williams asserts that his writings are modernist, as are most of the novels of the "Boom" period. He draws on the discussions of truth of Gadamer and Ricoeur, acknowledges the influence of poststructuralist thinkers such as Derrida and Foucault, and defines his concept of the postmodern around them. For him, postmodernism is not just about pluralism, but it is about a radical pluralism that very explicitly undermines all truth and meaning.

Carlos Rincón seems to understand the link between heterogeneity and democratization, as his article, "The Peripheral Center of Postmodernism: On Borges, García Márquez and Alterity," suggests (Rincón 1993). Rincón argues that Borges's "Pierre Menard" and García Márquez's works define a different vision of the world from their modernist, European, and North American predecessors and contemporaries. They show a way of experiencing the alien and its difference that others never realized.

Rincón has another article of some interest, "Posmodernismo, poscolonialismo, y los nexos cartográficos del realismo mágico" (Postmodernism, Postcolonialism, and the Cartographic Nexus of Magical Realism) (Rincón 1995). He summarizes the development of postmodern thought in the Americas and highlights some central expressions in both North and South America.

Ariel Dorfman's essay, "Borges and American Violence" in *Some Write to the Future: Essays on Contemporary Latin American Fiction* does not deal specifically with Borges and the postmodern, but has important implications (Dorfman 1981). Dorfman suggests that while Borges denies "reality," he portrays a concrete world of violence with a Latin American context that speaks to the problems of Latin

American societies, thus underscoring Borges's Latin American roots.

K. B. Conal Byrne in "Inventing the New World: Finding the Mythology of Jorge Luis Borges" emphasizes how Borges highlights the textuality of existence (Byrne 1999). In reading Borges, the reality demons of death and political and social horror creep in and confront you. He argues that Borges is in the penumbra between modernism and postmodernism. Byrne asserts that while his style is postmodern in decentering truth, his belief in an absolute truth is modernist. I would take issue with Conal Byrne here. Borges does not definitely believe in an absolute truth, although he does not rule out the possibility that it exists. Conal Byrne effectively draws together disparate points of view into a unity in his discussion and seems to note the distinctions Borges draws. However, his definition of postmodernism fails to make some important distinctions and would exclude many, including some of the very important critics who first helped define postmodern culture, as he would include only what I have called the radical postmodernists.

In "Modernism/Postmodernism in 'The Library of Babel': Jorge Luis Borges' Fiction as Borderland," Graciela Keiser uses the story "The Library of Babel" to decide whether Borges is a "modernist" or a "postmodernist" writer (Keiser 1995). She places him in a "borderland" area, asserting that he does not move into the realm of the postmodern, which is embodied by Barthes and Derrida. Her reading is close and thoughtful, but the difficulty with her analysis lies in her definition of the postmodern. Using the poststructuralist thinkers as models, she defines postmodernism as an absolute relativism. She senses that Borges has resisted that philosophical stance and defines that hesitancy as modernist.

In "Tlön, Pilgrimages, and Postmodern Banality," Ian Almond sees Borges as postmodern (Almond 1998). He states that Borges's story "Tlön Uqbar, Orbis Tertius" emphasizes that the world is construction and play and lacks truth and direction. Interestingly, he cites Derrida's rejection of truth and affirmation of play as a standard of sorts for the postmodern and underscores that it is very much in line with Borges. He either overlooks the differences between their visions or considers them unimportant. He sums up postmodernism with reference to Derrida. He says that postmodernism is a way of perceiving other "isms." It does not expect the neo-

Nazi, Islamic fundamentalist, or the Southern Baptist to change what they believe, but rather how they talk about them:

> (I)t simply wants them to "lighten-up" a little, to stop talking (as Tlön's innumerable doctrines did long ago) about words like Truth and Reality with such competitive seriousness, as if they were the only things that mattered. Like Tlön, Postmodernism wants the world's totalizers to acknowledge, once and for all, that one cannot arrive at any kind of "truthful knowledge about the world". Bereft of this ancient raison d'être, most totalities find themselves scratching their heads in a postmodern age, wondering why they should bother to exist at all. Tlön already had the answer long ago; truth-claims aren't supposed to convince, they were made to delight. Why bother chasing after boring old Truths and Realities? Astonishment and uncertainty, as both Tlön and Derrida might have said, are much more fun. (Almond 1998, 231)

Kate Fullbrook, in "The Godfather: Borges and the Ethics of the Labyrinth," calls Borges a precursor of the postmodern and highlights his emphasis on value (Fullbrook 1997). She states that his sense of value derives from Spinoza. As the title suggests, she considers him "the godfather" of postmodernism. The ethics of the labyrinth are what she calls "the ethics of intellection, and of its writerly signs," and "the ethics of the book" (Fullbrook 1997, 185). However, she doesn't explain more specifically what those ethics are.

Several critics have connected contemporary mathematics and science and postmodern theory. Thomas P. Weissert, in "Representation and Bifurcation: Borges's Garden of Chaos Dynamics," is an example of that (Weissert 1991). He explains how bifurcation theory and chaos theory and local theory have received a lot of attention in recent years in mathematics and scientific circles. He explains how Borges was there first. Working with "El jardín de senderos que se bifurcan," (The Garden of the Forking Paths), Weissert introduces the concept of bifurcation and levels of time and space that later become an important component of contemporary mathematical and scientific theory. Weissert argues that Borges's labyrinth shows a predilection for the determinism of modernism and concludes that Borges has not become a postmodernist. The problem with that logic is that it assumes that scientific thought alone defines the boundaries of postmodern thought and that postmodernism and chaos are synonymous. It fails to realize that an affirmation of chaos is an affirmation of a totality, a totality of negation. Rather than affirm a totality, Borges opts for skepticism. The labyrinth argues not for modernism, but for pluralism and our limitations in knowing.

LATIN AMERICAN POSTMODERNITY AND BORGES

In his book, *The Spanish American Regional Novel: Modernity and Autochthony,* Carlos Alonso defines perceptively the contradictions that have marked Latin America's relationship with modernity (Alonso 1990). His discussion provides a foundation for understanding Borges's relation to the modern and postmodern. He agrees with Octavio Paz that the emancipation movement in Latin America was inspired by those "two great political archetypes of the modern era," the French Revolution and the American Revolution. He distances himself from Paz when he contends that, while the rhetoric and discourse of Latin America affirmed these visions of modernism, Latin America did not experience modernity as a historical reality. This led its writers toward self-definition, to an explanation of how their cultures differ from the hegemonic European model. The authors' simultaneous tendency to both affirm and distance themselves from modernity in their writings runs through most of the cultural discourse.

While Borges is no exception, he confronts the modernist vision, subverts, and totally redefines the relationship between the Americas and Western culture. In doing so, he asserts the equality of the cultures, creates a space for himself and other Latin American writers, and lays the foundation for the postmodern.

A number of Borges's stories and essays deal with the conflict of cultures, with the relationship between colonist and colonizer, between hegemonic and developing countries, and, almost without exception, they all seek to affirm the values, vision, and culture of the Latin American, the colonist, and/or developing countries. They illustrate that Borges played a pivotal role in the development of the postmodern vision and values, and that he did so very much as a Latin American. For Borges, culture is not static, but rather a fluid, hybrid, ongoing process formed by both the dominant culture and the culture of the colony or developing country. "El escritor argentino y la tradición (1951)," (The Argentine Writer and Tradition), "El hombre en el umbral (1949)," (The Man on the Threshold), "La busca de Averroes (1949)," (Averroes's Search), "El informe de Brodie (1970)," (Brodie's Report), "La escritura del Dios (1949),"

(The God's Script), among others, all depict cultural interchange and conflicts of cultures, suggest that culture is historically and experientially created, and illustrate Borges's attempts to give a voice to the marginalized.

"El escritor argentino y la tradición" (The Argentine Writer and Tradition) most clearly and distinctly portrays how Borges views his role in regard to dominant Western culture, and illustrates his purposes in dealing with the Western cultural heritage. That essay, along with a number of his stories, highlights that he not only sought to create a space where Argentine and Latin American cultures could define their distinct qualities, but that he also viewed Latin American writers as playing a significant role in the redefinition of Western culture. Taking issue with those who claim that Argentine writers should focus on their indigenous material and their gaucho tradition, he argues that that self-reflexive attitude is limiting and artificial.[2] He refers to Gibbon's remark that there are no camels mentioned in the Koran because Mohammed, being an Arab, assumed that such an everyday item needed no special mention. Furthermore, he points out that no one challenges Shakespeare's right to draw on material from Scandinavia for *Hamlet* or from Scotland for *Macbeth* or from Italy. Nor would Racine understand someone saying he has no right to draw on Greek and Roman themes. He argues that the passions that Argentines felt about Europe during the war years underscore that Argentina is tied to Europe and is part of Western culture. He affirms: "Creo que nuestra tradición es toda la cultura occidental, y creo también que tenemos derecho a esta tradición, mayor que el que pueden tener los habitantes de una u otra nación occidental" (1974, 272). [I believe our tradition is all of Western culture, and I also believe we have a right to this tradition greater than that which the inhabitants of one or another Western nation might have] (1962, 184). Quoting from sociologist Thorstein Veblen, he compares the Argentine writer's relationship to Western culture to that of the Jews (and the Irish), and affirms the role of smaller cultures to engage with the hegemonic culture and try to innovate and change it. For Veblin, (and Borges), the Jews and the Irish have excelled and left their mark in Western culture because they have innovated from within, while not feeling totally tied to the culture. Borges argues that Argentine writers, similarly, are in a better position to innovate and change the vision and values of Western culture.

His stories illustrate how he creates a cultural space for Latin

America and other "Calibans" of the world and how he redefines the relationship between the dominant cultures and the marginalized one. In "La busca de Averroes" (Averroes's Search), Borges draws attention to the difficulty in understanding other cultures. Averroes, one of the foremost Islamic scholars of his time, sets out to understand Aristotle's concepts of tragedy and comedy. After much deliberation and discussion, he decides that Aristotle gave the name "tragedy" to panegyrics and "comedy" to satires and anathemas. One of the wisest men of his time is not capable of bridging the gap between the two cultures. The narrator states at the end that he chose this tale because "quise narrar el proceso de una derrota" (1974, 587). [I have tried to narrate the process of failure, the process of defeat] (1998, 241). Islamic culture, which does not permit such dramatic representations, limits Averroes. The children acting out their own invented drama outside his window do not help him. The problem is not the limits of the imagination. Rather, it is the limits of his experience. The narrator goes on to admit his own shortcomings in attempting to imagine Averroes while only having a little of Renan, Lane and Asín Palacios to draw on. Understanding another culture, another people, in their totality requires a great deal of personal effort, and borders on the impossible.

We see a similar pattern in "La escritura del Dios" (The God's Script). Borges narrates the story from the point of view of Tzinacán, the priest of the Pyramid of Qaholom, which Pedro de Alvarado burned. In search of the buried treasure, they have tortured and mutilated Tzinacán, but he has not relinquished the whereabouts of the treasures. He remembers that a secret text exists that will allow him to escape and make him omnipotent. Through much searching and concentration, he discovers this text in the spots of the jaguar, only to not make use of it. The mystical experience and the escape from the everyday and the individual to the universal and absolute so overwhelm and enthrall him and his sense of self that he loses interest in his own problems. "Quien ha entrevisto el universo, quien ha entrevisto los ardientes designios del universo, no puede pensar en un hombre, en sus triviales dichas o desventuras, aunque ese hombre sea él" (1974, 599). [Whoever has seen the universe, whoever has beheld the fiery designs of the universe, cannot think in terms of one man, of that man's trivial fortunes or misfortunes, though he be that very man] (1962, 173).

The way Borges handles this story tells us much about his attitude toward the conquest and the conflict of cultures. Indian/Mayan culture is depicted fairly positively. Certain magical/imaginative/exotic references, such as the jaguar with spots that hold the secret to the universe, capture our attention and fascinate us. Borges narrates the story from Tzinacán's point of view, which leads the reader to identify with the victim who is imprisoned and beaten. Both the Spanish and the Indian/Mayan cultures are shown to be barbaric in their practices. Tzinacán admits to having opened the chest of his victims with a knife, and Pedro de Alvarado and the Spanish have burned his temple and tortured and beaten him in order to get him to reveal the location of his treasure. Tzinacán's religious experiences are portrayed as equivalent to Christian ones. He demonstrates a pantheistic unity with his deity, suggesting a pantheistic attitude toward nature and the universe as well. He moves into a spiritual/mystical realm that seems to parallel mystical experiences in the Judeo-Christian tradition and in other religions.

Another of the stories in *El Aleph* collection, "El hombre en el umbral," (The Man on the Threshold), reflects a similar attitude toward other cultures in a colonizer/colony context. Set in a Muslim city, it pits the harsh colonialism of the British Empire against the Islamic culture of India, with Borges siding with the colonists. The story tells of the disappearance of a Governor, David Alexander Glencairn, who ruled with an iron fist. The narrator, Christopher Dewey, spends days searching for him. He happens upon a house where some sort of festival is occurring and where an old man is squatting. The man relates a tale of a tyrannical ruler whose story mirrors the one that is taking place inside. Locals kidnapped Glencairn, tried him for his abuse of the citizens, sentenced him to death, and executed him. The judge who oversees the trial and carries out the sentence is a madman, because it is believed that there are four honest men in every generation who secretly support the universe and justify it to God: "De un loco . . . para que la sabiduría de Dios hablara por su boca y avergonzara las soberbias humanas" (1974, 615). [A madman . . . so that the wisdom of God might speak through his mouth and bring shame to human pride and overweening] (1998, 272).

Here again, the handling of the narrative voice creates a certain attitude toward the relationship of the two cultures and tells us something about the authorial attitude. While Christopher Dewey, of the British Council, relates the story about the search for Glencairn, Dewey's story is related by another voice. That person is a friend of Bioy Casares, and could conceivably be Borges. In a number of other stories, such as "Tlön Uqbar, Orbis Tertius," the narrator refers to Bioy Casares, and that narrator is supposedly the fictional Borges. However, in this story it may be another person. The narrator states: "Mi texto será fiel: líbreme Alá de la tentación de añadir breves rasgos circunstanciales o de agravar con interpolaciones de Kipling, el cariz exótico del relato" (1974, 612) [My text will be a faithful one; may Allah prevent me from adding small circumstantial details or heightening the exotic lineaments of the tale with interpolations from Kipling] (1998, 269). Perhaps this is the fictional Borges playfully assuming the voice of a Muslim and/or an author of *1001 Nights,* or perhaps this narrator is meant to be Islamic. In either case, the narrator of the whole tale shows a tilt toward and a respect for Islamic culture. Furthermore, a sense of justice and a respect for the dignity and will of the oppressed people and culture come through in this story. David Alexander Glencairn, whose first names symbolize the rulers in the Judeo-Christian and Greek traditions, comes across as dictatorial and authoritarian. He appears to act unilaterally and often cruelly. In contrast, the citizens of the city set up a legal structure to try Glencairn. If one culture appears more barbaric in its treatment, it seems to be the British as represented by Glencairn.

In "El informe de Brodie," (Brodie's Report), these issues reappear. Borges draws on the satiric *Gulliver's Travels* in developing the story. In Book IV, Gulliver visits a utopian land of rational, serious, and virtuous horses called Houyhnhnms that rule the island. However, there is another group of people who do menial tasks and are vicious and disgusting. They are called "Yahoos." Gulliver is ultimately forced to admit that these Yahoos are human beings. He finds happiness with the Houyhnhnms, but is not accepted by them because he is simply an advanced Yahoo.

"El informe de Brodie" reveals a manuscript by a Scottish missionary who preached in Central Africa and the jungles of Brazil. He describes some of the primitive and disgusting practices of the Yahoos, including eating the raw flesh of their witch doctors and kings, and walking about naked. The Yahoos probably reside in South America, in Brazil. Their kings are gelded, blinded, and have their hands and legs cut off. However, Borges subtly and ironically suggests that the Yahoos may be the Argentines and/or the Latin Americans. He states that the kings are kept "en una caverna, cuyo nombre es Alcázar (Qzr)" (1974, 1074) [within a cavern, whose name is Citadel (Qzr)] (1998, 404). Since they use no vowels, the word "Qzr" that they use for fortress or castle is the Spanish word, which comes from the Arabic. He also mentions that the Yahoos only count to four using their fingers, and that infinity begins with the thumb. He then asserts that the same things happen with the tribes that raid and pillage around "Buenos-Aryes." Borges aims the satiric barbs in various directions. They are aimed at the narrator, who, as a representative of British/ Western cultures, sees and declares the barbarity in other cultures but not in his own. The narrator's call to convert and save the natives displays a sense of superiority that Borges subtly mocks and subverts. (The simplicity of the narrator is underscored when he is duped into believing that the Yahoos can foretell the future because the Yahoos predict that a fly will light on the back of your neck soon, or a bird will start singing.) In addition, they are aimed at the Argentines and Latin Americans, who are part of Western culture and have exhibited that sense of superiority toward other cultures. They are aimed at an intolerant mankind in general. We often note the barbarity in others but not in ourselves.

Cruelty and barbarity captured Borges's attention and imagination. He wrote extensively about it all his life, from the stories of *Historia universal de la infamia* (*Universal History of Iniquity*) (1935), to *El informe de Brodie (Brodie's Report)* (1970), *and El libro de arena (The Book of Sand)* (1975), linking it to epic visions, and often suggesting that none of us is free of it. His frequent depiction of knife fights and gauchos subtly calls attention to Sarmiento's *Civilización y barbarie (Civilization and Barbarity)*, while suggesting that Sarmiento's privileging of European culture may have been overdone, as all cultures have barbaric tendencies. Here again, Borges mocks those who marginalize and look with condescension on the Americas and suggest that they are not of the same stature as the European.

There are a number of other examples in Borges of conflicts of cultures and their difficulties. "Pierre Menard, autor del Quijote," satirizes the notion that one can totally understand another culture, since Menard, a Frenchman, reproduces Spain's greatest novel. In "El etnógrafo" (The Ethnographer), from *Elogio de la sombra* (1969) (*In Praise of Darkness*), Fred Murdock, who lives on the prairie in the United States to study a Native American language, learns some secrets that he cannot communicate but that change his life. Yet they are secrets that assist him wherever he may live. The story suggests that every culture has some truths to offer, and challenges the privileging of science, since Murdock comes to look upon science as frivolous. "Historia del guerrero y de la cautiva" (1949) (Story of the Warrior and the Captive Maiden), which I will discuss in more detail in chapter 6, also challenges the sense of cultural superiority.

Far from simply trying to be or to imitate the Europeans, Borges realized that the writers of the Americas have a special role and perspective in relation to Western culture. At the same time, because, as a culture, they were marginalized, they could use, innovate, subvert, and/or redefine Western culture to create a literary space and vision for their newly independent societies in a way that writers from the European countries could not. In doing so, he helped provide the framework and foundation for the postmodern. The central question may not be: "Why is Latin America accepting a Western or European concept in embracing postmodernism?" but rather: "Why are other countries, both Western and non-Western, embracing a concept that arose in Latin America?" One response to that question, which will be developed more thoroughly in the following chapter, is "because of its pluralism."

3
Pluralism, Meaning, Postmodernity, and Borges

THE EPISTEMOLOGICAL CRISIS WITH ITS RESULTING EMPHASES ON MULTI-plicity, ambiguity, randomness, fragmentation, indeterminacy, its challenge to privileged discourse, its democratic orientation, its questioning of what is reality and what is fiction, its re-exploration of the meaning of the self, and its re-examination of the nature of the literary work and of woman's/man's place in the universe, have marked the postmodern. They have helped produce a philosophical and cultural shift away from utopian models and monistic visions and toward philosophical and cultural pluralism. This philosophical pluralism and these challenges to the boundlessness of and the sources of our knowledge permeate the thinking and writing of Borges. A close reading of several stories and essay selections illustrates Borges's importance to the evolution of postmodern literature in challenging singular, totalistic, monistic visions and in affirming pluralism. However, it also shows that Borges was not a radical relativist, but that his orientation came closest to those postmodern writers and critics who affirm that positive knowledge is possible, to those who not only negate the One but also affirm the Many. Borges seems to suggest that one can create a sense of order within an impenetrable, chaotic labyrinth, and that with the help of certain manmade signposts, travel from one part of the labyrinth to the other may certainly be possible. However, deciphering the overall, ultimate structure and order of that labyrinth proves impossible.

BORGES, IDEALISM, EPISTEMOLOGY, AND PLURALISM

Borges's narrative challenges to a singular, totalistic vision derive in part from an idealistic conception of the world. His idealism sub-

49

verts the sense of a fixed reality, and the ultimate, objective authority of sensory data in defining objective truth. This questioning of material existence serves to undermine the cultural tendency to give privileged status to scientific knowledge. Borges states that, although he prefers not to define himself philosophically, if he had to, he would call himself an idealist (Dembo 1970, 317). He seems to identify especially with the idealism of Schopenhauer. He views the world as dreamlike and as a series of illusory mirror images. Along these lines, Borges asserts at one point in *Discusión* in "Avatares de la Tortuga" (Avatars of the Tortoise):

> Admitamos lo que todos los idealistas admiten:
>   el carácter alucinatorio del mundo . . . Nosotros (la indivisa divinidad que opera en nosotros) hemos soñado el mundo. Lo hemos soñado resistente, misterioso, visible, ubicuo en el espacio y firme en el tiempo; pero hemos consentido en su arquitectura tenues y eternos intersticios de sinrazón para saber que es falso. (1974, 258)

> [Let us admit what all idealists admit: the hallucinatory nature of the world . . . We (the undivided divinity operating within us) have dreamt the world. We have dreamt it as firm, mysterious, visible, ubiquitous in space and durable in time; but in its architecture we have allowed tenuous and eternal crevices of unreason which tell us it is false.] (1962, 208)

"Tlön Uqbar, Orbis Tertius" is one of the most thorough expressions of Borges's idealism. Here, as in other works, he employs mirror images as an expression of infinity and unlimited plurality (Barrenechea 1965, 39). He has stated that the fiction that creates its own world is the most creative, and he does just that in this story. The world of Tlön Uqbar is an idealistic world in which everything is imagined and nothing has material existence. Consequently, philosophy is considered to be a dialectical game, and metaphysics does not search for truth but rather for "el asombro" [amazement] (1974, 436).

The literary work and, by implication, the author and the self, are affected as well. In Tlön, all books derive from one author. Furthermore:

> Los de ficción abarcan un solo argumento, con todas las permutaciones imaginables. Los de naturaleza filosófica invariablemente contienen la tesis y la antítesis, el riguroso pro y el contra de una doctrina. Un libro que no encierra su contralibro es considerado incompleto. (1974, 439)

[Their fiction has but a single plot, with every imaginable permutation. Their works of a philosophical nature invariably contain both the thesis and antithesis, the rigorous pro and contra of every argument. A book that does not contain its counter-book is considered incomplete.] (1998, 77)

These comments highlight Borges's cultural and philosophical pluralism. He sets up a dynamic between the One and the Many through the reference to one plot with many permutations. A single, definitive plot has implications for a singular, determined world with little opportunity for choice. The multiple permutations offer a world of unlimited possibilities. The fact that all philosophies must give expression to opposing points of view also emphasizes that this world allows for multiple, competing perspectives, rather than exclusive, monistic visions. It has implications for a discourse on ideas and freedom of expression as well.

In effect, Tlön Uqbar is a world that challenges the very nature of reality and existence in our contemporary world. In Tlön, time exists but space does not. Furthermore, there are no nouns in the language of the imaginary planet, underscoring that there is nothing concrete. As cause and effect do not exit, reason is negated (McMurray 1980, 57). The imaginary world slowly begins to overtake the present world, which implies that existence is a fiction, since the present, past, and/or future are so easily modified (Barrenechea 1965, 9–10). As the story comes to a close, Borges's belief in the fictional nature of all systems, religions, and philosophies is underscored. The narrator conjectures that English, French, and Spanish will disappear. Nonetheless, he proceeds with a translation from English to Spanish of the "Urn Burial" of Browne. He knows that while all reality and philosophies are imaginative and fictional creations and that ultimate truth is beyond our reach, it is important we continue to make meaning, impose order, and search to define positive knowledge within our present bounds. Translating a poem is as meaningful as anything else, even though its importance and value may be altered in the future.

A number of other Borges stories also question the nature of reality by projecting an idealistic vision of the world, and, in doing so, underscore his indebtedness to Schopenhauer. The short story, "Las ruinas circulares" (The Circular Ruins), offers an example. This story, in which a wizard dreams a "son" into existence and then realizes that he too is an apparition that has been dreamed, underscores the indeterminacy that is so much a part of the postmodern. It emphasizes that we are dream images, that we exist because we are perceived, and that the line between sleeping and waking is indistinguishable. It serves to challenge the reliability and authority of sensory perception. Our senses do not define "the real world." They are subject to question, distortion, and misinterpretation. Subject and object roll and blend into each other as the line between creator and created, outside world and inner mind, dissolves.

There are numerous other direct and subtle references to this idealism, to the difficulty in distinguishing between waking and dreaming, fiction and "reality" in selections written throughout his life. In "El Sur" (1953) (The South), ambiguity permeates the second half of the story. The reader cannot know with certainty if Dahlmann actually dies in a knife fight with a gaucho, or whether the journey out of the hospital and into the South to his estancia or farm was actually a dream fabrication to help him accept his imminent death or an actual journey. In "La espera" (1950) (The Waiting), from *El Aleph*, as the man is waiting for his death, the main character, Villari, who assumes the name of his assassin, finds dream and reality blurring as he awaits the arrival of his killer. In "El jardín de senderos que se bifurcan" (1941) (The Garden of Forking Paths), Dr. Albert compares Yu Tsun and himself to characters within Yu Tsun's ancestor's novel, and conjectures they may exist in various time planes with different possible future relationships and endings. In "Tres versiones de Judas" (1944) (Three Versions of Judas), the narrator suggests an idealistic relationship between heaven and earth when he states "El orden inferior es un espejo del orden superior; las formas de la tierra corresponden a las formas del cielo" (1974, 515). [The lower order is a mirror of the higher; the forms of earth correspond to the forms of Heaven] (1962, 96). References run through his poetry as well. A poem such as "Las dos catedrales" (The Two Cathedrals), from *La cifra* (*The Limit*) (1981) refers to an archetype of the earthly cathedral; and "Descartes" from the same work, speaks of dreaming the world. In "La tarde" (The Afternoon), from *Los conjurados*, all afternoons are a reflection of one. In "Alguien sueña" (Someone Dreams), he catalogs what time has dreamed and suggests that it has dreamed virtually everything. In "Everything and Nothing," from *El hacedor* (*The Maker*) (1960), Shakespeare discovers that, as the Kabbalah suggests, God himself has dreamed him and the world, much as Shakespeare has dreamed his works. In another delightful, short, comical piece in *El hacedor*, "Diálogo sobre un diálogo" (A Dialogue

About a Dialogue), Borges plays with the line between life and death and dream and reality in discussing immortality. The narrator, A, describes a conversation with Macedonio Fernández, who strongly believes in immortality. The narrator suggests that they kill themselves to escape the noise in the background. When the other listener, Z, says mockingly that he assumes that they reconsidered, the narrator says that he doesn't remember. Although the list could go on, Borges summarizes his use of idealism nicely in a reference to Schopenhauer in an article "Cuando la ficción vive en la ficción" (When Fiction Lives in Fiction) (1939):

> Arturo Schopenhauer escribió que los sueños y la vigilia eran hojas de un mismo libro y que leerlas en orden era vivir, y hojearlas, soñar. Cuadros dentro de cuadros, libros que se desdoblan en otros libros, nos ayudan a intuir esa identidad. (1996, 435)

> [Arthur Schopenhauer wrote that dreaming and wakefulness are the pages of a single book, and that to read them in order is to live and to leaf through them at random, to dream. Paintings within paintings and books that branch into other books help us sense this oneness.] (1999a, 162)

Idealism, Objectivity, Limits, and the Fantastic

This idealism has profound implications. It challenges an objective vision of the world and the reliability of the senses, underscores our limits, and creates a space for magic and the supernatural. Aesthetically, magic, the fantastic, and the marvelous all become possible. In effect, it creates a world of possibilities, a world that in being bounded is aesthetically boundless.

"Funes el memorioso" (Funes the Memorious) (1944) illustrates how Borges's pluralistic vision challenges and subverts objectivity. Funes becomes paralyzed in an accident when he is thrown from a horse. Consequently, his faculties of perception and memory become extremely enhanced to the point that he records and remembers all details. However, he is unable to think. As the narrator suggests, he seems incapable of thought. To think is to forget differences, to generalize and abstract. In Funes's world, there was nothing but immediate details, something like camera or video shots of the past without any editing. Funes's remarkable ability underscores our own limitations in perceiving and observing the world. It challenges the division between subject and object. A truly objective observer would need such a gift. Funes's shortcoming, his inability to think and reason, suggests that we should not be too distraught by our inability to achieve that objective clarity, because true objectivity does not reason, generalize, and think. While these are more important gifts, they also are quite subjective, as they involve editing, selecting, and generally making subjective choices.

Along these same lines, "Pierre Menard, autor del *Quijote*" (Pierre Menard, Author of the *Quixote*) questions what we can know, challenges monistic certainty and also questions, in particular, what we can "know" objectively of the past. The story is a eulogistic essay written for Menard by his narrator friend. The narrator considers Menard's distinctive contribution to be a written recreation in the twentieth century of part of chapter 22 of *Don Quijote* in its original form. The piece has implications both for the elusiveness of truth and the act of reading.

This short piece is a parody of the essay form. The essay is a genre largely intended for the discussion of objective reality and fact. Like the narrator in the story, an author often incorporates footnotes into his essay to further support and develop the authority of his remarks. Traditionally, the use of footnotes suggests a different type of discourse, a nonfictional one. By converting this tool of objectivity and logic into a fiction, Borges challenges the authority of all truth and implies that reality is a fictional creation.

Pierre Menard's recomposition of the *Quijote* is a comment on the act of reading, which also has implications for the nature of truth. In highlighting the differences between the *Quijote* written in the seventeenth century by a Spaniard, and the same piece in the twentieth century by a Frenchman, the Argentine suggests that each reading of a work is different and is a subjective re-creation of the text by the reader. The irony is especially striking when the narrator cites Cervantes's and Menard's two identical passages from chapter 9 of the *Quijote*: "La verdad, cuya madre es la historia," (1974, 449), [truth, whose mother is history]. The implication of this passage is that one's time and place determine one's sense of reality, something that the twentieth-century Frenchman, Menard, seemed to overlook in undertaking his project on the *Quijote*. All of this suggests that our present context will always color our understanding of the historical past and literary works of the past. One's view of the past will always be subjective and fictional.

Borges pokes fun at the scientist's aura of objectivity as well, in a snippet in *El hacedor* (*The Maker*), entitled "Del rigor en la ciencia" (On Exactitude in Science). The narrator tells of an Empire that is so concerned with geographic precision in maps that it has one created that coincides directly with the towns and provinces. Future generations realized that it was useless, and it was discarded. Like Menard, these cartographers humorously believe they can achieve perfect objectivity and correspondence with nature.

Borges closes his epilogue to *El hacedor* (*The Maker*), with a narrative anecdote that expresses similar sentiments about subjectivity. He later expresses a very similar notion poetically in the poem "La suma" (The sum) from *Los conjurados* (1985). A man spends his life drawing the world, sketching in kingdoms, mountains, ships, islands, fish, and everything else. Shortly before death, he realizes that he has done nothing more than draw the lines and image of his face. The suggestion is that he has not been able to transcend his own subjectivity to obtain his desired objectivity. Of course, this underscores the futility and limitations of naturalism and realism and similar aesthetic movements that attempt mimesis, an imitation of nature and the world. The anecdote has implications for others who try to sketch the world objectively as well, the sociologist, the geographer, the anthropologist, the historian, the physical scientist, the journalist, and so forth. According to Borges, they will never transcend the labyrinth of their subjectivity.

Once one acknowledges the aesthetic futility of capturing "truth" through objectivity and mimesis, the options for literature open up. Borges realized this early in his career. In "El arte narrativo y la magia" (Narrative Art and Magic) (1932), he argues that magic is very much a part of good fiction. He asserts that causality based on magical and prophetic suggestions of what is to come in the plot is much more appropriate for the novel than natural causality based on incessant causes and effects. His stories abound with magical elements, miracles, and violations of physical laws. Borges loved to play with the creative possibilities that extended the limits "reality" offered, whether it is the immortality of Homer in the story "El inmortal" (The Immortal) (1949), the suspension of time and stopping of a bullet so that Jaromir Hladik could finish his play in "El milagro secreto" (The Secret Miracle) (1943), the various objects that contain the power and/or the secret of the universe, such as the Aleph, the tetragrammaton in "La muerte and la brújula" (The Death and the Compass) (1942), the spots on the jaguar in "La escritura del Dios" (The God's Script) (1949), the disk in "El disco," the book of sand in *El libro de arena* (1975), or the coins that defy mathematical laws or contain magical qualities in "Tigres azules" (Blue Tigers) (1983), or "El zahir" (1949). The list could go on. All of these open an aesthetic space for myths, legends, the marvelous, the magical, the supernatural, and the fantastic.

THE LABYRINTH, ORDER, AND CHAOS

The stories referred to above define certain epistemological problems that we face, and argue for a pluralistic perspective. They challenge and undermine monistic and totalistic visions yet do not necessarily draw a distinction between a chaotic and an ordered but unknowable universe. However, in some of his others writings, Borges emphasizes that the universe might be a cosmos rather than chaos, that is, that there may be an order to our world, albeit an indecipherable one. The image of the labyrinth figures centrally. While this labyrinth is a prominent and dominant image in Borges's thinking and writing, as mentioned above, it does not necessarily suggest the desperation and chaos that many associate with it.

Two well-known Borges stories, "La lotería en Babilonia" (The Babylonian Lottery) (1941), and "La biblioteca de Babel" (The Library of Babel) (1941), employ the image of the labyrinth to portray impenetrable, seemingly random, and pluralistic worlds, and suggest an ordered but unknowable universe rather than a chaotic one. Both of these stories deal more with metaphysical issues. Perhaps as a result, they focus on the labyrinth as symbol and tend to give a more complete view of Borges's larger vision.

"La lotería en Babilonia" stresses the workings of chance in our lives. In this story in which a lottery grows to control all aspects of a people's lives and in its silent functioning becomes "comparable al de Dios," [comparable to God's], the Company is a metaphor for God and Babylonia represents the world (1974, 460). The implication is that God works with a randomness that man will never comprehend. Jaime Alazraki has stated that the story, by its nature, has an ironic, mirror image twist. It is an effort to limit, define, and thus transcend the chaos that is our lives, but in doing so, it is attempting to order and explain what is, in effect, a labyrinthine disorder (Alazraki 1977b, 111). Borges might take issue with that statement. Alazraki assumes, it seems to me, that the labyrinth suggests chaos, that the choice is between a monistic and an absolutistic, relativistic stance, between a knowable truth and utter chaos. Alazraki implies that in trying to limit and define life in Babylon, the author sought to delineate an overarching monistic diagram or model to give order to the world. The story is set in ancient Babylon to counter this very assumption. By selecting a sight that is exotic, removed, and foreign in both time and place and, at the same time, very specific and particular as a symbol of the universe, Borges, in effect, creates "a" world, one of many. He implies that any attempt to understand, limit, and define the universe is determined by one's place and time, and thus, is subjective and open to multiple interpretations. The universe may have an order, but it is an order that we will never fathom. By offering an inclusive overview of Babylon's lottery, he suggests that there is merit in seeking to define an explanation, a vision, a truth, as long as we realize our ultimate limitations in actually attaining that end, an idea that he will state a little more explicitly in "El idioma analítico de John Wilkins" (The Analytic Language of John Wilkins) (1942).

While "La lotería en Babilonia" (The Babylonian Lottery), emphasizes the workings of chance and the inexplicability of our lives, the narrator in the closing lines offers multiple possible explanations of La Compañía, thus underscoring his limitations in understanding the overarching vision. At the same time, this passage suggests that Borges does not affirm a totally absurd world. In discussing different opinions about the existence and nature of La Compañía, the narrator states:

Otra, por boca de heresiarcas enmascarados, que no ha existido nunca y que no existirá. Otra, no menos vil, razona que es indiferente afirmar o negar la realidad de la tenebrosa corporación, porque Babilonia no es otra cosa que un infinito juego de azares. (1974, 460)

[Another, in the words of masked heresiarchs, that it (The Company) has never existed and will not exist. Another, no less vile, reasons that it is indifferent to affirm or deny the reality of the shadowy corporation, because Babylon is nothing else than an infinite game of chance.] (1962, 35)

While these lines reflect Borges's skepticism, and while there certainly is some irony in his use of the terms "heresiarcas enmascaradas" [masked heresiarchs] and "vil" [vile], his narrator, who has entertained those ideas, discredits them. They express a certainty about the nature of the lottery and the universe that runs counter to the narrator's and the author's viewpoints. This narrator is a sailor who must finish his tale quickly before his ship leaves: "Poco tiempo me queda; nos avisan que la nave está por zarpar" (1974, 459). [I don't have much time left. They tell us that the ship is about to weigh anchor] (1962, 33). He is a sailor who goes on traveling the journey of life in spite of all its hazards and random happenings. He continues without hesitation or defeat. This is a subtle comment on the line that Borges draws. Our "realities" are fictions of our own making. Our lives seem ruled by chance. Yet, there is still supreme importance in attempting to understand and create an order, even though we must ultimately admit that we will not ultimately succeed and that any creations will be fictions.

The image of the labyrinth is central to "La Biblioteca de Babel" (The Library of Babel) as well. Borges uses the library as a metaphor to contrast the knowledge of man/woman and the knowledge of the universe. The order of the universe is portrayed as being as impenetrable as the destiny of man. The opening words of the story tell us directly that the library is a symbol for the Universe. The story is a representation of man's effort to know the universe. The ambiguity and plurality of that universe are expressed through the statement that no two books are the same. The vain search for the one book that is the key to all other books symbolizes the inability of our minds to grasp the totality of the incredibly complex universe. There is a symmetry to this library, but it is illusory, suggesting that woman/man will never ultimately understand the universe through reason. As the narrator discovers, "La Biblioteca es ilimitada y periódica" (1974, 471). [The Library is unlimited and cyclical] (1962, 58). It is a paradox of opposites that can never be rationally resolved. Again, by connecting it with the biblical Babel, Borges achieves three interrelated effects. He links the library, symbol of knowledge and understanding, with the problems of language and of comprehending each other's languages. He calls attention to the gulf between the human world and the world of the divine, a theme connected with the biblical Babel and also with the labyrinth as a symbol. He sets it in a distant and exotic realm that further highlights our difficulty in understanding it, and thus suggests that this is an individual, subjective, worldview.

Here, the narrator, who is approaching death, admits that his search for the one book that will explain all others has been in vain. Yet, he affirms the importance of continuing such a search:

En aventuras de ésas, he prodigado y consumido mis años. No me parece inverosímil que en algún anaquel de universo haya un libro total[1]; ruego a los dioses ignorados que un hombre—¡uno solo, aunque sea, hace miles de años!—lo haya examinado y leído. Si el honor y la sabiduría y la felicidad no son para mí, que sean para otros. Que el cielo exista, aunque mi lugar sea el infierno. Que yo sea ultrajado y aniquilado, pero que en un instante, en un ser, Tu enorme Biblioteca se justifique.

[1] Lo repito: basta que un libro sea posible para que exista. Sólo está excluido lo imposible. (1974, 469–70)

[In adventures such as these, I have squandered and wasted my years. It does not seem unlikely to me that there is a total book on some shelf of the universe;[1] I pray to the unknown gods that a man—just one, even though it were thousands of years ago—may have examined and read it. If honor and wisdom and happiness are not for me, let them be for others. Let heaven exist, though my place be in hell. Let me be outraged and annihilated, but for one instant in one being, let Your enormous Library be justified.

[1] I repeat: it suffices that a book be possible for it to exist. Only the impossible is excluded.] (1962, 56–57)

The attitude of the narrator here seems inclined toward the belief in an ordered center to the labyrinth and to a Supreme Being. In stating "Tu enorme Biblioteca" with capital letters, [Your enormous Library], he appears to address God directly. While the story as a whole affirms the plurality and inexplicability of the universe, Borges's skepticism also leaves him skeptical about asserting that there is no God. However, he does maintain that if such a Divine Being does exist, our capabilities of comprehending It and understanding Its workings are very limited.

In one of Borges's finest stories, "La escritura del Dios" (The God's Script), we find a similar tendency and a somewhat mystical vision that parallels "El Aleph." The narrator, Tzinacán, the last in the line of shamans of an Indian tribe, in searching for that magical sentence to ward off the evils of the torturing and oppressing Spanish, represents all of us waiting for death. Unlike the old man in the Library, he finds the center of the labyrinth. Like the wizard in "Las ruinas circulares" (The Circular Ruins), he finds himself caught in a kaleidoscope of recurring dreams. He is struck by the difference between our world and the realm of God. It is a world in which there is no self, in which self and other are one, in which opposites are unified, as implied by his presence and that of his tormentor and enemy, Pedro de Alvarado. As readers, we may question whether that experience was a hallucination, a figment of his imagination, the result of his traumatic oppression, or an actual mystical experience. The narrator, Tzinacán, assumes the latter. In contrast to "El Aleph," the source or "reality" of the experience is not as important to the major thrust and themes of the narrative, so the tendency is to allow the author his poetic license. This story emphasizes the differences between the divine and the human and man's/woman's limitations in comprehending any divine scheme. The story does not argue that a divine scheme does not exist, but rather, its incomprehensibility and inexplicability.

"El jardín de senderos que se bifurcan" (The Garden of Forking Paths), is a story in which the line between reality and fiction is blurred and in which life is portrayed as a series of alternate times and possibilities. In this parody of the spy tale, Yu Tsun, a German spy of Chinese ancestry, meets Stephen Albert, a quiet, peaceful, knowledgeable sinologist living in England. Before killing Albert to convey the intended message to his German superiors, Yu Tsun discovers that his great-grandfather has written a labyrinthine novel with alternative pasts, presents, and futures and realizes that Albert, the labyrinthine garden that he oversees, and he are like creations of that novel. Time and life are portrayed as a myriad of diverging possibilities, and reality and existence dissolve into an idealistic fiction upon this realization. In "Tlön Uqbar, Orbis Tertius," all literature is portrayed as a single plot with all imaginable variations. Here, that image becomes a metaphor for life itself, a single plot with infinite variations. The One and the Many merge into an infinitude of possibilities. Like the wizard who created his son, these characters are products of a novelist with god-like powers. The story suggests the Kabbalistic vision of God dreaming the world.

Borges's short prose poem from *Los conjurados* (1985), "El hilo de la fábula," (The Thread of the Fable), recounts the tale of Theseus and the Minotaur and how Ariadne's thread provided him with an escape. He remarks that Theseus did not realize that there were other labyrinths, that time is the labyrinth on the other side of the labyrinth, and that Medea, with her anger and madness as the scorned lover also has a place in the labyrinth, and then comments on our present day attitude toward the labyrinth:

> El hilo se ha perdido; el laberinto se ha perdido también. Ahora ni siquiera sabemos si nos rodea un laberinto, un secreto cosmos, o un caos

azaroso. Nuestro hermoso deber es imaginar que hay un laberinto y un hilo. Nunca daremos con el hilo; acaso lo encontramos y lo perdemos en un acto de fe, en una cadencia, en el sueño, en las palabras que se llaman filosofía o en la mera y sencilla felicidad. (1989a, 481)

[The thread is lost; the labyrinth is lost also. Now we don't even know if a labyrinth surrounds us, a secret cosmos, or a haphazard chaos. Our beautiful duty is to imagine that there is a labyrinth and a thread. We will never find the thread; maybe we'll find it and lose it in an act of faith, in a rhythm, in a dream, in the words that they call philosophy, or in a mere and simple happiness.] (translation mine)

Here too, the labyrinth symbolizes the order that seems to exist but is beyond our comprehension.

The Argentine author always showed a fascination with the collection of stories *Mil y una noches*, known in English as the *Arabian Nights*. He includes a short narrative parable that imitates the form of that work, "Los dos reyes y los dos laberintos," (The Two Kings and the Two Labyrinths) (1949). In the 1952 Postscript to *El Aleph*, Borges playfully suggests that the story came from *Arabian Nights* but was left out of the Galland translation. This piece again highlights this attitude toward the labyrinth and emphasizes the difference between the divine and the human. Here the tension is not between the universe as labyrinth or the universe as chaos. The Islamic narrator assumes that the universe has an order although an indecipherable, labyrinthine one. Rather, the tension is between man/woman and Allah, between what are man's/woman's limits and what are Allah's prerogatives. The narrative voice highlights man's/woman's limits in relation to God in the opening line: "Cuentan los hombres dignos de fe (pero Alá sabe más)" (1974, 607). [It is said by men worthy of belief (though Allah's knowledge is greater)] (1998, 263). A Babylonian king has had his architects and wizards construct a labyrinth so subtle and perplexing that prudent men do not enter it. Again, the narrative voice underscores the tension between man/woman and God when it states that the labyrinth was a scandal, "porque la confusión y la maravilla son operaciones propias de Dios y no de los hombres" (1974, 607). [For it is the prerogative of God, not man, to strike confusion and inspire wonder] (1998, 263). The king invites an Arabian king to enter in order to ridicule him. The Arabian king does so, gets lost, and only exits after requesting help from Allah. Upon departing Babylonia, he tells its king that he too has a labyrinth, but without galleries, walls, or doors. He returns with his Army, conquers the kingdom, ties up the king of Babylonia, and abandons him in the middle of the desert to die. The story implies that death is a labyrinth, a labyrinth beyond man's/woman's comprehension that only God understands.

The gap between man and God reappears in a number of Borges stories. He addresses and challenges modernity's attitude toward time directly in the story "Los teólogos" (The Theologians), but underscores the futility of our efforts to understand and create dogma on such issues. As Matei Calinescu (1987a) and Octavio Paz (1981) have pointed out in their perceptive studies, modernity and time are closely linked. The term "modern" has a long history. It dates back to the Christian Middle Ages. It is essentially about time. The term posits that the present is different from the past. Consequently, it is founded on a sense of progress through time, or of "unrepeatable time." A society that does not have such a temporal, sequential concept of history employs mythical or recurrent models.

The postmodernist conception of time differs from modernism. Modernity rejects tradition, considers the present superior to the past, views society as moving into a utopian end of time. Time is linear, progressive, and not repetitive. This conception evolved from the Judeo-Christian conception of the universe as having a beginning of time and an end of time, a creation, and, in regard to Christianity, an apocalypse. Our society's faith in scientific progress and the sense of superiority of our age over the past ages derive from this utopian conception of time as well. In its conflicted way, aesthetic modernism, at the same time, undermines this sense of time as "progressive" with its view of the present as decadent, superficial, and materialistic. The postmodern reintroduces a mythical and circular time into our consciousness. Future progress is not necessarily a given as it is in modernism. Utopian visions come under challenge. Scientific and technological progress may have positive fruits, but they also have created the atomic and hydrogen bombs that, for the first time, could destroy the world as we know it, and ecological crises that could make the world uninhabitable.

Borges's story, "Los teólogos" (The Theologians) (1949), plays with these two conceptions of time. Aureliano and Juan de Panonia are ecclesiastical rivals in the Church in their theological writings. Both composed a treatise challenging a heretical sect that professed to believe in the concept of time as repeating itself, but Juan de Panonia's writing gains favor. Subsequently, the heretics are killed. However, as time passes, this concept of cyclical time becomes accepted doctrine, and both theologians accept it. When another sect challenges it, Aureliano writes a statement against that sect and brings to light that his rival, Juan de Panonia, had rejected the sense of time as repeatable. Consequently, Juan de Panonia is put to death. Then one night, Aureliano is startled by the sound of rain at dawn and remembers a previous time when he similarly felt startled, implying that time repeats itself. During the storm, lightning starts a fire in which he dies, in much the same manner as Juan did. He discovers in heaven that in God's eyes, his rival, Juan de Panonia, and he are one person.

The story underscores the provisional nature of philosophical positions by highlighting the shifting positions on the nature of time, emphasizing man's limits in understanding issues relating to the divine, and suggesting God's indifference to man's theological concerns. It projects a pantheistic conception of the self in which opposites are unified. Even more importantly, it challenges the notion of an unrepeatable time and affirms a mythical, cyclical conception of time, although in the fashion of Borges, it simultaneously problematizes that conception and hesitates to confirm it as the one correct conception of time. It also underscores the provisional, fictional nature of theology.

We see a similar undercurrent regarding theological understandings in his stories that are, in effect, a defense, of Judas, "Tres versiones de Judas" (Three Versions of Judas) (1944), and "La secta de los Treinta" (The Sect of the Thirty) (1975). The former suggests that perhaps God did not come to earth as Jesus, but rather as Judas, since if God became man, he must have all of man's qualities, including sin. The latter relates the discovery of a manuscript from a secret sect. It believed that Judas was a player on a stage acting out a divine scheme, much as Jesus was, and that no one is guilty. The fact that the members of that sect crucify themselves at age thirty-three, like Jesus and Judas, underscores our limitations in understanding the work of the Divine, and the limitations of our religions.

The theme is present as well in the story "El evangelio según Marcos" (The Gospel According to Mark) (1970). The thirty-three-year-old medical student, Baltasar Espinosa is, as his name suggests, a Christ symbol. He finds himself stranded on his cousin's ranch during a flood with the illiterate gaucho ranch hands, the Gutres. He begins reading them the "Gospel according to Mark." They entice him to sleep with their daughter, and then they construct a cross to crucify him for his sin. For Borges, all of us are Gutres, limited in our understanding and trying to make sense of the Divine.

In a masterful story, "La muerte y la brújula" (Death and the Compass), Borges uses the detective story to challenge the rational systems and reason in general as privileged modes for explaining the world. The world is portrayed as a chaotic, subjective, labyrinthine puzzle that reason cannot unravel. Police detective Lönnrot refuses to accept that the killing of Rabbi Yarmolinsky could have been an act of chance and mistaken identity. Instead, he seeks a rational explanation in the Kabbalah and in the tradition surrounding the tetragrammaton or the four letters in God's name. By planting clues, his alter ego and archenemy, Scharlach, manipulates him into coming to the Triste-le-Roy, the labyrinthine mansion filled with mirrors, where he is killed.

The nature of the self is explored again here as the dichotomy between pursuer and pursued, between detective and criminal, between rationalist and absurdist is played out. The "rot" at the end of Lönnrot's name and "Scharlach" both mean red in German and both men's minds function with the same rigid logic (McMurray 1980, 17). However, Scharlach has accepted the absurdity of existence.

The use of the detective story is significant, because that form is based on the assumption that the universe is ordered in such a way that reason and justice will prevail. However, Lönnrot's manipulation and undoing imply that those willing to violate the rules of ethics, religion, morality, and reason, sometimes have an advantage, or at least sometimes win. As Jaime Alazraki asserts, Lönnrot discovers that the center of the labyrinth is another labyrinth (Alazraki 1977b, 102). That labyrinth is the universe itself. The implications are far-reaching. Scharlach and Lönnrot are two sides of the same coins, alter egos. This raises questions about the role of reason in the universe. Reason is a tool that man/woman uses to order and understand the world. It is not necessarily a divine instrument nor the path to understanding divinity. That is not to say that God is irrational (although It might be), but rather non-rational. If there is an order to God's workings, it is not available through reason. Ultimately, Inspector Treviranus was correct when he suggested that the murder was a product of chance, a mistake, that the thief who was after the jewels, entered the wrong hotel room, implying again that our reason will not explain the workings of the world. The story also tends to problematize our understanding of justice and injustice and of good and evil. It is not that they do not exist, but that they coexist in a way that we cannot comprehend. The story as a whole, in its settings and descriptions, has a dream/nightmare-like quality that removes it from the realistic realm and emphasizes our inability to decipher and understand the world. This suggests that there are limits to our knowledge, and that the world is accessible through multiple modes.

In the essays of *Otras inquisiciones* (Other Inquisitions) (1952), Borges makes some prose comments on the nature of history, the universe, and the self that challenge the one, and thus illustrates postmodernity's indebtedness to him. At the same time, he separates himself from the stance of the radical relativist. In "La esfera de Pascal" (Pascal's Sphere), he refers to different commentaries on the image of God and of the universe as an intelligible sphere whose center is everywhere and whose circumference is indefinable, implying that God and the universe exceed our powers of definition. The metaphor has pantheistic overtones, suggesting a divinity that is everywhere. Yet Pascal, in using the metaphor, expresses a frightful sense of solitude that his predecessors did not. Borges attributes this to the Copernican redefinition of the cosmos in which human beings are no longer the center of that sphere nor the major interest, but rather, seemingly marginalized. Borges ends the essay by suggesting that universal history may be the history of the diverse intonation of a few metaphors. That closing line has definite implications for a pluralistic universe. If one assumes that that spherical image is a pantheistic metaphor for God, the implication is that there are numerous visions of that metaphor. It highlights the way in which the One and the Many depend upon each other in Borges, and how at times, that dichotomy dissolves into irresolution.

In "El tiempo y J. W. Dunne" (Time and J. W. Dunne) (1952), Borges elaborates on Dunne's sense of the immediacy of time. Dunne's concept fits well with Octavio Paz's notion of an eternity in the present and the future that is not necessarily religious. Dunne suggests that our nightly dreams capture eternity because the past, the present, and the future all flow together into an instant. As Borges states in explaining it:

Los teólogos definen la eternidad como la simultánea y lúcida posesión de todos los instantes del tiempo y la declaran uno de los atributos divinos. Dunne, asombrosamente, supone que ya es nuestra la eternidad y que los sueños de cada noche lo corroboran. En ellos, según él, conflu-

yen el pasado inmediato y el inmediato porvenir. En la vigilia recorre-
mos a uniforme velocidad el tiempo sucesivo, en el sueño abarcamos
una zona que puede ser vastísima. (1974, 648)

[Theologians define eternity as the lucid and simultaneous possession of
all instants of time and declare it a divine attribute. Dunne, surprisingly,
presumes that eternity already belongs to us, as collaborated by the
dreams we have each night. In them, according to him, the immediate
past and the immediate future intermingle. Awake, we pass through successive time at a uniform speed: in dreams we may span a vast zone.]
(1999a, 219)

The ways in which dream and "reality," the mysterious and the
mundane, and the divine and the human flow into each other en-
chant Borges. In his essays and stories he frequently tries to project
a milieu in which mystery, magic, and the marvelous can exist. That
is one of his purposes in highlighting Dunne's writing.

In "Magias parciales del *Quijote*," (Partial Enchantments of the
Quixote), Borges creates a space for mystery by questioning the certainty of our sense of self. While admitting that the *Quijote* was a realistic work in its time, he argues that Cervantes loved the
supernatural and that it was a subtle, nostalgic way to bid goodbye
to the era of the knight errant. He suggests that Cervantes's fascination with the line between the objective and the subjective has les-
sons for contemporary society. Borges introduces uncertainty, and
questions the fictional nature of us all as well as the tentative line
separating reality and dream when he asks rhetorically why it makes
us uneasy that Don Quijote is a reader of the *Quijote* and Hamlet a
spectator of *Hamlet*. He then answers that if characters of a fictional
work can be narrators or spectators, then we, the readers and spectators, can be fictions.

This has overtones of the short stories, "Las ruinas circulares"
(The Circular Ruins) (1941), and "Everything and Nothing
(1960)," and has suggestions of that Kabbalistic image of God
dreaming the world, and of human beings as dream images of a
larger being. That possibility does not threaten or challenge Borges.
Rather, it is a part of the wonder of the world, and he appears to
welcome and prefer it.

In "Kafka y sus precursores" (Kafka and his Precursors), he argues again for the fluidity and subjectivity of the past when he asserts
that each writer creates his own precursor. Thus, our understanding

of history, literary or otherwise, continuously changes with changing events in the present.

In this collection of essays, he twice quotes León Bloy to reinforce not only this notion of history, but also to suggest the indeterminacy of the self. Borges's fascination with this religious figure illustrates the balance that Borges seeks. He finds Bloy's skepticism fascinating, and yet distances himself from the religious affirmations that Bloy falls back on to overcome that skepticism. He quotes Bloy's statement in "El espejo de los Enigmas" (The Mirror of Enigmas) as well as in "Del culto de los libros," (From the Cult of the Books):

No hay en la tierra un ser humana capaz de declarar quién es, con certidumbre. Nadie sabe qué ha venido a hacer a este mundo, a qué corresponden sus actos, sus sentimientos, sus ideas, ni cuál es su *nombre* verdadero, su imperecedero Nombre en el registro de la Luz . . . La historia es un inmenso texto litúrgico donde las iotas y los puntos no valen menos que los versículos o capítulos íntegros, pero la importancia de unos y de otros es indeterminable y está profundamente escondida. (1974, 722, 716)

[There is no human being on earth capable of declaring with certitude who he is. No one knows what he has come into this world to do, what his acts correspond to, his sentiments, his ideas, or what his real name is, his enduring Name in the register of Light . . . History is an immense liturgical text where iotas and dots are worth no less than the entire verses or chapters, but the importance of one and the other is indeterminable, and profoundly hidden.] (1962, 211)

In "Del culto de los libros" (The Cult of the Books), Borges seems fascinated by Bloy's representation of the universe in metaphoric terms as a text. As is clear in "La biblioteca de Babel," (The Library in Babel), that metaphor resounds in many different ways. It has been adopted widely. However, Borges maintains a skeptical stance, while Bloy makes a leap of faith, as is clear in "El espejo de los enigmas" (The Mirror of Enigmas), when Borges writes:

Es dudoso que el mundo tenga sentido; es más dudoso aun que tenga doble y triple sentido, observará el incrédulo. Yo entiendo que así es; pero entiendo que el mundo jeroglífico postulado por Bloy es el que más conviene a la dignidad del Dios intelectual de los teólogos. (1974, 722)

[It is doubtful that the world has a meaning; it is even more doubtful that it has a double or triple meaning, the unbeliever will observe. I understand that this is so; but I understand that the hieroglyphical world postulated by Bloy is the one which best befits the dignity of the theologian's intellectual God.] (1962, 212)

Borges assumes the stance of the ultimate skeptic. When he says "it is doubtful" he does not deny the existence of meaning but rather, remains skeptical, at least intellectually. He realizes that such a denial is simply the flip side of an affirmation of meaning and derives from a similar desire for a singular, monistic view. In many ways, a passionate atheism does not differ from a passionate fundamentalism. Rather, Borges's position is one of doubt, of the agnostic, affirming that we simply cannot know whether such meanings exist. At the same time, he steps back just a bit from the stance of the "incrédulo," "the unbeliever." While Bloy becomes more affirmative, Borges remains the skeptic. His stance is not a denial nor an affirmation of a divine order, but is respectful and dignified in its statement that we must admit that our knowledge and ability to be certain are limited.

That skepticism, however, does not convert into a nihilism. In the lines from "El idioma analítico de John Wilkins" (The Analytical Language of John Wilkins) quoted earlier, Borges underscores the plural and indecipherable nature of the universe, but at the same time, emphasizes the importance of creating fictions to represent and comprehend it, and thus separates himself from the ranks of the nihilists: "La imposibilidad de penetrar el esquema divino del universo no puede, sin embargo, disuadirnos de planear esquemas humanos, aunque nos conste que éstos son provisorios" (708). [But the impossibility of penetrating the divine scheme of the universe cannot dissuade us from outlining human schemes, even though we are aware that they are provisional] (1981, 243).

In Borges's world we affirm our role as creators of fictions, of systems, of philosophies, of religions, of realities, of worlds, of knowledge, to give us direction. We realize that these creations are not "natural," but that they are our fictions to help us deal with our world. This is not a challenge to truth itself, but to our ability ultimately to arrive at it.

EPISTEMOLOGY AND THE POSTMODERN

Scholars and critics of the postmodern have drawn extensively on Borges's challenges to monistic visions in outlining and defining the qualities of postmodern culture. Some of these critics have argued, as Borges does, that positive knowledge and values are possible within a pluralistic context. The most widely agreed upon characteristics of postmodernity relate to a crisis of epistemology, a crisis of knowledge. To summarize this crisis briefly, we have lost our faith in the metanarratives on which our society has depended, and which defined our utopian visions (Christianity, Marxism, Capitalism, Reason, Science, Positivism). These metanarratives do not have the same "truth" value for us. The result is an indeterminacy, a decentering, a mixing of the highbrow and the lowbrow, a reaching out to the margins, and a challenge to the privileged status of knowledge and of authority in general.

Jean-François Lyotard defines the postmodern condition as an "incredulity toward metanarratives" (1984, xxiv). He explains that there are two types of great stories (grands récits) or metanarratives (meta récits) that have served to legitimize knowledge in the past. The first is mythical and the second is projective or modern. The former explains origins while the latter manifests a finalistic vision of universal history (i.e. Christianity, Enlightenment progress through knowledge, Marxism, Capitalism). In postmodern society, in postmodern culture, Lyotard asserts that the grand narrative has lost its credibility.

In many ways, science's confrontations with epistemological problems are at the forefront of the "crisis" of postmodernity. Lyotard underscores the crisis of knowledge when he contends in regard to science:

> Postmodern science—by concerning itself with such things as undecidables, the limits of precise control, conflicts characterized by incomplete information, 'fracta,' catastrophes and pragmatic paradoxes—is theorizing its own evolution as discontinuous, catastrophic, nonrectifiable and paradoxical. It is changing the meaning of the word knowledge while expressing how such a change can take place. (Lyotard 1984, 60)

Many scientists have acknowledged the limitations of their knowledge. As Norman Holland has asserted, non- scientists often assume that science is numerical, objective, rigorously confirmed, verifiable, and unmarred by the subjectivity of human emotions. However, the Fudge Factor and Murphy's Law are very much a part of their world (Holland 1985, 288–90). Max Planck stated that it is the passing of a generation rather than deep and compelling insight that engenders changes in scientific visions: "A scientific truth does not triumph by convincing its opponents and making them see the light, but rather because its opponents eventually die, and a new generation grows up that is familiar with it" (Holland 1985, 288–89).

Lay people assume, also, that science possesses a broad consensus. However, Nobel Laureate Percy Bridgman wrote:

> I believe that in society as at present constituted the possibility of consensus, except with respect to the simplest situations and as a first approximation, is a mirage. There is no such thing as true consensus, and any ostensible reality supposed to be revealed by the consensus does not exist. (Holland 1985, 289)

Postmodernists argue that science rests on personal, subjective elements. Evidence depends on the senses, and the perceptions of the senses change with the perceiver.

While the postmodern condition may reflect a crisis in the foundations of our knowledge, it does not necessarily eliminate knowledge. That knowledge still exists. Linda Hutcheon asserts that the postmodern represents change, but it is not a new paradigm (Hutcheon 1993, 247). In his article, "From the One to the Many: Pluralism in Today's Thought," Matei Calinescu argues that positive knowledge is still possible within philosophical pluralism (1991, 156–74). However, the postmodern offers a more honest assertion of the foundations of our knowledge.

For the postmodernist, what we call "knowledge" is our own creation. We are creators of worlds, of contexts, of fictions, and within those worlds we create criteria to confirm or deny that knowledge. Knowledge exists within those worlds. We set up standards and systems to verify it. It does not have a certain, transcendental foundation. If those transcendental truths, ideals, or values exist, we will never define them with certainty. When a theory or explanation stops working for us, we search for and create a new one, a new fiction, a new paradigm. It is not the invisible hand of Capitalism that will bring us utopian redemption, nor the Force of History as defined by Marxism, nor the singular objectivity of Science, nor the faith in Reason and progress, nor the end of time of Christianity. Postmodern culture does not destroy or totally reject "truth value," but simply redefines it as systems that we construct to meet our needs.

People who lament that the postmodern destroys meaning really mean that it challenges our narratives of knowledge. The humanistic principles are still operable but, for many, they are no longer seen as eternal and unchallengeable (Hutcheon 1993, 247). Postmodernity is about epistemology, about how we know what we know. It simply says we should be honest about the sources of our knowledge and our ability to accurately define concepts such as Truth, God, male and female roles, etc. In itself, the postmodern is not totally relativistic nor is it nihilistic.

This emphasis on epistemology is probably the most widely agreed upon characteristic for defining postmodern culture. The sense of indefinability, of disunity, of the breakup of center, and the repudiation of a totality or a utopia are central characteristics relating to epistemology.

PHILOSOPHICAL PLURALISM AND THE POSTMODERN

Borges's employment of the labyrinth as a defining symbol in his work and his discussion of the dichotomy between order and chaos that is inherent to the symbol resonates through many aspects of the postmodern debate. The postmodern represents a tilt away from modernist, monistic, utopian visions and toward philosophical and cultural pluralism. While modernism acknowledged the explosion of knowledge, the development and branching of different disciplines, and the pluralistic tendencies within the culture, it found them generally threatening. It viewed these as fragmentary and divisive tendencies, and often sought a monistic vision to recreate the lost unity. In contrast, postmodernity has defined the world as pluralistic. We are creators of worlds, of systems, of fictions, and we live with those fictions in those diverse worlds. Borges's story, "El Congreso" (The Congress), from *El libro de arena* (*The Book of Sand*), symbolizes some of the failures of monism and suggests the inevitability of pluralism. The references to monistic attitudes and past visions abound in the story. The president of the Congress, Alejandro Glencoe, seeks to create a political body to represent and thus unify the diversity of the world. As the narrator, Alejandro Ferri, discovers when he visits his ranch, Glencoe is autocratic in nature. Both their first names suggest a link to Alexander. The narrator is attracted to and wants to marry a woman named "Beatrice," suggesting the monistic vision of Dante. Glencoe's library contains the volumes of Carlyle. He preaches the Bible to his gaucho ranch hands who do not

understand it. Ultimately Alejandro Glencoe dissolves the Congress
and burns books. He has decided that the Congress is the world,
that it is impossible to restrain and homogenize the diversity of the
world.

The emphasis on the plurality of the world has produced competing pluralistic visions. There are two key contending postmodern
positions in the present literature.[1] One tends to affirm the possibility of positive knowledge, while the other tends toward absolute relativism and celebrates chaos. In this sense, they parallel Borges's
representation of the labyrinth as a symbol of order and contrasting
with a representation of the universe as chaotic. Hans Bertens expresses it as follows:

> . . . We can locate two major modes within Postmodernist literature in
> the criticism that I have reviewed here: one mode that has given up refer-
> entiality and meaning, and another that still seeks to be referential and
> sometimes even tries to establish local, temporal and provisional truths.
> (Bertens 1986, 65)

In regard to the mode that affirms some provisional truths, it affirms pluralism, but it argues that pluralism has limits and that certain small truths are possible. Those proponents, who include some
of the leading figures who have theorized the concept of the postmodern, assert that truth, history, objectivity, and art, are virtually
impossible to define singularly. We are limited by our psychological
makeup, our cultural and historical moment, and our individual
subjectivity. Truth is like the center of a wheel with an infinite number of spokes approaching it but never exhausting it. Yet, we still
may be able to define some positive knowledge and values. Ihab Hassan discusses how indeterminacy leads to fragmentation. He also
argues that a certain "immanence" exists that tends toward unification, but in a nonreligious sense. Examples of this tendency include
the image of the world as a "global village" and the movement
toward globalization and economic consolidation. Hassan emphasizes the importance of defining values or finding a place for the
spirit in his references to William James and Ralph Waldo Emerson
(Hassan 1987b). Lyotard discusses "petite histoires." While truth
may very well exist beyond us, we are limited in what we can ultimately know of it with certainty. "Reality" is not objective, but rather
is composed of various and competing representations. Calinescu
suggests that this pluralistic shift ultimately may permit new dia-

logues on puzzling cultural issues and among the sciences, the arts, and other disciplines (Calinescu 1991, 172–73). As is clear from the discussion above, I believe that Borges's vision and perspective on most postmodernist issues correspond closely with this mode that sees positive knowledge as possible.

The second facet includes those who reject all referentiality and meaning. These are what I would call the radical relativists or absolute relativists. The most controversial are the poststructuralists, Barthes, Derrida, Foucault, et al. Their initial writings predated the wide-spread acceptance of the term and the concept of the postmodern, and they tend not to use the term, but they are usually included, because as cultural critics, their texts have mapped out some of these changes and dealt with many of the same issues. However, Andreas Huyssen wrote a widely disseminated article that cogently argues that poststructuralists are not postmodernists, but rather, represent the last breath of modernism.[2] Matei Calinescu takes issue with deconstructionist tendencies, which he characterizes as monistic rather than pluralistic in their negation and radical agnosticism (Calinescu 1991, 162–63). He links Derrida and other imitators to modernism, and contends that deconstructionism is a "negative monism" or a "monism of absence." He asserts that they create a unity or totality that challenges totalities, and that they negate and subvert the One without affirming the Many (Calinescu 1991, 163–64) Linda Hutcheon also argues that the "non-mimetic, ultra-autonomous, anti-referentialist" tendencies are not postmodernist (Hutcheon 1988, 51–52).

As a culture, we have entered an era that is different from the Modern period. It is marked by a crisis of epistemology. The monistic pillars that previously supported our sense of meaning and understanding of the world: Reason, Science, Marxism, Christianity, Capitalism, have come under sharp criticism. An undecidability permeates many aspects of our intellectual and artistic landscapes. The theoretical orientation has shifted from monistic to pluralistic models. The tendency in literature has been to question the nature of reality and of the literary work of art. That is exactly what Jorge Luis Borges has done. In reintroducing the labyrinth, the dream and other qualities of idealism, the mirror image, the fantastic, and the exotic into contemporary literature, he has established a new set of metaphors and symbols for capturing the pluralism, the uncertainties, and the indeterminacies of the world. He has helped alter the structure of the literary work and the traditional vision of the artist.

Yet, while pluralism, ambiguity, and diversity figure centrally in his writing, his intellectual stance avoids affirming an absolute and radical relativity. Rather, it assumes the stance of the skeptic and argues for being aware of the limits of what we can know and being cognizant of the sources of our knowledge. The prevalence of these new metaphors, visions, and forms underscores that he is one of the first of the postmodernists, or one of the principal precursors of postmodern literature. This mark is quite evident, as well, in the postmodern concept of the self.

4
Borges, the Self, and the Postmodern

RECENTLY, THE SELF AND ITS NATURE HAVE BECOME THE CENTER OF CRITI-cal attention. Writers and critics have questioned whether a single, essential subject exists and whether that subject is a unified whole. The issue has diverse implications for our understandings and definitions of ourselves, for the portrayal of character in literature, for the study of the social sciences, and for many aspects of our lives. Postmodern writers and critics have argued for the uncertainty of knowledge and the indeterminacy of the universe. Much of the discussion of the self derives from the extension of this postmodernist discussion. A study of some of Borges's short stories, essays, and poems underscores his centrality in this debate on the self and provides insights into Borges's writings as well.

POSTMODERNISM AND THE SELF

Poets, philosophers, writers, and artists have questioned the nature of the self for some time. During the last 150 years, the thinking and writing of Freud, Marx, Joyce, Faulkner, Dostoevsky, Eliot, Kierkegaard, and Kafka, among others, have profoundly affected our conception of the traditional self and our understanding of the subject as an entity. Such challenges to the self are not new. They have occurred during much of Western literary and intellectual history. What is different are the many and varied claims that the self does not exist. Particularly today, one hears a lot about the self as a fiction, as nonexistent, as surface, as a series of masks. The issues have important implications for feminism and gender studies, which I will discuss in chapter 5, as well as for postmodern culture's attempt to redefine reality. As Enrico Garzilli asserts, to question what the real "I" is, in effect, is to ask: what is real? (Garzilli 1972, 6).

The traditional self has come under attack from many fronts, but not all challenges argue for totally eliminating our concept of the self. While a fluid and indefinable self may permit more equality between the races and sexes, its total elimination creates legal problems relating to individual responsibility and identity problems for both groups and individuals. This lack of an identity and agency makes social and political action and change theoretically quite difficult, as a number of feminist critics have contended. In regard to the questioning of the nature of the self, Linda Hutcheon distinguishes between modern and postmodern attitudes toward the self:

> The challenges to the humanist concept of a coherent, continuous, autonomous individual (who paradoxically also shares in some generalized universal human essence) have come from all sides today: from poststructuralist philosophical and literary theory, Marxist political philosophy, Freudian/Lacanian psychoanalysis, sociology, and many other domains . . . Where modernism investigated the grounding of experience in the self, its focus was on the self seeking integration amid fragmentation. In other words, its (for many, defining) focus on subjectivity was still within the dominant humanist framework, though the obsessive search for wholeness itself suggests the beginnings of what would be a more radical postmodern questioning, a challenging brought about by the doubleness of postmodern discourse. In other words, postmodernism works both to underline and to undermine the notion of the coherent self-sufficient subject as the source of meaning or action. (Hutcheon 1989, 108–9)

Hutcheon underscores that, in her view, the postmodern problematizes the nature of the self rather than calls for its elimination. This suggests an indeterminate subject that permits multiple definitions. A number of other critics have sought to define a similar self.

Normand Holland, for one, defines a subject that bridges that gap between the traditional self and a totally non- existent self. In his book, *The I,* he brings together psychoanalytic, literary, and postmodern theory. He acknowledges that all ways of construing the world may be fictions, human inventions, but asserts that one fiction is not as good as another, that not all fictions are equal. He draws on the work of Heinz Lichtenstein and argues for a concept of "theme and variations" that runs through identity questions. Lichtenstein (and Holland) distinguish between "primary identity" and "identity theme." Primary identity is a style, a way of being, that is in a person. "Created in the earliest relationship between baby and its first caretaker, it is a way of being that is in, even is, that person" (Holland

1985, 144). However, it is formed before words and can never be "known" in that sense.

Identity theme involves the interaction of the "I" with literature, culture, politics, society, people, even ourselves, and others. The assumption is that we are constantly doing something new, but in the same style that we have done things previously. Holland states:

> This theme and variations concept of identity decenters the individual in a distinctly Postmodern, metafictional way. You are ficted, and I am ficted, like characters in a Postmodern novel. The most personal, central thing I have, my identity is not in me, but in your interaction with me or in a divided me. (Holland 1983, 304–5)

Holland's definition of subjectivity allows for a self that seeks and attains fulfillment, awareness, and self-realization through its interaction with cultural or ethnic, religious, communal, or group identities.

Critics who have taken issue with the dismantling of the self often seem to defend it, using certain precepts of Borges as well. Robert Young suggests that the undermining of the self was a foolish act by the postmodernists, one that derives from a pessimism of the will. Referring to Richard Rorty, he argues that narrative is the basis of reality, and that we live in a world of stories layered upon stories (Young 1989, 71). He contends that "the self is an imputed concept, but so are subjectivity, totality, fragmentation, Kantian schematia, socialism, and for that matter the external world—fragment or coherent" (Young 1989, 76). One need only recall Borges's belief that all systems are fictions, and his affinity for idealism and acceptance of reality as emanating from a dream to make the connection. Ihab Hassan, a defender of redefining of the self from a pluralistic theoretical perspective, states: "The self may rest on no ontological rock; yet as a functional concept, as a historical construct, as a habit of existence, above all, as an experienced or existential reality, it serves us all even if we deny it theoretically" (1988, 422). While Borges may not agree totally with that comment, he acknowledges a similar inevitability of the subject in "Nueva refutación del tiempo" (New Refutation of Time) (1944–47), in the poem, "El otro tigre" (The Other Tiger) (1960), and in certain references to the relationship between love and the self, as I shall point out later in this chapter.

Borges's preoccupation with the nature of the self derives from the realization that one can never really understand the universe if one does not understand oneself. As the above examples suggest, Borges perceives the self as he does the universe: as an indecipherable labyrinth. It is a dream image, a fiction. Postmodern literature and literary theory follow his lead in this regard. Peter Currie (1987) offers two explanations for the undoing of the self in postmodern fiction: (1) It is the result of the dehumanization in society, the subordination of the individual to the commercial and the growth of mass culture; and (2) It reinstates the role of the individual by attacking the ideology of abstract individualism. A third reason might have to do with the link between the traditional self and sexist and racist attitudes that that definition of the self has helped perpetuate. Borges's purposes seem closer to the second explanation and perhaps the third. The major thrust of his writings on the subject emphasizes the faces, shadows, and ambiguities that compose what we call the self. He rejects a search for a recovery of its lost unity. In fact, he suggests that that unity exists in a pantheistic relationship with the world around us. He calls for a rethinking of our nature and our capabilities.

Borges and the Indefinable Self and Pantheism

Borges has certainly helped to define the parameters of this debate over subjectivity. His essays and stories repeatedly project two different, and in some ways, contradictory images about the subject, one suggesting binary oppositions, but at the core, a fluid, indefinable self, and the other implying a pantheistic unity. Some critics and some of his successors have focused on the fluid and indefinable nature of subjectivity, and have overlooked or ignored the inevitability and the pantheistic unity he suggests. To understand how Borges views the self, we once again return to the image of the labyrinth that Borges employs as a metaphor for the universe and the world. It represents the ultimate incomprehensibility of existence. Stories such as "La biblioteca de Babel" (The Library of Babel), "La lotería en Babilonia" (The Babylonian Lottery), and "Tlön Uqbar, Orbis Tertius," underscore the ultimate limits of man's reason and understanding. His representation of the self and of human personality figures centrally in this message. The labyrinth serves not only as a metaphor for the world, but also as a maze that challenges man's uniqueness (Garzilli 1972, 105). Form and content are one in his stories. The content suggests that the universe and man are a maze in which personal identities are elusive, and the form reaffirms this. Storytellers are both hunters and hunted, creators and created.

The exchange of roles suggests the myth of the Minotaur and the labyrinth. Borges plays on this exchange of roles between hunter and hunted, between victim of the labyrinth and maker of the labyrinth, between the Minotaur and Theseus, in portraying human personality. We are both slayer and slain, lover and monster. Similarly, the interchange between wizard and son in "Las ruinas circulares" (The Circular Ruins) (1941), between murderer and victim in the stories "La espera" (The Wait) (1949), and in "Abenjacán el Bojarí, muerto en su laberinto" (Ibn-Hakam al-Bokhari, Murdered in His Labyrinth) (1949), between narrator and antagonist in "La forma de la espada" (The Form of the Sword) (1942), is the key to human personality or sense of self. Human personality is composed of its characteristics and its opposite. Hero becomes coward, and creator becomes created. Yet the labyrinth remains. It allows for shifting identities. Man's / woman's need to create fictions and labyrinths is more real than a personality, and thus the maze subsumes it (Garzilli 1972, 89–92, 100–106).

These oppositional characters figure in a number of key stories, and imply that the self is not hard and fixed, but rather provisional and fictional. In "La muerte y la brújula" (Death and the Compass) (1942), Lönnrot and Scharlach are detective and criminal, pursuing each other through time. Their similarities, marked by the plays on the word "red" in their names and their rational tendencies, are as marked as their differences. Similarly, in "El jardín de senderos que se bifurcan" (The Garden of the Forking Paths) (1941), oppositions exist between pursuer and pursued, Richard Madden and Yu Tsun, and between Yu Tsun and Stephen Albert. In "Tema del traidor y del héroe" (Theme of the Traitor and the Hero) (1944), Fergus Kilpatrick is both hero and traitor, as not only the nature of the self, but also, of truth and of history becomes ambiguous. In "El duelo" (The duel) from El informe de Brodie, (Dr. Brodie's Report) (1970), Clara Glencairn and Marta Pizarro play off against each other in defining different literary movements. In "Los teólogos" (The Theologians) (1949), Aureliano and Juan de Panonia assume oppositional roles in attempting to define the nature of time. They find their belief systems shifting along with their identities. In "El Sur" (The South) (1944), which I will discuss and analyze in more detail in chapter 8, Juan Dahlmann creates and confronts his own double while lying on his deathbed. Dahlmann's decision to die in a duel

on the plains rather than in a hospital underscores that we create
our fictional worlds, and implies that the self contains its opposite
and is determined by what we imagine it to be.

In discussing postmodern characterization, Hans Bertens states
that motivation, causality, and consistency govern the actions of the
traditional, realistic character (Bertens 1987, 143–45). Although
Dahlmann certainly exhibits a changing self, motivation and causality are offered for his actions through his family lineage and his two
very different grandfathers. Thus, from that perspective, he does not
seem to be a totally "postmodern" character.

En *El libro de arena*, (*The Book of Sand*) (1975), Borges raises yet
another aspect of the oppositional self in the story, "El otro" (The
Other). This prose piece relates an encounter between the younger
and the older Borges. Space and time are superseded, as the narrator, Borges, in 1969, in Cambridge, Massachusetts, sits on a bench
next to the Borges of 1918, who is in Geneva, Switzerland. The story
questions how a unitary self can exist when an individual grows and
changes over time. To convince the younger Borges that he is talking to his elder self, the narrator refers to secrets relating to his sexuality: a hidden book about the sexual practices in the Balkans, an
evening on a certain second floor in Place Dufour. These allusions
not only call attention to the secretive aspects of sexual experience,
but also suggest that sexual awareness and maturity change the self.
Had the young Borges not yet experienced sexuality, the differences
between him and the elder Borges might have been even greater.

Nevertheless, profound differences do exist between the two.
While the younger Borges celebrates the brotherhood/sisterhood
of humanity and feels obligated to address the oppressed and alienated masses as Borges did in his early poetry, the elder calls these
notions abstractions and states that, if anyone exists, he/she is only
an individual, not part of a mass. While the younger Borges has accepted the role of social forces in the definition of the self, the elder
Borges has rejected this as rather meaningless. Then the elder
Borges questions how the self could be one through time when he
quotes "algún griego" [some Greek] who remarked that "El hombre de ayer no es el hombre de hoy. Nosotros dos, en este banco
de Ginebra o de Cambridge, somos tal vez la prueba" (1989a, 14).[1]
[*Yesterday's man is not today's,* as some Greek said. We two, here, on
this bench in Geneva or in Cambridge, are perhaps the proof of
that] (1998, 414). The story underscores how the traditional concept of the self does not allow for growth, development, and change.

The elder Borges, who is the narrator, elaborates on this difficulty when the two disagree in their discussion of Whitman. Their disagreement over Whitman is appropriate, as he defined a literary self in "Song of Myself" that was pantheistic in nature and sought to speak for the nation. He concludes that a half century has made it impossible for the two to understand each other, yet acknowledges the fascinating dilemma of the self, that it changes, yet does not change through time: "Éramos demasiado distintos y demasiado parecidos" (1989a, 15). [We were too different, yet too alike] (1998 416). But shortly thereafter, he seems to reverse himself when he thinks: "No hemos cambiado nada, pensé" (1989a, 16). [We haven't changed a bit, I thought] (1998, 416). Borges affirms here that the self is a labyrinthine conundrum that both changes through time and remains the same.

In all of these references, Borges suggests that we perceive that our "self" is unitary and definitive through such oppositions. They provide a touchstone, a contrasting element to make it seem whole. Yet, as many of Borges's characters discover, those oppositions are simply two sides of the same coin. We are those oppositions that we consider "other."

Borges draws on certain pantheistic conceptions in developing this notion of the self, as well. Our "selves," to the extent that they exist, are a part of a larger, unified being or self, or the dream of such a being. This conception of the "self" or of "personality" finds expression in *Otras inquisiciones* (*Other Inquisitions*) (1952) and in other essays, in his poetry, as well as in his short stories. In an early essay, "La nadería de la personalidad" (The Nothingness of Personality) (1922), he states several times that there is no whole self and that the self does not exist. He later rejected the prose from this period, but still considered this one of his first fully realized essays. The same theme runs through his works repeatedly in his life, although he seems more direct, assertive, and certain about it in that early piece than in later writings.

In the selection, "Magias parciales del *Quijote*" (Partial Enchantments of the *Quixote*), he underscores the pantheistic, idealistic, fictional nature of the self. As cited in the previous chapter, Borges asks rhetorically why the scenes in *Hamlet* and the *Quijote*, where the characters see themselves as characters in a novel or play, make us uneasy. He then answers that it implies that we are fictions as well.

Similarly, in "Las ruinas circulares" (The Circular Ruins), a wizard dreams his son or double into existence, only to discover that he, too, is an apparition, a figment that someone else is dreaming. The story implies, as do Schopenhauer and Hume, that what we sense as an essential self is nothing more than a dream image. Furthermore, it suggests the Kabbalah, and the notion that God dreams the world, and that we are dream images of a Creator.

Throughout his writings, he highlights how a number of different authors have expressed or manifested similar notions of the self. In his essay from *Discusión*, "Nota sobre Walt Whitman" (Note on Walt Whitman) (1932), Borges contends that Whitman creates a similar pantheistic effect, not in identifying a divinity, but in identifying with all of mankind. In his essay on Nathaniel Hawthorne, Borges suggests that the American novelist believed in the fluid, pantheistic nature of the self: "también se nota en los bosquejos que he señalado, que propendía a la noción panteísta de que un hombre es los otros, de que un hombre es todos los hombres" (1974, 674). [And in the sketches that I have mentioned we observe that he leaned toward the pantheistic notion that one man is the others, that one man is all men] (1981, 221). This universalizes his portrayal of the self. It implies that the divide between self and other, between subject and object, has disappeared, and that we are the best and the worst of which man/woman is capable.

Borges wrote a poem on Robert Browning's discovery of his poetic voice, and his decision to become a poet where this pantheistic vision of the self appears to be the poetic self. The poetic voice of the poem, which is fictionalized as Browning's, in "Browning resuelve ser poeta," (Browning Resolves to Be a Poet), sets certain goals for his poetic vision. They include reaching out and identifying with others pantheistically, much as Whitman did. He will only half achieve a sense of identify, and then will forget himself. Instead, he will see the world as Judas in accepting the destiny of traitor, and like Caliban, and others:

> Viviré de olvidarme,
> Seré la cara que entreveo y que olvido,
> seré Judas que acepta
> la divina misión de ser traidor,
> seré Calibán en la ciénaga . . .
> [I will live by forgetting myself,
> I will be the face I half-see and forget,
> I will be Judas who accepts
> the blessed destiny of being a traitor,
> I will be Caliban in the swamp . . .]

(1999b, 350–51)

He will weave his fate with those who wear masks, suffer agonies and resurrections:

> Máscaras, agonías, resurrecciones,
> destejerán y tejerán mi suerte
> y alguna vez seré Robert Browning.

> [Agonies, masks and resurrections
> will weave and unweave my fate,
> and at some point, I will be Robert Browning.]

(1999b, 350–51)

Borges's Browning succeeds in defining himself as a poet by identifying with, and in some sense, becoming others.

The prose selection "Everything and Nothing" in *El hacedor* helps further define Borges's pantheistic vision of the self and especially the poetic self as a Godlike dreamer of his creations. In this piece, Borges imagines Shakespeare struggling with the unreality of the self. The narrator opens the parable by asserting that Shakespeare did not sense himself within himself. Behind his copious, fantastic, and agitated words there was just a little coldness, an undreamt dream. These opening lines capture the sense of emptiness, of a shifting center, of an indefinable core, and at the same time an individuality represented by a unique appearance and emanating from a personal dream. Shakespeare attempts to overcome this vacuum, first by sharing his feeling with a companion who eyes him strangely, later through love with Anne Hathaway, and still later, through his acting and writing of dramas. In his diverse role-playing, "Nadie fue tantos hombres como aquel hombre, que a semejanza del egipcio Proteo pudo agotar todas las apariencias del ser" (1974, 803). [No one has ever been so many men as this man, who like the Egyptian Proteus could exhaust all the guises of reality] (1962, 249). Some of the characters that he creates reveal this fluid, shifting self. Ricardo admits that he plays the part of many people in being himself. Iago states that he is not who he is. The narrator relates that this quest for a unified sense of individual being continues until Shakespeare's death. At that moment, he finds himself in God's presence and expresses his desire to be himself. The voice of God answers him: "Yo tampoco soy; yo soñé el mundo como tú soñaste tu obra, mi Shakespeare, y entre las formas de mi sueño estás tú, que como yo eres muchos y nadie" (1974, 804). [Neither am I anyone; I have dreamt the world as you dreamt your work, my Shakespeare, and among the

forms in my dream are you, who like myself are many and no one]
(1962, 249).

This narrative highlights several key points. It illustrates the pantheistic and idealistic tendencies of Borges. We are dream images of
a Creator much as literary characters are images of the imagination.
God also is portrayed as an emptiness without a definable Self. Once
again, this selection links Borges to the writings of the Kabbalah.
Salomón Lévy states in this regard, "The idea of God conceived as
Nothingness is fundamental to the doctrines of the Kabbalah" (Lévy
1976, 158). To be nothing is to be pantheistic, to be linked to one.

This story draws a connection between the role of the creative artist and that of the Creator. Borges's concept of pantheism seems to
draw heavily on this Kabbalistic image of some sort of God dreaming
the world. It allows for an integration of his pantheism and idealism,
of the One and the Many, and of the binary oppositions around
which the self revolves. Yet, this image seems to conflict with the agnosticism that Borges has professed at various times. In an interview,
Borges admits that his concept of God is neither traditional nor an-
thropomorphic, but closer to a sort of ethical force in the universe
(see chapter 9). One can assume that this pantheistic, larger self is
part of such a force. Furthermore, in affirming that Shakespeare,
the symbol and spirit of Western culture, actually believed in an indefinable, pantheistic, pluralistic self, he implies that this notion of
subjectivity is as much a part of the foundation and thinking of our
culture as the unitary, readily definable self, which has been traditionally associated with the West.

This pantheistic sense of self is linked to his conception of immortality as well. Immortality is a theme that runs throughout his works.
It figures in his expression of idealism and the concepts of time and
history as well as in his concept of the self. Immortality links to the
fantastic or magical, because it challenges our understanding of the
physical laws and the material world. It touches tangentially on
many stories. The spirits of the gauchos that live on through their
weapons such as in "El encuentro," (The Encounter), or "Juan
Muraña" from *El informe de Brodie (Brodie's Report)* (1970) are but two
examples. Borges delivered a lecture, "La inmortalidad" (Immortality), on June 5, 1978 at the University of Belgrano in Buenos Aires
(Borges 1999a, 546). In the lecture, he surveys differing perspectives
on the issue. He asserts that the language we use is the same that
others have used, and that language lives on in us. When we speak
or write it, in some sense we become the dead ancestors who used

it. When we repeat a verse from Dante or Shakespeare, we become Dante or Shakespeare, for a brief moment. He concludes by stating that he believes in immortality in a general or cosmic sense, but not in a personal one (1979b, or 1996, 172–79).

The story, "El inmortal" (The Immortal), focuses on the issue and many of its ramifications. As Ronald Christ has pointed out in his perceptive analysis of the themes and allusions of the piece, the epigraph to the story has four authors, Plato, Solomon, Bacon, and Borges, all affirming the Eternal Return in an intellectual or mental sense (Christ 1986, 49–50). Homer is the immortal, the Wandering Jew, everyone and nobody. The narrative voice shifts subtly between the "we" ("ofrecemos" [we offer]) and the I ("Que yo recuerde" [As I recall]) at the beginning as well as at different points throughout the story (Christ 1986, 51). Man / woman is immortal, like the universe. While the story's title is singular, Homer is the universal author (Christ 1986, 49–55). The self is, pantheistically, the One and the Many; it is everything and nothing; it is Shakespeare (or Homer) dreaming his world, and God dreaming Shakespeare.

Borges also turns his search, investigation, and analysis of the self directly on himself in his parable / poem, "Borges y yo" (Borges and I). In the piece, he focuses on binary oppositions of his being and in particular, on a division between a public self and a private self. The "yo" turns inward and is pensive, while "Borges" turns toward the outside world and is more dramatic. While the "yo" strolls slowly and examines things thoughtfully, "Borges" finds his name on a roster of professors or in a biographical dictionary. The poem is written from the perspective of the "yo" voice. It has certain tastes and preferences, and states that Borges, the public face, does also, "de un modo vanidoso que las convierte en atributos de un actor" [but his vanity transforms them into theatrical props] (1999b, 92–93). In a comic twist, he suggests that he is not sure from which self the poetic inclination derives when he states: "No sé cuál de los dos escribe esta página" [I don't know which of us wrote this] (1999b, 92–93).

Three short poems from La rosa profunda (The Unending Rose) (1975), take up this issue of the self from different points of view: "Al espejo" (To the Mirror), "Soy" (I am), and "Un ciego" (A Blind Man). All of them are fourteen line sonnets with a rhyme scheme of "abba," the last two lines being "aa." In all of them, also, the emphasis shifts away from the pantheistic unity that he often suggests, toward the frustration of not knowing. His poem to the mirror was first published in *El oro de los tigres* (*The Gold of the Tigers*) (1972). He portrays the mirror as both obsessive and persistent and as a "misterioso hermano" [mysterious brother], for its incessant duplication. Being blind compounds the horror in knowing that he is being duplicated. Not even death offers relief, for the multiplication of the self will continue. In this poem, he expresses the haunting feeling that mirrors and an unstable subjectivity bring to him.

The other two poems are more positive. The poem "Soy" (I Am), also captures the narrator's search for the self and for meaning. The reflection in the mirror here is again referred to as a brother. He questions certain theological notions about revenge and pardon when he asserts that he knows that there is none other than oblivion. Much like the narrator of "La biblioteca de Babel" (The Library of Babel), this voice has not been able to decipher the labyrinth of existence:

> Soy el que pese a tan ilustres modos
> De errar, no ha descifrado el laberinto
> Singular y plural, arduo y distinto,
> Del tiempo, que es de uno y es de todos.
>
> [Despite my many wondrous wanderings,
> I am the one who never has unraveled
> the labyrinth of time, singular, plural
> grueling, strange, one's own and everyone's.]
>
> (1999b, 356–57)

Our limitations and inability to know are highlighted here. He then focuses on the nature of his self and states: "Soy el que es nadie, el que no fue una espada / En la guerra. Soy eco, olvido, nada." [I am no one. I did not wield a sword / in battle. I am echo, emptiness, nothing] (1999b, 356–57) Here, the narrator picks up on the theme from "Everything and Nothing." The pantheistic suggestion is that in nothingness is oneness, but the poem stops short of actually affirming that.

"Un ciego" (A Blind Man), functions both as an expression of his personal blindness and as a metaphor for the impossibility of knowing the self. Again, the mirror comes into play in the duplication. The blind narrator is looking at himself in the mirror. He asserts that he does not know what face is looking back at him. This blind man is all of us trying to comprehend who and what we are. He slowly explores the invisible characteristics of his face, which he cannot really see. There is a suggestion that love gives him some insight when a flash of light allows him to see the ash and golden hair of another person. He takes some comfort in a comment by Milton about only losing the inconsequential surface of things. But his thoughts turn to letters and roses, and the loss of sight seems more dramatic. The poem closes with a wish to know what the self is: "Pienso que si pudiera ver mi cara / Sabría quién soy en esta tarde rara" [I think, too, that if I could see my features, / I would know who I am, this precious afternoon] (1999b, 356–57). The ending expresses an unquenchable thirst to know but does not despair. The expression, "esta tarde rara" [this precious afternoon] suggests a sense of wonder before the world.

The Argentinian author expands, elaborates, and limits his concept of the self in some short stories as well and suggests a resolution to the conflict between the binary opposition and his pantheistic vision. In "La forma de la espada" (The Form of the Sword), the sword of the title serves as symbol of the double-edged self. Yet here, form and content flow together, first person and third person focalizations merge, and self and other become one when el Inglés reveals that he is the coward and traitor, John Vincent Moon. The narrator of this tale within a tale, el Inglés, asserts:

> Me abochornaba ese hombre con miedo, como si yo fuera el cobarde, no Vincent Moon. Lo que hace un hombre es como si lo hicieran todos los hombres. Por eso no es injusto que una desobediencia en un jardín contamine al género humano; por eso no es injusto que la crucifixión de un solo judío baste para salvarlo. Acaso Schopenhauer tiene razón; yo soy los otros, cualquier hombre es todos los hombres, Shakespeare es de algún modo el miserable John Vincent Moon. (1974, 493–94)

> [This frightened man mortified me, as if I were the coward, not Vincent Moon. Whatever one man does, it is as if all men did it. For that reason it is not unfair that one disobedience in a garden should contaminate all humanity; for that reason it is not unjust that the crucifixion of a single Jew should be sufficient to save it. Perhaps Schopenhauer was right: I am all other men, any man is all men, Shakespeare is in some manner the miserable John Vincent Moon.] (1962, 70)

These lines highlight the conscious universal tendency of Borges's vision. He has projected a sense of subject in which we all are capable of the best and worst of human beings. It is a pantheistic vision in which we all are communally intertwined in each other's fate. It sidesteps the conflict between the individual and the universal that accompanies the traditional notion of the self. It creates a sense of understanding for and identification with others that sometimes was lacking in traditional conceptions of the self.

In the story, "La escritura del Dios" (The God's Script), the relationship between Borges's pantheistic vision and the binary self becomes even clearer. Tzinacán, the last of the Mayan Indian magicians, has been imprisoned and is awaiting death. He remembers that his god had devised a magical, secret statement for a time such as this that would ward off these evil conditions. He searches and finds it in the spots of the jaguar that is encaged next to him. It permits him to see the eternal. In its complexity and unity in diversity, it has certain overtones of the experience of Ezekiel. It is worth looking at this passage in some detail to see how it relates to the sense of self. The image is that of a wheel that contains all things and all places within it:

Esa Rueda estaba hecha de agua, pero también de fuego, y era (aunque se veía el borde) infinita. Entretejidas, la formaban todas las cosas que serán, que son, y que fueron, y yo era una de las hebras de esa trama total, y Pedro de Alvarado, que me dio tormento, era otra. Ahí estaban las causas y los efectos y me bastaba ver esa Rueda para entenderlo todo, sin fin. ¡Oh dicha de entender, mayor que la de imaginar o la de sentir! Vi el universo y vi los íntimos designios del universo. Vi los orígenes que narra el Libro del Común. Vi las montañas que surgieron del agua, vi los primeros hombres de palo, vi las tinajas que se volvieron contra los hombres, vi los perros que les destrozaron las caras. Vi el dios sin cara que hay detrás de los dioses. Vi infinitos procesos que formaban una sola felicidad y entendiéndolo todo, alcancé también a entender la escritura del tigre. (1974, 598–99)

[That Wheel was made of water, but also of fire, and it was (although the edge could be seen) infinite. Interlinked, all things that are, were and shall be formed it, and I was one of the fibers of that total fabric and Pedro de Alvarado who tortured me was another. There lay revealed the causes and the effects, and it sufficed me to see that Wheel in order to understand it all, without end. Oh bliss of understanding, greater than the bliss of imagining or feeling! I saw the universe and I saw the intimate designs of the universe. I saw the origins narrated in the Book of the Common. I saw the mountains that rose out of the water, I saw the first men of wood, the cisterns that turned against the men, the dogs that ravaged their faces. I saw the faceless god concealed behind the other gods. I saw infinite processes that formed one single felicity and, understanding all, I was able also to understand the script of the tiger.] (1962, 172–73)

Through this experience, he discovers the fourteen words that would allow him to rule the universe. However, through the contact with the eternal, he has lost his individual sense of self. The paradoxical images of water and fire, of being limitless yet bounded, of interweaving his self with that of his tormentor, Pedro de Alvarado, imply that irresolvable paradoxes and the binary oppositions become part of a unified whole. They are part of the symmetry that suggests an order, but one that is beyond our abilities to explain or understand.

Tzinacán becomes aware that the eternity in which his god lives dissolves our individual oppositional selves and our everyday lives into meaningless details. The Aleph-like experience that he undergoes makes him lose all designs for power and makes him realize the trivial nature of man's existence, even if he is that man. Borges chooses as his voice a Native American with a belief system very different from the Judeo-Christian tradition to affirm a pluralistic theological stance. At the same time he expresses a concept that has broad implications for that Western tradition, that the traditional concept of the individual self is at odds with the nature of the divine.

THE NONEXISTENT SELF, LOVE, AND THE INEVITABLE SELF IN BORGES

One other opposition seems to exist in Borges's thinking and writings on the self: a tension between a sense of an inevitable self and a nonexistent self. While Borges lays the foundation for the postmodern undoing of the subject, he acknowledges a certain inevitability in the notion and steps back a bit from a total rejection of the concept. Although the self is a fiction, Borges implies that it must be reckoned with. Certain references and comments in stories and poems about intimacy, love and meaning, in the poem, "El otro tigre" (The Other Tiger) (1960) and the prose essay, "Nueva refutación del tiempo" (New Refutation of Time) (1944–47), all capture that sense of inevitability of the self.

Love, sexuality, and intimacy were infrequent themes in Borges's work. Garzilli's contention that to understand the self is to comprehend the universe and thus give meaning to life runs through this treatment of love. Traditionally, love has been defined as the union of two selves with the accompanying purpose and fulfillment for both. This is the definition to which I am addressing most of my comments. It is a definition that expects and demands a great deal of the love bond, but one which is quite pervasive in our culture. Some of his poetry displays confessional qualities and deals with this theme fairly directly. He approaches the topic indirectly in certain other stories as well, such as "El Zahir," (The Zahir) (1949), "El Aleph," (The Aleph) (1949), and "La casa de Asterión," (The House of Asterion) (1949), and depicts how the search for the self, the desire to understand the universe, and the discovery of love and happiness interrelate.

In the short story, "El Zahir" (The Zahir), love, personal meaning, and universal meaning find themselves inextricably intertwined. Borges, the narrator, cannot break his fixation on a coin, the Zahir. Borges's fascination and obsession with this coin begin immediately after the funeral of a woman he loved, Teodelina. To make the connection between the miniscule, the material, and the universal, the narrator quotes Tennyson, who says that if we could understand a flower, we could understand the world. The narrator interprets this as meaning that there is no fact that does not encompass universal history with its infinite causes and effects, and goes on to assert:

Tal vez quiso decir que el mundo visible se da entero en cada representación, de igual manera que la voluntad, según Schopenhauer, se da entera en cada sujeto. Los cabalistas entendieron que el hombre es un microcosmo, un simbólico espejo del universo; todo, según Tennyson, lo sería. Todo, hasta el intolerable Zahir. (1974, 594–95)

[Perhaps he was trying to say that the visible world can be seen entire in every image, just as Schopenhauer tells us that the Will expresses itself entire in every man and woman. The Kabbalists believed that a man is a microcosm, a symbolic mirror of the universe; if one were to believe Tennyson, *everything* would be—*everything*, even the unbearable Zahir.] (1998, 248)

The narrator closes the story by asserting "Quizá detrás de la moneda esté Dios" (1974, 595). [Perhaps behind the coin is God] (1998, 249). The Zahir symbolizes the divine, who is creator and integral part of an idealistic and dreamlike universe that consumes and subsumes everything. Thus, he links the desire for love with a thirst to comprehend the nature of the cosmos. To grasp it is to find meaning and give purpose to existence, to find the unity of the self.

Yet such a union seems impossible, at least in this world, as Teodelina, the focus of his love, has died, and he seems destined to self-dissolution because of his obsession with the Zahir, and with attaining that traditionally defined wholeness.

Returning to the short story, "La casa de Asterión" (The House of Asterion), Borges provides a further clarification of the self, the other, love, and fulfillment. In the story Theseus or Teseo succeeds in killing the Minotaur and escaping because his lover, Ariadne, provides him with a thread that leads him out of the labyrinth. Love defeats the monster, conquers the labyrinth, and thus gives purpose to life. To understand its full implications, however, one must read it both from the perspective of Teseo and Ariadna, and from that of the Minotaur. We are all this "pobre protagonista" [poor protagonist] as Borges refers to him in the epilogue to El Aleph (The Aleph). Self-deception, limited perception, delusions of grandeur, solitude, and loneliness mark his narrative. Like us, he longs for "el otro Asterión," the other, the lover and companion with whom he can share his world and who will make him complete. This desire for "the other" allows him to be deceived by Theseus.

The poem, "Adam Cast Forth," from El otro, el mismo (The Self and the Other) (1964), offers further insight into Borges's attitude toward love, the self, and the universe. In the poem, the narrator questions whether the Garden of Eden actually existed. He concludes that, although he himself might be largely excluded, that he is destined to live not in the garden, but on the earth, that garden does exist. Furthermore, he suggests that love and happiness are implicated in the symbol of the Garden and suggests that he has experienced it briefly: "Y, sin embargo, es mucho haber amado. / Haber sido feliz, haber tocado / El viviente Jardín, siquiera un día." [Nevertheless, it means much to have loved, / To have been happy, to have laid my hand on / The living Garden, even for one day] (1996, 232–33). This garden, this paradise, this union appear to have touched the narrator, but only fleetingly.

One may conclude from these references that the otherness that we seek, that love which will provide purpose and meaning to our lives and order and meaning to the world lies beyond our reach and may be really nothing more than death. Such a love is inextricably linked to the greater universe and the inner self, both of which ultimately prove impenetrable and indecipherable. However, such a conclusion does not do justice to Borges and does not account for Teseo's conquest of the Minotaur and the labyrinth with Ariadna's assistance. We are both the Minotaur and Teseo and Ariadna seeking to conquer it. Because of the self's fluid, indefinite nature, overcoming its labyrinth and finding that personal meaning, much like finding the meaning in the universe, proves to be an elusive, monumental task. However, the suggestion is that it is not impossible, and that love can give definition and meaning to the self and the world.

BORGES AND THE INESCAPABLE SELF

So the search for love interweaves with the search for the self. The poem, "El otro tigre," (The Other Tiger), elaborates on the search for the self and plays a sense of material existence off against the world as fictional dream impression. At the same time it treats the creative artist's relationship to her/his material. Also, it approaches the nature of the self from a somewhat different point of view. As dawn surrounds the narrator, he imagines a tiger, a symbol of the self, treading, stalking, moving purposefully through a nameless world. But as afternoon spreads over his soul, that is, in more enlightening and clarifying moments, or perhaps in his later years, he realizes that this tiger of symbols and shades is not the deadly tiger, but: "Una serie de tropos literarios / Y de memorias de la enciclopedia" [A set of literary images, / scraps remembered from encyclopedias] (1996, 116–17). Here, Borges acknowledges a material existence that differs from this dream-like image that he conceives in the first part of the poem. However, as he creates the circumstances through which this "real" tiger moves, he realizes that he intertwines his imagination with that reality and "Lo hace ficción del arte y no criatura / Viviente de las que andan por la tierra" [creates a fiction, not a living creature, / not one of those that prowl on the earth] (1996, 118–19). In the third verse, he is determined to search for a third tiger. He concedes that it will be a construction of language, and not of flesh and bones:

> Un tercer tigre buscaremos. Éste
> Será como los otros una forma
> De mi sueño, un sistema de palabras
> Humanas y no el tigre vertebrado
> Que, más allá de las mitologías
> Pisa la tierra. Bien lo sé, pero algo
> Me impone esta aventura indefinida,

Insensata y antigua, y persevero
En buscar por el tiempo de la tarde
El otro tigre, el que no está en el verso.

[Let us look for a third tiger. This one
will be like a form in my dream, like all the others,
a system, an arrangement of human language,
and not the flesh and bones tiger
that, out of reach of all mythologies,
paces the earth. I know all this; yet something
drives me to this ancient, perverse adventure,
foolish and vague, yet still I keep on looking
throughout the evening for the other tiger,
the other tiger, the one not in this poem.]

(1996, 118–19)

The poem speaks to the problems inherent in representation. One can not represent the world without the play of the imagination. As a symbol of the self, that tiger of flesh and blood represents an unambiguous inner core of being. At the same time, it is a metaphor for an objective reality and a definable truth. While that definable self, with all its implications for the larger world, remains an elusive fiction and a product of our imagination and our perception, the narrator feels compelled to continue the search for its essence and its being.

Similarly, in the closing lines of "Nueva refutación del tiempo" (New Refutation of Time), Borges, through a complex mixture of self-reflexive images, implies that the sense of self is inescapable:

Negar la sucesión temporal, negar el yo, negar el universo astronómico, son desesperaciones aparentes y consuelos secretos. Nuestro destino . . . no es espantoso por irreal; es espantoso porque es irreversible y de hierro. El tiempo es la sustancia de que estoy hecho. El tiempo es un río que me arrebata, pero yo soy el río; es un tigre que me destroza, pero yo soy el tigre; es un fuego que me consume, pero yo soy el fuego. El mundo, desgraciadamente es real; yo desgraciadamente soy Borges. (1974, 771)

[And yet, and yet—to deny temporal succession, to deny the ego, to deny the astronomical universe, are apparent desperations and secret assuagements. Our destiny . . . is not horrible because of its unreality; it is horrible because it is irreversible and ironbound. Time is the substance I am made of. Time is a river that carries me away, but I am the river; it is a tiger that mangles me, but I am the tiger; it is a fire that consumes me, but I am the fire. The world, alas, is real; I, alas, am Borges.] (1981, 190)

Here again, the oppositions dissolve. The self, like death, proves inescapable. Borges senses that the concept of irreversible time and the traditional concept of the self are linked. Death brings us back to a sense of a separate being. Similarly, the Minotaur's sense of his own uniqueness in "La casa de Asterión" (The House of Asterion), the narrator's expression of both the differences between the younger Borges and himself, and their similarities, in "El otro" (The Other), Shakespeare's desire to be himself, and Borges's need to search for the flesh and blood tiger, rather than the dream tiger in "El otro tigre" (The Other Tiger), all suggest that, while the self may be a fiction, it is an unavoidable and perhaps necessary one. Once again, we are confronted with the labyrinth, this time highlighting the indecipherable nature of the self, or of being. Explaining the nature of the subject, like explaining the universe, proves ultimately impossible. Again, we are drawn back to the broad implications of those lines in "El idioma analítico de John Wilkins" (The Analytical Language of John Wilkins). Although we may not be able to penetrate the divine scheme, that does not preclude searching, reaching, creating fictions. Similarly, although we may never be able to define and understand the self, we should still attempt to create schemata relating to it, and to use our concepts, while acknowledging our limitations and their provisional nature.

5
Women, Feminism, Postmodernity, and Borges

JORGE LUIS BORGES'S PORTRAYAL OF WOMEN AND HIS RELATIONSHIP TO feminism are curious and paradoxical. One could point to the lack of female characters in the Argentinean's stories and to his tendency to idealize some of those women whom he does depict (Brodski 1990, Hughes 1979). Or one could examine his epic tales, which reinforce traditional, macho, patriarchal, values. One would conclude, as a number of critics have, that he has little respect for the role of women and little concern with equality for women. Yet, as Nancy Kason Poulson (1997), illustrates in her article, "Del margen al centro: La voz femenina en la cuentistica de Borges" (From the Margin to the Center: The Feminine Voice in the Stories of Borges), the women whom he portrays as central figures show themselves to be strong, willful, determined, and heroic. They often confront inordinate odds and display values that traditional, patriarchal culture has considered masculine. We also know that Borges considered himself a feminist. In a dialogue with Osvaldo Ferrari, the two are discussing Virginia Woolf's *A Room of One's Own*. Borges explains why he finds it a less interesting work than *Orlando*:

> El tema es . . . un mero alegato a favor de las mujeres y el feminismo, pero, como yo soy feminista, no requiero alegatos para convencerme, ya que estoy convencido. Ahora, Virginia Woolf se convirtió en una misionera de ese propósito, pero como yo comparto ese propósito, puedo prescindir de misioneras. (Borges and Ferrari 1986b, 232)

> [The theme is . . . a mere summary defense on behalf of women and feminism. But as I am a feminist, I do not require a summary defense to convince me, as I am already convinced. Now, Virginia Woolf became a missionary of that aim, but as I share that aim, I can do without missionaries.] (translation mine)

To understand fully how Borges viewed women and feminism, one must consider the repercussions of his representations of the

95

world. While we can not know for certain whether he foresaw all of the implications of the vision that he projected, his facility with ideas and familiarity with philosophy would suggest that he did. As aspects of Borges's vision became widely accepted, they provided a framework that indirectly proved quite helpful to feminists. A culture that already questions general order and meaning is more disposed to accept specific challenges to patriarchal ordering. For instance, his problematizing of the self and his undermining of the certainties of our knowledge open the way for a redefinition of the traditional feminine self. Stories with women characters such as "Emma Zunz," "El duelo" (The Duel), and "Historia de guerrero y de la cautiva" (Story of the Warrior and the Captive Maiden), as well as "Tlön Uqbar, Orbis Tertius" and some other short pieces show how Borges helps subvert the traditional sense of order and meaning and challenges the limitations Western society has placed on women. They suggest that he was probably quite conscious of the implications of his writings and vision, and underscore that one must consider his role as a precursor of postmodern culture in evaluating his relation to women's issues and contemporary feminist thought. Furthermore, the balance he strikes between monism and chaos, and his search for a new understanding of the self suggest ways of balancing agency and pluralism with that evolving self, an important issue to the feminist/postmodernist debate.

Feminist activities and thought have not been confined to the fully industrialized countries. Feminism has been one of the most important forces for democratization in much of Latin America in the last thirty years (Ortega 1997, 31). Its role, reception, and success have been different in every country. While in some countries there have been antifeminist movements, in countries such as Chile during the Pinochet years, a group of women who didn't call themselves feminists were responsible for a large part of the resistance (Ortega 1997, 45–46). Similarly, in Argentina, the weekly mother's march demanding information about their disappeared children helped bring an end to the military dictatorship.

FEMINISM AND THE POSTMODERN

Current feminist/postmodernist discourse either has vigorously affirmed or has contested the link between feminist thought, feminist movements, and the postmodern. A review of some of that debate proves useful in understanding the questions facing feminist scholars, provides a heightened awareness of current postmodernist issues, and underscores Borges's contribution to this discourse. Much of the debate focuses around the nature of truth, of history, and of the self or subject. Borges has been widely recognized as an important precursor of postmodernism or one of the first of the postmoderns because of his treatment of those very issues in his fiction, prose, and poetry. To appreciate Borges's relationship to feminist thought, one must consider the relationship between the postmodern and feminism.

A definition of feminism is probably as impossible as a definition of the postmodern. Nevertheless, some statements are possible to circumscribe what is known as the women's movement. As Linda Hutcheon has asserted, "feminisms" rather than "feminism" is the more appropriate term to capture the diversity of beliefs and methods commonly referred to as the feminist movement (1989, 141). Catherine R. Stimpson argues that "feminism offers an analysis of history and culture that foregrounds gender, its structures and inequities; a collective enterprise that foregrounds women's resistance to inequities; and utopian visions of a different, and better future that enables and ennobles that resistance" (1989, 140). In comparing feminist and postmodern writings, she asserts that both trust differences and distrust hierarchies, that the postmodern prosecutes ideological and representational codes even more rigorously than feminism, but that postmodern discourse seem to forget actual women (Stimpson 1989, 139).

Nancy Fraser and Linda Nicholson take issue with Stimpson's attitude toward the postmodern. They argue that both the postmodern and feminism have deep and far-reaching criticisms of philosophy. Both have been critical of the relation between philosophy and culture. Furthermore, both have "sought new paradigms of social criticism which do not rely on traditional philosophical underpinnings" (Fraser and Nicholson 1990, 19). However, while postmodernists have focused on the philosophical side of the problem, feminists have been interested in social criticism. They assert that Lyotard, who was central in initially defining postmodernism, leaves little room in his universe for social theory. The local theories that he proposes simply cannot grasp the subjugation of women. Larger theories are necessary. However, since the 1980s, women have stopped looking for the grand social theory that cuts across race, class, and cultural differences. Frazer and Nicholson assert that, while large theories are necessary, they should be sensitive to cultural and historical differences. They would replace unitary and simplistic theories with plural and complexly constructed conceptions of social identity. They call for pragmatic approaches that fit the methods to the task and that tailor their approaches for different cultures, groups, and classes (Fraser and Nicholson 1990, 19–38). Fraser's and Nicholson's positions strike a similar balance to the one that Borges does, as I have explained earlier. It is a balance between the One and the Many, between monism and pluralism, between an inability to act or know in the face of uncertainty and chaos, and a need to create visions and define positive knowledge while acknowledging that they may be provisional.

In her article, "Postmodernism and Gender Relations in Feminist Theory," Jane Flax (1990) takes an approach similar to Frazer's and Nicholson's. She states that while some have argued for aligning the feminist movement with the ideals of the Enlightenment, feminist thinkers generally accept a concept of knowledge and of the self that more appropriately belongs to the terrain of the postmodern. She outlines how various feminist scholars have sought a defining, totalizing quality of gender that cuts across historical and cultural boundaries, but that the result has been and inevitably will be the exclusion of certain groups of women. She argues that sex and gender are different, and that while some claim that gender is "natural," this does not mean that change is out of the question. After all, science has constantly challenged "the natural" with medical innovations, technology, etc. She asserts that feminists must rethink values, but that they must also insist that all relations of dominance are social. She calls for using certain investigative tools of modernist activity, such as "history, reason, progress, science, some transcendental essence," to rescue us from partiality, but that feminist theories must accept and encourage tolerance, ambivalence, ambiguity, and multiplicity (Flax 1990, 56).

By contrast, Christine Di Stefano (1990), in her article, "Dilemmas of Difference: Feminism, Modernity, and Postmodernism," challenges the link between feminism and postmodernity. She asserts that three different approaches have surfaced within feminist scholarship: a rationalist, an antirationalist, and a postrationalist. One may substitute "modernist" for "rationalist" here. She critiques and finds shortcomings with all of the categories. In regard to the postrationalist or the postmodern, she agrees with Nancy Hartsock. Hartsock questions why, at this moment when marginalized subjects have begun to speak in their own voices on behalf of subject and subjectivities, the sense of subject and of liberating truth becomes suspect. Hartsock views postmodern discourse as the expressions and assertions of white, privileged, Western men and argues that the theory has ignored gender. Hartsock sees risks in the uncertain promise of postmodernity, and argues for a conception of self in which identity is fragmented but healthy, and in which there is a solid and nondefensive core identity. Also, Di Stefano suggests that gender differences may be more universal than we may think when she states:

> By reference to postmodernism's own championing of an alternative to unified theoretical coherence, we should insist that the theoretical and political dilemmas of difference are well worth pondering. As yet, they remain stubbornly persistent and elusive, suggesting that gender is basic in ways that we have yet to understand, that it functions as "a difference that makes a difference" even as it can no longer claim the legitimating mantle of the difference. (Di Stefano 1990, 78)

Di Stefano resists the redefinition of the self that Borges undertakes because she privileges gender differences. However, the traditional self in its fragmented form that she champions may limit the parameters for individual change.

Judith Butler questions the whole concept of gender and suggests that it helps impose an oppressive, heterosexual orientation. In her article, "Gender Trouble, Feminist Theory, and Psychoanalytical Discourse," she argues that gender identity and sexual orientation are formed at the same time. She asserts that all gender is based on fantasy or fabrication. With that realization, we might then understand gender coherence "as the regulatory fiction it is—rather than the common point of our liberation" (1990, 339). In her book, *Bodies that Matter: On the Discursive Limits of "Sex,"* (1993) she develops this argument even more thoroughly, contending that all notions of gender are fictional constructions. While Borges would certainly feel some affinities with Butler's concept of the self, there seems to be a certain monistic certainty in her deconstructing of the self that, I suspect, would trouble Borges.

The book, *Feminist Contentions,* by Seyla Benhabib, Judith Butler, Drucilla Cornell, and Nancy Fraser, (1995), highlights and further defines some of these central issues of conflict between feminism and postmodernism. The authors of the book offer different viewpoints on issues relating to postmodernism, the self, and feminism. Seyla Benhabib draws on Jane Flax's characterization of the postmodern as affirming the Death of Man, the Death of History, and the Death of Metaphysics. She argues that extreme positions on these issues create problems for feminists. She asserts that a certain version of postmodernism would undermine a feminism that calls for the emancipation of women. This happens because a "strong" postmodernism is committed to "the death of man" or the death of the independent, self reflective subject; "the death of history," implying that groups seeking emancipation cannot write their own history; "the death of metaphysics," which means that it becomes impossible to criticize or legitimize practices, institutions, or traditions, other than through "small narratives" (Benhabib 1995, 29). This "strong" postmodernism, thus, subverts the commitment to women's agency, undermines efforts to define a feminist self, to define women's history so as to highlight a emancipated future, and to undertake a radical social criticism that uncovers gender in all its roles and amplifications (Benhabib 1995, 29). Benhabib argues for a "weak" postmodernist position on these issues that would prove compatible with those feminist goals.

In response, Judith Butler challenges the existence of a concept known as "postmodernism." She contends that appropriate criticism does not necessarily deny the existence of the subject or authorial "I," but rather, questions its use as taken for granted. Similarly, in regard to foundations, she admits that "theory posits foundations incessantly and forms implicitly metaphysical commitments as a matter of course, even when it seeks to guard against it" (Butler 1995, 39). She asserts that the point is not to eliminate foundations or to assume a stance that shows you are antifoundationalist. Rather, she seeks to question moves that cut off debate from the nature of the foundations and attempts to show what it excludes and forecloses. She asserts that criticism must continually deconstruct or call into question the subject because identity is, by nature, repressive.

Nancy Fraser stakes out a middle position that allows for an engaged feminism and at the same time incorporates the pluralistic attitudes of postmodernity. She contends that both Benhabib and Butler express false antitheses, and that the strong points of each are theoretically and critically possible. She argues that Benhabib "overlooks medium strength versions that do not pose a false antithesis between Critical Theory and poststructuralism and are theoretically defensible and politically enabling" (Benhabib et al. 1995, 61).

Like Calinescu, she argues that positive knowledge is possible within a pluralistic, postmodern context. She asserts that Linda Nicholson and she have argued for a "postmodernist, pragmatic, fallibilistic mode of feminist theorizing" that avoids foundational statements but allows for social and critical action that can be emancipatory (Fraser 1995, 62). They distinguish between "metanarratives" that have provided truth claims in history and other disciplines, and large scale empirical narratives that are nonfoundational and fallibilistic.

Fraser takes issue with Butler as well and, in particular, with her view of identity in regard to women, and then further defines her vision of a postmodern feminist criticism. She asserts that Butler goes too far in her assertion that "woman" or "women" are the sign of the "non-identical." She admits that claims about "woman" or "women" in general are unavoidable but always subject to change and revision. She states that they should be "advanced nonfoundationally and fallibilistically" (Fraser 1995, 70). Fraser goes on to assert that she is not for "anything goes." Feminist should make normative judgments and offer emancipatory alternatives. She suggests that the proliferation of "identity-dereifying images and significations" is as great a threat to women's liberation as are "the fixed fundamentalist identities" and argues that they are two sides of the same coin and require a double response:

> Feminists need both deconstruction and reconstruction, destabilization of meaning and projection of utopian hope. . . . Thus, instead of clinging to a series of mutually reinforcing false antitheses, we might conceive subjectivity as endowed with critical capacities and as culturally constructed. (Fraser 1995, 71)

Fraser goes on to argue for a view of history that is not foundational but politically engaged, and of collective identities that are constructed and complex.

Here again, Fraser stakes out a position almost identical to what I have argued Borges defines in regard to the postmodern debate. It is a balance between extremes that allows for both pluralism and agency. In effect, she seeks a feminist theory that incorporates postmodern pluralism into a theory of positive knowledge and of emancipatory action. She seems to recognize that an open, flexible, balanced, pluralist culture and evolving, enduring feminist movements symbiotically assist each other.

BORGES AND FEMINISM

The critics above argue over the nature of the self, of history, and of truth and foundational positions because they realize that, ultimately, the acceptance or rejection of these ideas and issues may affect the success or failure of the feminist movement. They realize that ideas are important, that people act on their ideas, and that changing ideas can change behavior. Borges was very aware of this as well. While women's issues are certainly not the central theme of his works, some of his stories suggest that they were part of his thinking and writing.

Postmodern theorists and critics, drawing on Borges, have focused attention on topics such as the self and pluralism, and now these issues are at the crux of the postmodern debate. While by no means alone in bringing about these changes, Borges proves to be an important player in the cultural transitions of the last forty years that have helped to bring women's issues to the fore. In many ways, postmodernity and feminism have helped sustain each other. In rethinking and redefining the self, history, and foundations of our truths and our utopian visions, postmodern discourse has helped bring women and women's issues in from the margins and has encouraged feminist thought. These feminist discourses have opened, challenged, and changed the culture so as to feed the postmodern debate. Together, they have helped initiate a rereading and a redefinition not only of the role, place, and image of women in the society, but also of many of the foundations and assumptions of Western culture as well. It is in this interaction that Borges's contribution to the development of various feminisms becomes clear.

One of Borges's stories that best exemplifies his vision of the world as fluid and changeable is "Tlön Uqbar, Orbis Tertius." It is worth revisiting it from this perspective. This story is often considered important in a discussion of Borges because it contains so many different aspects of his vision with themes that appear in other stories. The narrator, Borges, along with Bioy Casares, has discovered an effort to superimpose a new world upon the existing one. A group of scholars has undertaken the writing of an encyclopedia that redefines reality. They are creating a planet, named Tlön, based on idealism. They change the language, the understanding of material reality, of metaphysics, of truth, and of literature. In effect, they transform the total sense of self, of being, and of order and meaning. As the story closes, it becomes clear that this new order is super-imposing itself on the old.

In some ways, this story provides a blueprint for what many feminists hope to accomplish, as it shows an old conception of the cosmos and of reality being replaced by a new one. It offers a vision of a world that is textual, a world defined by ideas and words and changed by them. The world is portrayed as "una enciclopedia" an encyclopedia, with all the implications for knowledge as the foundation and circumscriber of consciousness and/or our sense of reading the world as we read a book. In this idealist world, reality is a projection of the mind. All the nations are idealist and all of its systems that derive from language, religion, letters, metaphysics, are idealist as well. The world is not material, not a group of objects in space. It is successive and temporal, but not spatial.

In effect, the planet challenges the present sense of material reality. The language reflects that, because there are no nouns. Neither is there any sense of cause and effect.

This altered sense of reality has implications for metaphysics, for the role of literature, and for the sense of the self. In regard to metaphysics, it is considered a branch of fantastic literature. Philosophical systems are considered fictions that are constantly being replaced by other fictions. Again the implication is that this is a world that is changeable, that is fluid, that is constantly being redefined, and in which truth may have different meanings. Similarly, on this planet, all literary plots contain all imaginable permutations, and all philosophical theses and arguments contain their antitheses and opposites. It is a world that breaks out of the confines of singularity and opens itself to diversity and plurality.

This is reflected in the sense of being and of self or subject as well, and has pantheistic implications. As suggested in chapter 4, the self is a fluid and indefinable entity for Borges. His attitude toward authorship captures this. He contrasts Tlön with contemporary society:

En los hábitos literarios también es todopoderosa la idea de un sujeto único. Es raro que los libros estén firmados. No existe el concepto del plagio: se ha establecido que todas las obras son obras de un solo autor, que es intemporal y es anónimo. (1974, 439)

[Within the sphere of literature, too, the idea of the single subject is all-powerful. Books are rarely signed, nor does the concept of plagiarism exist; It has been established that all books are the work of a single author who is timeless and anonymous.] (1998, 76–77)

There is no sense of individual identity here. Borges believes that we contain the potential for being the best and the worst of what woman/man can be. This malleable sense of self offers the possibility of change. Roles are not embedded in stone and unchangeable. Character and personality are fictional constructs that are created and can be altered. Generalizations about the nature of women or of men are ungrounded. He envisions a world of options and choices rather than of limitations and deterministic restrictions. A look at some other stories, especially ones dealing with women, illustrates this.

One such story of two women artists, "El duelo" (The duel), from *El informe de Brodie, (Dr. Brodie's Report)* (1970), has interesting implications for feminism as well as the relationship between the modern and the postmodern and for the ways in which artistic tastes change and evolve. The two friends, Clara Glencairn and Marta Pizarro, have a competitive relationship that feeds each other's creative and artistic energies. Clara practices abstract, formless art, while Marta devotes herself to a more mimetic, realistic mode. The story is interspersed with ironic comments on the nature of artistic tastes and the jargon used to discuss art.

These ironic comments prove important because they problematize the sense of objective criteria for judging art. There are numerous references. For instance, in 1954, Clara gives an exhibition which was considered vanguard:

> Ocurrió un hecho paradójico: la crítica general fue benigna, pero el órgano oficial de la secta reprobó esas formas anómalas que, si bien no eran figurativas, sugerían el tumulto de un ocaso, de una selva o del mar y no se resignaban a ser austeros redondeles y rayas. Acaso la primera en sonreír fuera Clara Glencairn. Había querido ser moderna y los modernos la rechazaban. (1974, 1054–55)

> [The result was paradoxical: general opinion was kind, but the sect's official organ took a dim view of the painting's anomalous forms—forms which, while not precisely figurative, nonetheless seemed not content to be austere lines and curves, but instead suggested the tumult of a sunset, a jungle or the sea. The first to smile, perhaps, was Clara Glencairn. She had set out to be modern, and the moderns rejected her.] (1998, 383)

Similarly, the narrator mocks the critical language and the way in which prizes are bestowed. He states that around 1970, " 'dos pinceles a nivel internacional'—séanos perdonada esta jerga—se disputaban un primer premio" (1974, 1055). ["Two world-renowned artists" (if we may pardon the cliché) were competing for a single first prize] (1998, 383). Because the judges cannot decide, they select Clara as the unanimous compromise choice. Other similar ironic statements are scattered throughout the narrative.

Against this backdrop of very subjective criteria for art, Clara and Marta's relationship develops. In many ways their "duel" mirrors the interaction between competing literary movements, such as modernism and the postmodern, or naturalism and modernism. The two artists work in different, competitive modes, one emphasizing realism, and thus form and order, and the other practicing abstract art, implying a disdain of language and logic. This "duel" gave them meaning:

> La vida exige una pasión. Ambas mujeres la encontraron en la pintura o, mejor dicho, en la relación que aquélla les impuso. Clara Glencairn pintaba contra Marta y de algún modo para Marta; cada una era juez de su rival y el solitario público. En esas telas, que ya nadie miraba, creo advertir, como era inevitable, un influjo recíproco. (1994, 1056)

> [Life must have its consuming passion. The two women found that passion in painting—or rather, in the relationship that painting forced them into. Clara Glencairn painted against and in some sense for, Marta Pizarro; each one was her rival's judge and solitary audience. In these canvases that no one any longer looked at, I believe I see, (as there inevitably had to be) a reciprocal influence.] (1998, 84–85)

This "duel" moves on several levels. On the one hand, it is the story of two individual women seeking to establish their professional identities in a male-dominated world. As Andrew Hurley points out, the narrator plays with Claira Glencairn's name to underscore the difficulty she has in gaining recognition separate from her husband (Borges 1998, "Note to the Fictions," 556). The narrator refers to her initially as Clara Glencairn de Figueroa, the wife of Argentina's ambassador to Canada, rather than as Clara Glencairn. When she is awarded the compromise prize, the judge slights her by referring to her as Clara Glencairn de Figueroa. It seems that it is given because she was "distinguida, querible, de una moral sin tacha y solía dar fiestas, que las revistas más costosas fotografiaban, en su Quinta de Pilar" (1974, 1055). [Distinguished, lovable, of impeccable morality, and tended to give parties, photographed by the most costly magazines, at her country house in Pilar] (1998, 384). Later, Marta rejects an offer of marriage because only her battle interests her. She wishes to maintain her identity as an artist, and senses that marriage would make that more difficult, as she would be shadowed by her husband in society's eyes, as Clara has been. The "duel" of the title is not only between Clara and Marta, but also about the two of them seeking acknowledgement of their talents and accomplishments, however major or minor they may be, and a society that will not give them due professional recognition because they are women and thus must fulfill other social expectations. Together, they support each other in that "battle."

That "duel" also speaks to the way in which artistic modes and movements compete and define themselves and the shortcomings of critical judgments of them. Like two literary periods or movements, the existence of one helps define the other. While the critical judgment may be basically unreliable, their individual identities derive from their need to define themselves against their opposite. In a universe in which objective standards for taste do not exist, they acquire purpose through their artistic interaction. Each "self" contains her/his opposite in Borges's world, and so does each literary movement.

In much the same way, real pluralism needs monism and takes it quite seriously. The postmodern defines itself against modernism, and modernism defined itself against Romanticism and the Enlightenment. Borges implies here that artistic tastes and artistic visions create identities for themselves as much by what they challenge as by what they profess.

As depicted in this story, aesthetic values and tastes are very whimsical and defiant, and follow few standards. Thus, these mores can be altered, redefined, enlightened, and broadened. Again, the sense of possibility, of options, of malleability, comes to the fore. Set boundaries and restrictions do not delimit Borges's fictional world. It is a world in which competing modes and methods exist together. As the narrator states in the final paragraph:

En aquel duelo delicado que sólo adivinamos algunos íntimos no hubo derrotas ni victorias, ni siquiera un encuentro ni otras visibles circunstancias que las que he procurado registrar con respetuosa pluma. Sólo Dios (cuyas preferencias estéticas ignoramos) puede otorgar la palma final. La historia que se movió en la sombra acaba en la sombra. (1974, 1057)

[In that delicate duel (perceived only by those few of us who were intimate friends) there were no defeats or victories, nor even so much as an
open clash—no visible circumstances at all, save those I have attempted
to record with my respectful pen. Only God (whose aesthetic preferences are unknown to us) can bestow the final palm. The story that
moved in darkness ends in darkness.] (1998, 385)

Aesthetic movements, periods, canons, approaches, and orientations do not have intrinsic values. Rather, they are defined by men
and women and can be redefined by them. The final line contains a
veiled reference to Plato's image of the cave: "La historia que se
movió en la sombra acaba en la sombra." "Sombra" has the suggestion of "shadow" as well "darkness" here. If there are such intrinsic
values as beauty and truth in art, human beings, from their limited
perspectives in the shadows or darkness, are not capable of defining
them with certainty. Those are the tenets of the postmodern and
they also play a role in many of the discussions and efforts of feminism.

At the same time, this story speaks to the nature of the self or subjectivity. When Clara dies, the narrator states that Marta realized that
her life now had no meaning. She paints one last portrait and never
paints again. Without her double, she ceases to exist. Each woman's
sense of identity depended on her "other." Similarly, literary periods or literary movements define each other by their contrasts.

This sense of the "other" as part of the self is especially evident in
the story "Emma Zunz (1949)," where Emma shows that she can
become the opposite of what she was and of what everyone perceived her to be. Critics have generally overlooked that the self and
"other," the nature of identity in general and of the feminine identity in particular, are significant to this story. It concerns the differences between public and private lives and boundaries that may
circumscribe female behavior. It draws upon the patterns of the Judith and Holophernes story in the Book of Judith.

On January 14, 1922, mild-mannered Emma Zunz receives a letter
informing her that her father who is in prison dies from an acciden-
tal overdose. After recovering from the shock, she blames Aaron
Loewenthal, the owner of the factory where she works, for what she
suspects was her father's suicide. It seems that Loewenthal had
framed her father for embezzlement and sent him to prison while
he himself had committed the crime. Consequently, Emma plots an
elaborate scheme to attain divine and/or poetic justice while keep-

ing herself out of prison. Posing as a prostitute, she gives herself to a Scandinavian sailor who will depart the next day, thus preventing him from testifying that he, not Loewenthal, had had intercourse with her the night before. She arranges to see Loewenthal in private under the pretext of giving him some information on an upcoming strike, shoots him with his own gun, and then calls the police to report that he had raped her, so she killed him. While she had hoped to confront him with her identity and why she sought vengeance before killing him, when the time comes all her thoughts focus on the sailor who used her the night before as a sexual object. Consequently, Loewenthal never learns her motive.

Critics of this story have emphasized what she accomplishes or the ambiguities, but have largely ignored how the story relates to Borges's sense of character and self. Jaime Alazraki highlights that an ulterior motive replaces her initial reason for killing Loewenthal (Alazraki 1977b, 65). Edna Aizenberg (1983) sees the conflicting characters as allegorically representative of the Kabbalah and Emma as symbolic of the female aspect of the Godhead. J. B. Hall (1982) calls attention to the extended ambiguities that permeate the narrative and make a definitive reading impossible—the fact that we do not know who actually committed the initial crime or whether her father actually did die of a suicide or an accident. George McMurray sees Emma as a rationalist who gives in to passion in her pursuit of justice. He emphasizes that justice itself is not always rational and that reason can be manipulated to camouflage truth (1980, 35–37).

Many women in history and mythology have defended their honor in this manner. One particularly close analogue is the biblical story of Judith. Both protagonists, Emma and Judith, deceive men who have some degree of control over them into meeting with them privately under a false pretext. When the men least suspect it, the women marshal epic courage and kill them—supposedly in God's name—acting out a role that is out of character for a traditional woman.

Emma's ability to assume a totally different character and to act in a totally different way creates a major part of the fascination and intrigue in this narrative. In order to carry out her elaborate plan, she must do something that is totally contrary to her normal patterns of behavior. This topsy-turvy sense, this condition of totally altering her self, that is, the sense of who she is and how she interacts with her world, finds expression in her actions. She is a quiet nineteen-year-old girl with few concrete interests in men. When Emma and her friends talked of boyfriends, "nadie esperó que Emma hablara" (1974, 565). [No one expected Emma to speak] (1962, 133). She possesses certain romantic notions of love, as her Sunday afternoon visit to the movies and her saving a picture of a movie star, Milton Sills, suggest. When talk of a strike arises, "Emma se declaró, como siempre, contra toda violencia" (1974, 565). [Emma declared herself, as usual, against all violence] (1962, 133). Yet she leaves the security, safety, and seeming certainty of her home and identity and enters this labyrinth of mirrors and fog and reflections, which allows her to become her opposite. As the narrator describes it:

> Un atributo de lo infernal es la irrealidad, un atributo que parece mitigar sus terrores y que los agrava tal vez. ¿Cómo hacer verosímil una acción en la que casi no creyó quien la ejecutaba, cómo recuperar ese breve caos que hoy la memoria de Emma Zunz repudia y confunde? Emma vivía por Almagro, en la calle Liniers; nos consta que esa tarde fue al puerto. Acaso en el infame Paseo de Julio se vio multiplicada en espejos . . . (1974, 565)

> [One attribute of a hellish experience is unreality, an attribute that seems to allay its terrors and which aggravates them perhaps. How could one make credible an action which was scarcely believed in by the person who executed it, how to recover that brief chaos which today the memory of Emma Zunz repudiates and confuses? Emma lived in Almagro, on Liniers Street: we are certain that in the afternoon she went down to the waterfront. Perhaps on the infamous Paseo de Julio she saw herself multiplied in mirrors.] (1962, 134)

Even her name reflects this mirrorlike nature of her being. Zunz backwards and inverted so that the "u" and the "n" are turned upside down is still Zunz.

She senses that she is traversing a labyrinth as the sailor takes her through doors and up stairways and down passageways and into vestibules. She is inside a labyrinth that will come to dominate her actions. "En aquel tiempo fuera del tiempo, en aquel desorden perplejo de sensaciones inconexas y atroces" (1974, 566) [During that time outside of time, in that perplexing disorder of disconnected and atrocious sensations] (1962, 135) the horror of the thought that her father had done the same thing to her mother overtakes her, and she almost loses her will to act. Ultimately, the outrage at that act rather than the desire for justice and vengeance for her father lead her to follow-through on the killing. Yet, this outrage derives not only from the shock of naiveté and innocence in discovering the lurid, physical nature of sexuality, nor from the sense of being robbed and cheated of her virginity, but also from the sense of being used as an object by that sailor, of being relegated to a role that greatly limits her actions, movements, and possibilities, thus letting people use her as the sailor did. It is also an outrage at a reality that is predetermined and restrictive, not open and fluid, a reality that tells her what and who she is and is not. A need to challenge these prohibitive limits of her life leads her to create a new and incredible reality about Loewenthal abusing her and to relay it convincingly to the police. As the narrator explains at the end, "verdadero era el tono de Emma Zunz, verdadero el pudor, verdadero el odio. Verdadero también era el ultraje que había padecido; sólo eran falsas las circunstancias, la hora y uno o dos nombres propios" (1974, 568). [True was Emma Zunz's tone, true was her shame, true was her hate. True also was the outrage she had suffered: only the circumstances were false, the time and one or two proper names] (1962, 137).

A number of Borges's pieces portray strong, determined, assertive women as characters. While Borges often did not seek to portray characters in the traditional sense, he does on occasion depict what is called a well-rounded protagonist or antagonist. From *Historia universal de la infamia* (1935), (*Universal History of Iniquity*), there is a short biographical sketch, "La viuda Ching, pirata" (The Widow Ching, Pirate), that describes a female in this rather unconventional male role. In this same collection, "Hombre de la esquina rosada" (Man on Pink Corner) he portrays a barmaid, La Lujanera, who is strong and assertive and who prefers similar men. Also, from *El informe de Brodie* (1970), (*Brodie's Report*), the selection, "Juan Muraña" offers another example. The narrator's Aunt Florentina marries the gaucho Juan Muraña to the dismay of her sister. Muraña dies an early death. However, the aunt takes justice into her own hands by killing the unjust and insensitive landlord who was about to evict the narrator and his mother. Florentina claims that it was Muraña's spirit alive in his knife that performed the deed. Furthermore, from *El libro de arena* (*The Book of Sand*), Ulrica, in the story of the same name, is the willful and independent woman from Norway who makes love to the narrator as the two reenact the Nibelungenleid episode.

Another Borges story that very directly relates to issues of the self and of women is "Historia del guerrero y de la cautiva" (Story of the

Warrior and the Captive Maiden) (1949). At the beginning of the piece, the narrator, "Borges," briefly relates the story of Droctulft, "bárbaro que murió defendiendo a Roma" (1974, 557), [a barbarian who died defending Rome] (1962, 127). This leads him to recall the experience of his grandmother who lived a rather isolated life on the pampas with his grandfather who was a soldier. She felt very much alone as an Englishwoman exiled to the edge of the world. One day she meets another English woman whose parents had died, and who, consequently, had been raised by Indians and became the wife of a chief. The two seem to identify as sisters at once. Borges's grandmother tries to convince her to leave her life, but she states that she is happy. The grandmother sees her only one other time when she is drinking the blood of an animal. The story closes with the narrator asserting that while the two stories—of the barbarian defending Rome, and of the European woman taking to a life in the desert—may seem antagonistic: "El anverso y el reverso de esta moneda son, para Dios, iguales" (1974, 560). [The obverse and the reverse of this coin are, for God, the same] (1962, 131).

Those closing lines make the connection between the nature of the self and its implications for women. Borges quite consciously challenges the separation between the civilized and the barbarian, a dichotomy that dates back to ancient Greek philosophy and Plato, and is very much linked to the traditional definition of the self. It has important implications for the Argentine as well. In *Civilización y barbarie o vida de Juan Facundo Quiroga* (1845) (*Civilization and Barbarity or the Life of Juan Facundo Quiroga*), Domingo Faustino Sarmiento applied this duality to Argentine society in arguing for the need to control and tame the gauchos. One of the basic assumptions of the concept as used by the Greeks is that one is either a civilized person or a barbarian, that the nature of the soul distinguishes you as either one or the other. The examples of Droctulft and of the woman suggest that the nature of the self is much more fluid, and that we all have the potential for "civilized" or "barbarian" behavior.[1]

The traditional sense of self, as suggested by the dichotomy between the civilized and the barbarian, has relegated women to a second-class status as well. If not barbarians, women were thought to lack the rational capacity of men and were not men's equals. By using the examples of a man and a woman —Droctulft and the English woman living with the Indians—to suggest that the "civilized" can become barbarian, and the "barbarian" can become civilized,

Borges underscores that fluid sense of self. His redefinitions of the self have important implications for redefining gender issues. As barbarians can become civilized and vice versa, so too the weak can become strong, the irrational can become rational, the emotional can become controlled, and stereotypes for women and for men can be remade.

Borges's relationship to women, feminism, and postmodernity raises some interesting questions. Borges's stories, in general, portray very few women. Nor are his writings generally "compromet-idos," politically committed, in dealing with women's issues, although there are some instances of that. As Sharon Magnarelli (1983) suggests, for the most part Borges does not concern himself with characters and individuality in the traditional sense. Rather, many of the women in the narratives are everywoman, everyman, representatives of all of us. The issues he raises and the statements he makes cut across gender lines. Even more importantly, Borges realizes that ideas are important because people act on their ideas, and that changes in ideas can change the world. In this sense he is an activist. His treatment of the self, his discussions of the nature of reality, representation, knowledge, and truth, and his tendency toward philosophical pluralism, helped open doors for marginal-ized groups and move them toward the center. While not the only actress/actor in this unfolding drama by any means, his role proves fairly important. Furthermore, the balance he strikes between chaos and totalizing visions offers many advantages in seeking social justice and agency in a plural world. In certain ways, he underscores con-structively how postmodernity and feminist thought have nourished each other.

6

Borges, Universal History, and
Historical Representation

ONE OF THE MOST SIGNIFICANT OF THE POSTMODERN TURNS CONCERNS
universal history and historical discourse, and the shift in general in
the way historians, scholars, and writers view and represent the past.
Postmodern discourse has problematized the writing of history. It
has questioned the ability to distinguish between "fact" and "fiction" as well as between the objective and the subjective. It has emphasized that the historical period, the culture, the nationality, and
the background of the historian influence any historical perspective.
It has underscored that the writing of history is a subjective undertaking, and that the language, the literary tropes, and the style of
the historian are part and parcel of the "truths" of the historian's
texts. In doing so, it has opened the discourse to marginalized
groups whose histories were not previously heard or whose histories
were written for them. At the same time, it has challenged the basic
assumptions of universal histories. This debate has broad political
implications as well. Borges's writings have played a significant role
in this shift of focus in historical discourse. His stories and essays
challenge the representations of universal history and affirm the
subjective nature of all historical narrative. Borges expressed an
even more skeptical attitude toward historical representation than
some poststructuralist or postmodernist critics. A number of those
critics have wandered from the idealistic vision that Borges defined.

HISTORY AND THE POSTMODERN

An overview of some of the key critical commentaries on history
and the postmodern provides insight into Borges's place in the current discussion of postmodern discourse. Fredric Jameson has un-

dertaken one of the most far-reaching discussions of history and the postmodern. Jameson defines postmodernity as a cultural/historical period in which there is a lack of historicity. Jameson's most comprehensive statement on the subject is his book, *Postmodernism, or, The Cultural Logic of Late Capitalism* (1991). The title itself suggests that Jameson attempts to place the postmodern within a Marxist-historical context. In this work, Jameson defines the postmodern as an age that has forgotten to think historically. His book is an attempt to present this "ahistorical" time in an historical context. As he writes in the introduction to the book: "It is safest to grasp the concept of the postmodern as an attempt to think the present historically in an age that has forgotten how to think historically in the first place" (1991, ix). Jameson states:

> In the postmodern, then, the past itself has disappeared (along with the well-known "sense of the past" or historicity and collective memory). Where its buildings still remain, renovation and restoration allow them to be transferred to the present in their entirety as those other, very different and postmodern things called simulacra. Everything is now organized and planned; nature has been triumphantly blotted out, along with peasants, petit-bourgeois commerce, handicraft, feudal aristocracies and imperial bureaucracies. Ours is a more homogeneously modernized condition, we no longer are encumbered with the embarrassment of non-simultaneities and non-sychronicities. Everything has reached the same hour on the great clock of development or rationalization (at least from the perspective of the "West"). (Jameson 1991, 309–10)

Part of his mission is to preserve the concept of utopia and to argue that utopian visions are a component of the postmodern.[1] He defines postmodern parody as pastiche, as surface without depth. Thus, Jameson imposes a Marxist sense of history onto the postmodern.

From the historian's standpoint, Hayden White has written extensively on the representation of history and on its link to literature in a way that differs from that of Jameson. Much like Borges, he emphasizes the link between literature and history. In "Fictions of Factual Representation," he asserts:

> What should interest us in the discussion of the "literature of fact" or, as I have chosen to call it, "the fictions of factual representation" is the extent to which the discourse of the historian and that of the writer of

imaginative fictions overlap, resemble or correspond with each other. (White 1976, 21)

He explains that, prior to the French Revolution, historiography was regarded as a literary art, as a branch of rhetoric, and its fictive nature was generally recognized. The need to fall back on fictive methods in representing real events was acknowledged. However, early in the nineteenth century, historians began to identify truth with fact and regard fiction as the opposite of truth (White 1976, 24–25). He asserts that the difficulty with the notion of the truth of past experience is that it can no longer be experienced. Consequently, history becomes a construction of the imagination although the historian may be convinced himself and may attempt to persuade the reader that his account is true. History becomes rhetorical in its performance and must assume an attitude toward textuality that gives it neither more nor less authority than literature (White 1987, 147). He argues that the present implots the meaning of the past and that historians project backward and reformulate accounts of the past to fit into the present. Consequently, the past is endowed with different meanings (1987, 150–52).

White also challenges the objectivity of the historian. He asserts that one of the things one learns from studying history is that it is never innocent ideologically. Our notion of discriminating between left, right, and center in part disciplines the study but rules out the possibility that history may be meaningless (1987, 82). Furthermore, although the historian may profess objectivity, as he projects himself into the minds of the historical figures and assumes motives, intentions, and values that may be totally contrary to his own, the imagination comes into play (1987, 67).

Linda Hutcheon, in her book, *A Poetics of Postmodernism: History, Theory, Fiction* (1988), draws on White in defining a postmodern poetics and answers some of the challenges of Jameson and others. She defines postmodern fiction as very historically conscious. In fact, what she calls "historiographic metafiction" is the defining literary mode of the era. She asserts that modernism's formalist attitude in which artist, audience, and critic would stand outside of history has created the postmodern responses. Basically, these reassessments have problematized history, but, she argues, historical knowledge is still possible:

To speak of provisionality and indeterminacy is not to deny historical knowledge, however . . . What postmodern writing of both history and literature has taught us is that both history and fiction are discourses, that both constitute systems of signification by which we make sense of the past . . .

The postmodern, then, effects two simultaneous moves. It reinstalls historical contexts as significant and even determining, but in so doing, it problematizes the entire notion of historical knowledge. This is another of the paradoxes that characterize all postmodern discourses today. And the implication is that there can be no single, essentialized, transcendent concept of "genuine historicity" (as Fredric Jameson desires: 1984a), no matter what the nostalgia (Marxist or traditionalist) for such an entity. (1988, 88–89)

Hutcheon also argues that the parody of which so much postmodern fiction partakes is not superficial pastiche, as Jameson argues, but rather, a redefinition of the meaning of the term parody (1988, 26). She contends that "to include irony and play is never necessarily to exclude seriousness and purpose" (1988, 27).

In *The Politics of Postmodernism*, Hutcheon considers the contemporary narrative implicated in much of the self-conscious questioning surrounding the nature of history. She argues that historiographic metafiction, like that of Gabriel García Márquez's *Cien años de soledad*, (*One Hundred Years of Solitude*), Augusto Roa Bastos' *Yo el Supremo*, (*I the Supreme*), and E. L. Doctorow's *The Book of Daniel*, shows how turning events into facts is a process of turning traces of the past into historical representation (1989, 57).[2] One of the by-products of this examination of how we understand the past relates to the word "reality." The indeterminacy that is so much a part of postmodern culture, coupled with this scrutiny of the nature of history and its depiction, has engendered the substitution of the word "representation" for what used to be called "reality" in much of contemporary discussion of the topic.

Hutcheon also argues that postmodern fiction questions the totalizing narrative structure of the novel and other fictional and historical representation. The narrative form that we know well, with its beginning, middle, and end, raises questions about meaning, teleology, and closure, issues that both literary and philosophical theorists have scrutinized intensely in recent times. Many critics consider totalizing narrative representation to be the defining quality of the traditional novel. This self-conscious subverting of the totalizing tendency of narrative not only undermines the totalizing, universal, and historical visions of thinkers such as Marx and Kant, but also questions the manner in which we structure and thus give order to our world. In the mode of Borges, she asserts that "knowing the past becomes a question of representing, that is, of constructing and interpreting, not of objective recording" (1989, 74).

Hutcheon argues that postmodern writers have parodied the footnote to undermine the sense of authority of narration (1989, 85). Again as critics have frequently noted, this is a technique that Borges employs extensively. Stories like "Pierre Menard, autor del *Quijote*" (Pierre Menard, Author of the *Quixote*), "El jardín de senderos que se bifurcan" (The Garden of the Forking Paths), "Tlön Uqbar, Orbis Tertius," and "El Zahir" (The Zahir), contain such references from a fictional editor or narrator. In Borges, this device not only subverts the nature of narrative authority, but also works to blur the line between critical/objective and fictional/subjective discourse. In so doing, it challenges the very foundation of objectivity.

Matei Calinescu affirms postmodernity's historical character but cautions Jameson and others against an overly reductionist historical reading. He outlines two common fallacies in discourse on the postmodern, what he refers to as the mimetic and the theatrical fallacies (1987b, 3–16).

With regard to the mimetic fallacy, Jean François Lyotard and Umberto Eco, among others, have attempted to define the postmodern in transhistorical terms, yet history creeps in. Eco tries to remove history from his definition when he asserts that the postmodern, rather than being a trend is an ideal category. However, he cites how the avant-garde comes to an end, and defines postmodern writing as a revisiting of the past, although ironically: "The postmodern reply to the modern consists of recognizing that the past, since it cannot be really destroyed, because its destruction leads to silence, must be revisited: but with irony, not innocently" (Eco and Rossi, 1991, 243). This shows that postmodernism does indeed have unavoidable historical connotations. Similarly, Jean François Lyotard attempts to ground his definition ahistorically and thus speaks of Rabelais and Montaigne as postmodern. Yet, Lyotard often has been understood in historical terms.

In his article, Calinescu takes issue with the Marxist tendency to apply in excess to an analysis of postmodernity certain dramatic dimensions of Marxism, such as its totalizing historical belief in the demise of capitalism and the success of socialism. He refers to that overly dramatic tendency as the "theatrical fallacy." In effect, he challenges the notion of defining the postmodern in solely historical terms. In referring to an article by Fredric Jameson, Calinescu asserts that, when the theatricality becomes too pronounced, dogmatic, and totalistic, it undermines its own critic and robs the literary as well. Calinescu argues for a conception of the postmodern that accepts certain ahistorical qualities and at the same time acknowledges its periodic and historical nature as well (Calinescu 1987b).

A fundamental difference exists between some postmodern conceptions of history and those of Borges. For much of postmodern historiographic metafiction, the issue is not the nature of the past and of "reality," but rather how we understand and represent it. As Hutcheon states:

> The question is never whether the events of the past actually took place. The past did exist—independently of our capacity to know it. Historiographic metafiction accepts this philosophically realist view of the past and then proceeds to confront it with an anti-realist one that suggests that, however true that independence may be, nevertheless, the past exists for us now—only as traces on and in the present. The absent past can only be inferred from circumstantial evidence. (1989, 73)

BORGES AND HISTORY

The difference between Borges and these historiographic metafictionalists proves subtle but significant. We cannot know exactly how Borges would feel about the historical or ahistorical nature of the postmodern. However, the Argentine writer clearly and extensively engages questions dealing with historiography and fiction and with the nature of universal history. Probably, Borges would express more skepticism toward a sense of an empirical past than has occurred. The past is not only illusory from the vantage point of the present but also as it is occurring. It is filled with the repetition of both historical and literary myth and legend. Time is not necessarily progressive but rather cyclical in that certain mythic patterns reappear. There seems to be a level of skepticism beyond what some postmodernists bring to the discussion. The "empirical past" simply cannot be separated from how we know all "reality." And, all reality is a dreamlike illusion, tainted by the limitations of the senses, by our abilities to comprehend, and by the nature of material existence. No perception, no empirical experience proves trustworthy.

There is always another way of viewing events, of seeing things. In a world in which all knowledge is subjective and provisional, is molded by time and place, and is confined by human limitations, to speak of the past as actually having occurred, to speak of truly objective and empirical historical data has little meaning. Like Juan Dahlmann in "El Sur" (The South), whom we cannot definitely place either in the Sanatorium or in the South, like the narrator trying to resolve exactly competing and totally contradictory explanations of who Pedro Damián was and what he did, like the narrator of "El Aleph" who wonders if what he saw was the authentic Aleph, like Asterion, who closes his eyes and pretends to sleep and discovers that sometimes he does sleep, we cannot quantify, objectify, nor even confirm at times, that the past actually occurred.

Borges deals with two different aspects of history: the way in which we comprehend historical events and the nature of universal history. Central to an appreciation of both inquiries is the divide between the divine and the human. As with other metaphysical questions, the Argentine underscores the human limitations in understanding its world. Yet, he does not question the value of human constructs and historical knowledge but rather their ultimate universality and objectivity.

Borges has a number of stories, poems, and prose selections that address how we know the past. His prose poem, "Dreamtigers" from *El hacedor* (*The Maker*) (1960) captures this. Here, Borges explains how he worshipped the royal, Asiatic tiger as a child. Although his passion has faded, he still dreams of the animal. In his dreams, he is all powerful and attempts to conjure the tiger, only to fail. Now the tiger he dreams is feeble or stuffed or imperfect in form, looking more like a bird or a dog. This poem underscores the limits of mimesis and representation, the impossibility of accurately recreating the world.

The story, "La otra muerte" (The Other Death), from *El Aleph* (1949), imaginatively challenges the deterministic qualities of historical studies. The story is about the past of Pedro Damián, about different people's recollections, about whether he was a hero or a coward, about changing recollections by certain people, and about resolving those differences. The narrator decides that Damián originally acted in a cowardly way, but, because he is granted another chance, was given his wish to undo the past and the infinite causes and effects that accompany it. He relives the battle and dies bravely in it. The story suggests, like "El jardín de senderos que se bifurcan," (The Garden of the Forking Paths), that perhaps there are alternative realities where alternative choices are played out. It also problematizes the writing of empirical history. Memories are short and often inaccurate. Perspectives often differ on what actually occurred. Historians seek a "rational" explanation when memory and history are edited, imprecise, inexplicable, and/or unverifiable.

"Deutsches Requiem" from *El Aleph* also deals with historical discourse. The story relates the final days of an anti-Semitic, German Nazi as World War II is coming to a close and Germany is facing certain defeat. A man who was certain of the future of the Third Reich and the direction of history is forced to confront the errors of his vision. The narrator, Otto Dietrich zur Linde, emphasizes that our individual actions work in ways that we do not and cannot expect. This story also highlights that history is written by the victorious, that there are other stories and other histories.

"El espejo y la máscara" (The Mirror and the Mask) (1975), also speaks to how the effect of time alters the truths of history and of literature. The Irish king commissions Ollan, his poet, to sing the praises of his triumphs regularly. The poet does so but, as fortune turns against them, his words become fewer, and the structure and meaning more difficult to decipher. The king bestows some gifts upon him: a mirror, a mask, and finally a dagger. The story ends with the poet taking his life, his poem never repeated, and the king becoming a beggar. The mirror and the mask represent the mutability and uncertainty of one's fortunes, both historical and literary. The fact that Ollan's poems are never sung again, and that the king becomes a beggar suggest again that the victors write history, both literary and political. Time will often turn history on its head.

The essay "Kafka y sus precursores" (Kafka and his Precursors) (1951) offers similar insights into many aspects of Borges's conception of history. In considering Kafka's forerunners, Borges arrives at the conclusion that we create our precursors and our past, that the present makes the past through its reading of it. This has profound implications for the study of history. It underscores the subjective nature of historical studies. It stresses that the past is not a frozen entity but is constantly in flux as our times and our understanding of them change.

"Pierre Menard, autor del *Quijote*" (Pierre Menard, Author of the *Quixote*), echoes this theme, and in some ways, speaks to the Kafka essay. Menard, the Frenchman, totally transcends his place and time in recreating the Spanish classic. Menard's ability to transcend his period in time comments ironically on our own inability to do so.

The story, "Avelino Arredondo," from *El libro de arena* (*The Book of Sand*) (1975), emphasizes how the line between fiction and history often dissolves, but from a different perspective. The story relates the elaborate preparations that Arredondo takes by withdrawing from all social contact before assassinating Juan Idiarte Borda, the President of Uruguay. The narrator here has entered the mind of this historical figure and imagined and depicted his thoughts, motives, and emotions, much as a novelist, poet, or dramatist does with characters. In doing so, he implies that there is very little difference between the fiction and history.

Although the Arredondo story is drawn from a collection published later in his life, this blurring of the line between history and fiction appears in some of his earliest writings. *Historia universal de la infamia* (*A Universal History of Iniquity*), was published in 1935. The work purports to be biographical sketches of a number of indecent characters. However, in the prologue to the 1954 edition, he admits changing and fictionalizing those biographies for aesthetic purposes: "Son el irresponsable juego de un tímido que no se animó a escribir cuentos y que se distrajo en falsear y tergiversar (sin justificación estética alguna vez) ajenas historias" (1974, 291). [They are the irresponsible sport of a shy sort of man who could not bring himself to write short stories, and so amused himself by changing and distorting (sometimes without aesthetic justification) the stories of other men] (1998, 4).

The prose selection discussed earlier, "El escritor argentino y la tradición" (The Argentine Writer and Tradition) (1951), also has significant implications for the study of history. Borges suggests that history is fluid and changeable and refuses to accept the history written by the colonizing or hegemonic culture as the only acceptable one. He discusses how the Jews in Western culture or the Irish in English have innovated within the culture and then asserts that Argentine and South American situations are similar: "Creo que los argentinos, los sudamericanos, en general, estamos en una situación análoga; podemos manejar todos los temas europeos, manejarlos sin supersticiones, con una irreverencia que puede tener, y ya tiene, consecuencias afortunadas" (1974, 273). [I think we Argentines and South Americans, in general, find ourselves in an analogous situation. We can handle all the European themes, handle them without superstitions, with an irreverence that can have and already does have fortunate consequences] (1962, 184). Borges calls attention here to the problems of finding a voice for a culture or a people who have not had the opportunity to define their own voice, past, and history. He argues that the way to do that is to accept the tradition of the imposing culture or cultures, but to treat it with a certain distance and irreverence for one's own ends (See Aizenberg 1992).

The story "Tema del traidor y del héroe" (Theme of the Traitor and Hero) (1944) highlights further the similarities between history and fiction. Historian and biographer Ryan investigates the mysterious death in 1824 of Fergus Kilpatrick, an Irish national hero and Ryan's great grandfather. He learns that Kilpatrick was actually a traitor. Kilpatrick's companions, led by James Nolan, try him and find him guilty. So as not to dishearten the rebellion, they act out his death sentence along the lines of a Swiss Festspiele imitating Shakespeare's portrayal of the assassination of Julius Caesar. Consequently, the general public believes that Kilpatrick dies at the hands of an unknown assassin while sitting in a theater.

The story underscores the fictional and textual nature of history. It emphasizes the link between the dramatic and the historical. It suggests that the actors of the historical stage are acting out scripts. It stresses the impossibility of arriving at an objective, definitive history. Historians are detectives trying to piece together missing parts of a past, partially lost puzzle. That Nolan planned the details such that a future historian would discover the truth stresses how one's time confines and shades one's view of history. (Some have seen Nolan as symbolic of God in writing universal history for his role in this regard.) Like the Kafka essay, it suggests that the present creates the past through its perspective on it. The mirrorlike reflection of Kilpatrick's execution and Julius Caesar's assassination, and the foreshadowing of the Lincoln assassination in the theater suggest the repetitive nature of history.

Ryan decides not to reveal his discovery of his grandfather's duplicity for both personal and national reasons. This suggests that historical knowledge does have political and personal ends, although skepticism should and subjectivity must pervade any such investigation and discovery. The fact that the story is set in a struggle for independence and that Kilpatrick's grandson discovers his betrayal proves significant. Borges states that the action occurs in "un país oprimido y tenaz" (1974, 496) [an oppressed and tenacious country]. It underscores that every national history is an individual, personal history, and it stresses the link between individual, familial, and national identity. It emphasizes that in power struggles, the powerful write history. Ryan realizes that his historical study, like the elaborate Festspiele that Nolan arranged, is playing a role in defining the voice and the history of his nation that was a subjugated people, a colony. As a subjugated people, its oppressor defined its history and its past. Both Nolan and Ryan conceal Kilpatrick's betrayal for similar reasons: to keep alive the spirit that engendered and sustained the revolution. Ryan also has personal reasons, since the information on Kilpatrick's betrayal would reflect on his family as well as the national identity.

The repetitiveness of history in "Tema del traidor y del héroe"(Theme of the Traitor and the Hero) calls attention to this theme in a number of his other works. This sense of eternal return defines history as well as a sense of time. It challenges the notion that time is progressive and unrepeatable. "Las ruinas circulares" ("The Circular Ruins") highlights this theme where the wizard discovers that he is a dream image like the son that he has dreamt into existence. Similarly, at the end of "La muerte y la brújula" (Death and the Compass), Lönnrot suggests that Scharlach and he will pursue each other in many future labyrinths. Cyclical events reach back toward a mythical conception of time, a sense that certain rhythms and patterns reappear regularly. Thus, they challenge the concept of a definable universal history, a notion that all history is moving in a predictable and undeniable direction.

Along these lines, in a variety of different prose and poetic pieces, Borges invokes legendary figures from Argentina's literary and historical past: Rosas, Quiroga, Martín Fierro, and others. The references have an epic quality about them. Knife fights and similar settling of scores among gauchos are part of that heritage that keeps playing itself out in stories and poems such as "El Sur" (The South), "El muerto" (The Dead Man) "Biografía de Tadeo Isidoro Cruz (1829–1874)," (A Biography of Tadeo Isidoro Cruz [1829–1874]), "Martín Fierro," "Diálogo de muertos" (Dialogue Between Dead Men), "El Fin" (The End), and numerous others.

This historical/mythical repetition is particularly emphasized in three selections from El hacedor (The Maker), "In Memoriam J. F. K.," "La trama" (The Plot), and "El simulacro" (The Mountebank), and in a short story from El libro de arena (The Book of Sand), "Guayaquil." In "In Memoriam J.F.K.," the narrator suggests that the bullet that killed J.F.K. has reappeared throughout history in various forms and describes some infamous killings through time including that of Idiarte Borde, the Uruguayan president; Lincoln, killed by a Shakespearean actor who thought he was Brutus; Jesus of Nazareth, Gustavus Adolphus, Socrates, and reaching back to the Cain and Abel story. The transformed bullet symbolizes the unfortunate, repetitive tendency of human beings to spill the blood of some of their greatest leaders.

In "La trama" (The Plot), the narrator recalls Caesar's assassination and his recognition of his ward and perhaps his son, Brutus, with the words "Et tu Brute." That recognition leads him to stop resisting. The narrator comments then that fate appreciates symmetries, variations, and repetitions. He proceeds to describe an incident in the province of Buenos Aires nineteen centuries later when a gaucho is similarly pursued and recognizes his godson as an accomplice with the words "Pero che!" The man dies not knowing that he has died in order to repeat the scene.

"El simulacro" (The Mountebank) relates how a man or men have reenacted the funeral of Eva Duarte Perón in small villages. Both the actors involved and the responses of the public amaze the narrator who seems to reflect Borges's voice. The narrator raises all kinds of questions about the nature of history, reality, and myth that are at work here. He wonders what kind of man would carry out such a fake funeral playing the role of General Perón, a cynical imposter? A fanatic? He also wonders whether this actor believed himself to be Perón. The narrator compares the scene to the play within the play in Hamlet, and then comments that Perón was not really Perón either, nor was Eva actually Eva. They were unknown, or anonymous people acting out a crass mythology.

There are multiple implications of this reenactment of the Peróns. Certain historical events take on ritual and mythic proportions because they continue to speak to people who need to reenact them. Political and historical figures are actors on a stage who wear masks to play roles and disguise their identities, as most of us do.

The short story "Guayaquil" (1970) takes on a historical mystery: why San Martín turned his forces over to Bolivar after meeting with him in Guayaquil, thus letting Bolívar receive the glory as the liberator. In the story, original documents explaining what happened at the Guayaquil meeting have suddenly appeared. Dr. Eduardo Zimmerman and the narrator are the two candidates nominated by their universities to receive the documents and to publish their contents. The contest between the two and their encounter to resolve who shall actually go to get the letters parallel the meeting between Bolivar and San Martín. The implications are that history is embodied in men and their wills and that certain historical events keep repeating themselves in various forms.[3]

The poem "La dicha" (Happiness) (1981), reiterates this theme of eternal return and mythic repetition, but on a personal level. The narrator lists a series of diverse events, from embracing a woman where the two become Adam and Eve, to playing with a dagger and foreshadowing Caesar's death, to descending into the Ganges river, to spotting the recently sculpted Sphinx on the desert, to reading Borges's words on a page. As the last two lines state: "Todo sucede por primera vez, pero de un modo eterno. / El que lee mis palabras está inventándolas." [Everything happens for the first time but in a way that is eternal. / Whoever reads my word is inventing them.] (1996, 440–41). The title of the poem suggests a link between happiness and the ability to experience the mythical as new. Much as each rereading of a text is a new reading and new invention, so too if we can experience repeated events as if we are involved in them for the first time, a sense of awe and wonder and happiness become associated with them.

BORGES ON UNIVERSAL HISTORY

"La esfera de Pascal" (Pascal's Sphere) (1951) with the frame lines: "Quizá la historia universal es la historia de la diversa entonación de algunas metáforas" (1974, 638) [Perhaps universal history is the diverse intonation of a few metaphors] (1981, 242) echoes this Eternal Return theme as applied to universal history. In this essay, Borges demonstrates not only how the sphere has served as a metaphor for the universe, but also how that conception has changed. While that sphere once represented the fullness of God's presence, with Pascal it comes to symbolize a labyrinth, isolation, fear, and solitude. The spherical image has not changed. Rather, its intonation and interpretation have changed with the time period and the individual representing it. Thus, "universal history" is not "universal" in the sense of being fixed and eternal. Or, if it is, our minds cannot grasp its total significance. The sphere's metaphoric sense underscores its inexactitude and its fictional nature. It is a fiction in the sense that it is through our imagination that we comprehend it. This image of universal history stands as a criticism of Kantian and Hegelian attempts at divining a universal history. Once again, it emphasizes the symbiotic relationship between the One and the Many in Borges, with the sphere symbolizing the singularity, and the intonations representing the diversity of our interpretations and understandings.

In "El espejo de los enigmas" (The Mirror of the Enigmas), Borges cites passages from León Bloy. While Bloy says that everyone is on earth for a purpose, he also states that no human is capable of knowing with certainty who he/she is and what his/her mission on earth is, and then asserts, "La historia es un inmenso texto litúrgico donde las iotas y los puntos no valen menos que los versículos o capítulos íntegros, pero la importancia de unos y otros es indeterminable y está profundamente escondida" (1974, 722). [History is an immense liturgical text where the iotas and the dots are worth no less than the entire verses or chapters, but the importance of one and the other is indeterminable and profoundly hidden] (1961, 211). This image of history as a text suggests that we "read" history, that it is textual, that it is intertwined with language and the indeterminacy of language, and thus is neither a science, nor objective.

The notion of the textual nature of universal history and of knowledge appears in the short story, "La biblioteca de Babel" (The Library of Babel).[4] In this story, the universe, which is compared to a library, is portrayed as an indecipherable labyrinth. Again, the emphasis lies on the gulf separating the sacred and the profane, and on the limits of man's/woman's ability to comprehend the totality that is the universe. To state this highlights a tension between competing desires in Borges: an intellectual and a spiritual quest of profound dimensions to understand the nature of the universe and the godhead coupled with an equally deep and profound skepticism about our ability to fathom and confirm that.

Borges resolves this conflict between the spiritual search and the skepticism through an idealistic pantheism, the belief that the divine spirit is present in all things and that God is the essence and extension of the universe and universal history.[5] As mentioned earlier, while Borges does not subscribe to any particular philosophy, as all philosophies are fictions, he has stated that, if he had to define himself philosophically, he would associate himself with idealism, particularly the idealism of Schopenhauer (Dembo 1970, 317).

In his essay on Nathaniel Hawthorne, Borges expresses this concept of history and the universe when he discusses Schopenhauer and Emerson. He states that Schopenhauer compares:

la historia a un calidoscopio, en el que cambian las figuras, no los peda-
citos de vidrio, a una eterna y confusa tragicomedia en la que cambian
los papeles y máscaras, pero no los actores. Esa misma intuición de que
el universo es una proyección de nuestra alma y de que la historia universal está en cada hombre, hizo escribir a Emerson el poema que se titula
History. (1974, 679)

[history to a kaleidoscope, in which the figures, not the pieces of glass,
change; and to an eternal and confused tragicomedy in which the roles
and masks, but not the actors, change. The presentiment that the universe is a projection of our soul and that universal history lies within each
man induced Emerson to write the poem entitled "History."] (1981,
225)

The way in which the One and the Many flow together in this image
of the kaleidoscope underscores how Borges balances the two, as
well, in his historical conception. Similarly, in "La esfera de Pascal"
(Pascal's Sphere), Borges suggests an idealistic, pantheistic, paradoxical concept of the universe when he traces the evolution of the
notion, as Alain de Lille states it, or Analus de Insulus, that "Dios es
una esfera inteligible, cuyo centro está en todas partes y la circunfer-
encia en ninguna" (1974, 636). [God is an intelligible sphere whose
center is everywhere and whose circumference is nowhere]) (1981,
240).

A pantheism also figures centrally in two stories I discussed earlier.
In "El Zahir" (The Zahir), the coin symbolizes the pantheistic vision
of the universe, as the references to Schopenhauer, Tennyson, and
the Kabbalah suggest. The narrator states that the Cabalists understood that man is a microcosm and mirror of the universe. He then
asserts that according to Tennyson, everything, even the Zahir,
would be such a microcosm. In "El Aleph" (The Aleph), that magical, unified sphere contains the chaotic multiplicity of the universe.
Both have broad implications for universal history as a mystical, indecipherable, genetic code that plays itself out in all things.

Critics have generally overlooked or ignored the references to certain mystical encounters in Borges's writings. They have focused on
the chaos, the despair, the emphasis on human limitations, and the
absurd in his stories, poems, and prose. These qualities assume a
very prominent position, in part because his challenges to the One
have been of such importance. Critics have mentioned his idealism
and his pantheism but usually in the context of our limitations in
comprehending the cosmos. They have acknowledged the influ-

ences of the Kabbalah and of Buddhism.[6] They stress that he uses their metaphors in a non-religious sense.[7]

Nonetheless, a kind of spiritual quest and a quasi-religious quality permeates his vision. Borges's world is not one in which spirit is absent, as it is with some poststructuralist critics. Rather, it is an idealistic world in which a sense of spirit is everywhere, but indefinable and unknowable. This spiritual quest is evident also in his fascination with conceptions of universal history, with his frequent reference to Christian and Jewish writers who explore pantheistic and idealistic ideas, with his references to Moslem and Buddhist theologians and writings, and in his continuing quest into the existence of God and the nature of the universe.

In an otherwise relativistic world, his writings define certain values. In the heroic and epic gaucho stories, one encounters values such as courage, loyalty, and a passion for life. In other texts, one finds an indefatigable quest to create and to understand, as well. Still others offer subtle criticisms of cruelty and injustice. His sense of the self de-emphasizes individual identity but stresses that we embody the best and the worst of humanity. This expresses a certain universality or a brotherhood/sisterhood of all people.

In "Tema del traidor y del héroe" (Theme of the Traitor and the Hero), the grandson Ryan discovers that history imitates drama and the theater. In "El hombre en el umbral" (The Man in the Threshold), Christopher Dewey discovers that history is story and, like a good story, finds itself repeated. In these and other stories, Borges underscores that the line between fact and fiction, between the real and the illusory, converges into a skeptical, idealistic haze. The events of history are not only not recoverable, but they never were objective and empirical, as the world is ideal rather than material. History does not proceed in a linear, chronological direction toward an ultimate, utopian end, but is repetitive in its mythical patterns. Historical meaning, like all meaning, is constructed, but constructed meaning is not to be disparaged.

Borges's writings include a deep respect for literary and fictional creations and a heroic search for meaning in a seemingly indecipherable world. Throughout his work, he affirms our creative potential and recognizes the existence of a nonmaterial world. He admits that we will never discover the essence of the self, of Universal History and of Universal Truth, but he affirms that there is much merit in continuing to create our fictions and in trying to represent them, as long as we are aware that they are illusory dream images, and not Universal Truth.

Furthermore, while Borges's universe is more skeptical than that of many postmodernists' because all perceptions prove unreliable, it is also imbued with an idealistic and pantheistic spirit. Many poststructuralist and postmodern critics seem aware of the cultural conventions that set "culture" against "nature" in a way in which culture is connected to "spirit," and "nature" is linked with matter. Barthes, Foucault, and others then seek to de-spiritualize "culture," while not challenging material nature. They assert that objectivity is impossible and acknowledge certain limitations, but do not really subvert any underlying material assumptions. This dilemma proves greater for Borges. Most poststructuralists do not seriously consider any sort of metaphysics. However, Borges, with his grounding in Schopenhauer, idealism, and pantheism, challenges and undermines monistic visions and material nature as well.

7

Borges, Politics, and the Postmodern

CRITICS AND POLITICAL ACTIVISTS FREQUENTLY HAVE SOUGHT TO DEFINE the political posture of Jorge Luis Borges, usually while ignoring the biographical details of his life or the political and philosophical implications of his work. Borges's writings in particular contain many overtones that suggest a political attitude. Critics have not looked seriously at his epic tales from the standpoint of politics. Nor have they thoroughly considered the nature of the self as it relates to politics. Perhaps most importantly, they have not considered how his attitude toward all systems suggests a certain political stance. Some have attacked Borges's writings for being apolitical, and others for being reactionary. While some of this may be to the point, much of it is polemical and off the mark.[1] A review of certain biographical material and of some statements by Borges, as well as a look at certain stories captures some of his own political beliefs and has implications for the relationship between politics and postmodernity, in general, and Latin American politics and culture, in particular.

A number of critics have challenged Borges on ideological grounds. Alicia Borinsky takes issue with the suggestion that Borges's writings are neutral and apolitical. She contends that, in effect, this neutrality becomes "re-inscribed as the interested discourse of an ideological elite" (Borinsky 1986, 160). In so doing, the writings create an opposition between intelligence and ignorance, and feed the Sarmentista dichotomy between "civilización y barbarie" [civilization and barbarity]. She argues that these "neutral" discourses work against themselves and assume a political message. Borges certainly respected Sarmiento. However, Borinsky fails to see that a skepticism that undermines all systems also questions what is ignorance and what is intelligence, and what is civilization and what is barbarity. She also loses sight of the way in which certain of Borges's stories project and embody the epic qualities of the gauchos rather than undermine them as ignorant and barbaric, as Borinsky suggests. As pointed out in chapter 2 and the end of chapter 5, stories such as "El informe de Brodie" (Brodie's Report), "El hombre en el umbral" (The Man on the Threshold), "La escritura del Dios" (The God's Script), and "Historia del guerrero y de la cautiva" (Story of the Warrior and the Captive Maiden) subvert the privileging of European civilization and suggest that all cultures have their barbarous qualities.

A few comments on Borges's expressed political positions may be helpful. When the Spanish Civil War broke out in July, 1936, the Argentine intellectual community split in its support of the liberal, allied cause and in its allegiance to the Catholic and the Fascist establishment. Borges, along with Victoria Ocampo and Eduardo Mallea, supported the Allies. While Mussolini and Hitler had considerable support in Argentina before and during World War II, Borges was outspoken against the Fascists and against anti-Semitism.

Many of the essays written against Fascism were never printed in the *Obras Completas* (*Complete Works*). Recently, most of them have been reprinted in *Selected Non-Fictions*. In 1934, Borges wrote an article, "Yo, judío" (I, a Jew), in *Megáfono*, (no. 12, 1934), in which he responds to an accusation that he has Jewish ancestors but has hidden them. He mentions that his full name is Borges Acevedo and some Acevedos are Jewish, and states that he wishes he had more complete proof of a link to the tradition that he considers culturally very rich and respectable. In "Una pedagogía del odio" (A Pedagogy of Hate), *Sur* (no. 32, 1937), he expresses his outrage at an anti-Semitic book intended for children. His pieces "Una exposición afligente" (A Disturbing Exposition) (*Sur* no. 49, Oct. 1938) and "Ensayo de imparcialidad" (An Essay on Neutrality) (*Sur* no. 61, Oct. 1939), call for Hitler's defeat and express dismay at how the Fascists have demeaned and distorted German culture. In the latter work as well as in "Definición de un germanófilo" (Definition of a Germanophile), *El Hogar* (13 December 1940), he tries to separate authentic German culture from Fascists who ruled them at that time. He published another article entitled "1941" in *Sur* (no. 47, Dec. 1941), where he states that people who think that South America is far away from Germany do not realize that colonies are always far away, suggesting that Hitler no doubt would eventually invade the Americas if not stopped. Also in 1941, he reviews two books that take aim at Fascism, one by H. G. Wells and one by Bertrand Russell. The reviews were originally published as "Dos libros de este tiempo" in *La Nación*, but were later republished in the *Obras Com-*

pletas in *Otras Inquisiciones* as "Dos libros" (Two Books). His "Anotación al 23 de agosto de 1944" (Comment on August 23, 1944) was also republished in *Otras Inquisiciones.* He expresses his joy at the liberation of Paris and speculates that Hitler may perhaps want to be defeated. After the war ended, he published "Nota sobre la paz" (A Note on the Peace) in *Sur* (no. 129, July 1945), where he asserts that the victory of the Allies was not only a victory for Western Civilization, but also for England.

Juan Domingo Perón's subsequent rise to power greatly upset the Argentine poet and short-story writer as well. Perón's brand of nationalism, his emphasis on mass movements, his links to Mussolini and Hitler, Fascism and Nazism, and his lack of respect for democracy all incensed Borges, and he spoke out against them. Perón humiliatingly repaid him by relieving him of his post as third assistant at the Miguel Cané Library and appointing him chicken inspector. Borges refused the appointment and became a popular figure in the resistance.

Later, the same regime had Borges's mother and sister arrested and imprisoned for a month for passing out pamphlets. They permitted his mother, who was elderly, to serve her time in her apartment under house guard, while his sister was placed in a prison for prostitutes. This distrust and dislike of Perónism led him to support a right wing dictatorship later in his life, for which he was often rebuked.

His writings show quite clearly that he did not hold strong dictators in high regard. This is evident in the prologue which he wrote to Thomas Carlyle's work on heroes. Borges mentions that Carlyle perceived the world around him as disintegrating and saw no remedy other than the dissolution of parliaments and the surrender of power to strong and powerful men. Germany, Russia, and Italy eagerly sought that panacea; Borges expressed his disapproval: "los resultados son el servilismo, el temor, la brutalidad, la indigencia mental y la delación" (1996, 39) [the results are servility, fear, brutality, mental indigence, and treachery] (1999a, 416).

Similarly, in "Pedro Salvadores," he relates the tale of a man whom his grandfather Acevedo supposedly knew. He calls it "uno de los hechos más tristes de nuestra historia" (1974, 994) [one of the strangest and saddest events in the history of my country] (1998, 336). When Rosas's "mazorca" or the secret police come looking for him, he hides out in his cellar and never reappears until Rosas flees the country. The selection highlights the people's terror of the dictator and their willingness to put up with it.

However, Borges expresses reservations about democracy as practiced in the United States, as well. In "Nota sobre la paz" (A Note on the Peace), he mentions that the military might of the three countries that won World War II is more admirable than the cultures they represent. He asserts that the United States has not fulfilled the great promise of its nineteenth century. His prologue to Whitman's *Leaves of Grass* expands on this notion. He states: "América era entonces el símbolo famoso de un ideal, ahora un tanto gastado por el abuso de las urnas electorales y por los elocuentes excesos de la retórica, aunque millones de hombres le hayan dado, y sigan dándole su sangre" (1996, 157). [America, at the time was the famous symbol of an ideal, now a little worn down by an excessive dependence on the ballot box and by the eloquent excesses of its rhetoric, though millions of men have given and continue to give it their blood] (1999a, 446).

Borges made some comments on his approach to art and political commitments as well that should have helped clarified his political stance in regard to art, but did not. In the prologue to *El informe de Brodie* (*Brodie's Report*), he states:

> sólo quiero aclarar que no soy, ni he sido jamás, lo que antes se llamaba un fabulista o un predicador de parábolas y ahora un escritor comprometido. No aspiro a ser Esopo. Mis cuentos como los de las *Mil y una noches*, quieren distraer y conmover y no persuadir. Este propósito no quiere decir que me encierre, según la imagen salomónica, en una torre de marfil. Mis convicciones en materia política son harto conocidas; Me he afiliado al Partido Conservador, lo cual es una forma de escepticismo, y nadie me ha tildado de comunista, de nacionalista, de antisemita, de partidario de Hormiga Negra o de Rosas. Creo que con el tiempo merecemos que no haya gobiernos. No he disimulado nunca mis opiniones, ni siquiera en los años arduos, pero no he permitido que interfieran en mi obra literaria, salvo cuando me urgió la exaltación de la Guerra de los Seis Días. (1974, 1021)

> [But I do wish to make clear that I am not, nor have I ever been, what used to be called a fabulist or spinner of parables, what these days is called an *auteur engagé*. I do not aspire to be Aesop. My tales, like those of the *Thousand and One Nights,* are intended not to persuade readers, but to entertain and touch them. This intention does not mean that I shut myself, as Solomon's image would have it, into an ivory tower. My convic-

tions with respect to political matters are well known; I have joined the Conservative Party (which act is a form of skepticism), and no one has ever called me a Communist, a nationalist, an anti-Semite, or a supporter of Hormiga Negra or of Rosas. I believe that in time we will have reached the point where we will deserve to be free of government. I have never hidden my opinions, even through the difficult years, but I have never allowed them to intrude upon my literary production, either, save that one time when I praised the Six-Day War.] (1998 345–46)

In an interview with Rita Guibert, he elaborates upon some of these statements. He explains that to be a conservative in Argentina is not to belong to the right, but to belong to the center. He asserts that he detests the Nationalists and Fascists as much as he does the Communists, and that has been, basically his consistent position. He continues:

[I more or less believe in democracy, and of course I've always been against Perónism. Perón's government never had any doubts about that. They attacked me by throwing me out of a small post I held, and my mother, sister, and one of my nephews were imprisoned.] (Guibert 1973, 112–13)

During the "dirty war" of the 1970s, Borges signed letters asking for an accounting of the "disappeared." He refers to those government actions as clandestine terrorism, and opposed them (Borges 1984a, 147–48). Furthermore, while neither a Marxist nor a socialist, he affirms that economic inequality is the worst enemy of liberty, and that luxury is as offensive as poverty (Borges 1984a, 142–43).

In the same interview with Rita Guibert, he reiterates that he considers his literary views and his political views to be separate. In regard to literature, politics, and skepticism, he asserts:

[I have tried never to let my opinions intrude into my work; I would almost prefer people to be unaware of what these opinions are. If a story or a poem of mine is successful, its success springs from a deeper source than my political views, which may be erroneous and are dictated by circumstances. In my case, my knowledge of what is called political reality is very incomplete. My life is really spent among books, many of them from a past age, so that I may well be mistaken.] (Guibert 1973, 114)

There are two key aspects here. One has to do with his skepticism in regard to politics, and the other concerns not letting his political views find their way, (interferir) into his literary works. As for his skepticism, it is important to note that his affiliation with the Conservative Party was his way of affirming the stance of the skeptic. He makes clear that he views this affiliation as an alternative to certain dogmatic, ideological stances (Fascism, Communism, Anti-Semitism, etc.). It should come as no surprise that he would prefer a skeptical political stance, since it very much corresponds with his literary and philosophical writings. A political skepticism that challenges monistic attitudes toward justice, truth, freedom, right and wrong etc., by nature is antiauthoritarian and antidictatorial. As such it emphasizes pluralistic models and governments that allow for diversity and local control. In short, his general, anarchistic vision comes much closer to pluralistic democratic models of government than to monistic, authoritarian ones. Postmodern political expressions have favored such pluralistic, democratic models.

Borges's attempt not to introduce politics into his literary writings has, in part, led some to define his writings as "apolitical." An important difference exists between not being politically committed and being totally apolitical, between not having a political agenda and being neutral politically. Borges falls into the former categories. His writings have defined precise intellectual and philosophical themes. Some have argued that all writing is ideological and political. That assumption, like the mirrors in Borges, basically reflects upon itself. If one seeks to find ideology in everything, one will. But that tells more about the person wanting to find it than it does about the universal or truth-value of ideologies. Borges's general stance argues that all philosophical systems, all ideologies, are fictions that will be replaced in the future by other constructs. They are all temporary constructs with no universal truth-value. That said, it must also be stated that there are political overtones in some of his writings. He would argue that to transcend the social, political, cultural, and historical milieu of one's time proves impossible. Yet, those political themes are not the central defining message of his works. Understanding them, however, makes for a clearer conception of his writings and thoughts. I propose to re-examine three of Borges's stories that contain certain political or ideological undercurrents from a different perspective with different emphases from previous discussions: "La forma de la espada" (The Form of the Sword) (1944), "La biblioteca de Babel" (The Library of Babel) (1941), and "El hombre en el umbral" (The Man on the Threshold) (1949). I will also examine the essay from *Otras inquisiciones* (*Other Inquisitions*),

Nuestro pobre individualismo" (Our Poor Individualism) (1946) and refer to several other stories.

"La forma de la espada" (The Form of the Sword), contains some of Borges's most explicit comments in story form about his political ideas.[2] While not a dogmatic political statement, the story implicitly criticizes Marxist dogma and sets it off against a more pluralistic vision.

This story subtly calls into question dogmatic and monistic clarity. Juxtaposed against that certainty is a murky, pluralistic, dreamlike narrative in which nothing is as it seems. The narrator of the story within the story, who is called "el Inglés" [the Englishman] actually is Irish. Borges is quite drunk when he asks about the scar on El Inglés's face and then hears the story that we read. El Inglés tells his story in a combination of English, Spanish, and Portuguese. Borges comments that "su español era rudimental, abrasilerado" (1974, 491). [His Spanish was rudimentary, cluttered with Brazilian] (1962, 67).

That backdrop helps sharpen the contrast to the supposed clarity of Marxist thought. John Vincent Moon, who enters a cell that is fighting for Irish independence, represents that Communist perspective:

> Había cursado con fervor y con vanidad casi todas las páginas de no sé qué manual comunista; el materialismo dialéctico le servía para cegar cualquier discusión. Las razones que puede tener un hombre para abominar de otro o para quererlo son infinitas: Moon reducía la historia universal a un sórdido conflicto económico. Afirmaba que la revolución está predestinada a triunfar. (1974, 492)

> [He had studied with fervor and with vanity nearly every page of Lord knows what Communist manual; he made use of dialectical materialism to put an end to any discussion whatever. The reasons one can have for hating another man, or for loving him, are infinite: moon reduced the history of the universe to a sordid economic conflict. He affirmed that the revolution was predestined to succeed.] (1962, 68–69)

The dogmatic tone that Moon brings to his belief disturbs the narrator of this imbedded tale more than anything. The certainty of his truth leads him to scorn the opinions of others: "Los juicios emitidos por Moon me impresionaron menos que su inapelable tono apodíctico. El nuevo camarada no discutía: dictaminaba con desdén y con cierta cólera" (1974, 492). [The judgments Moon emitted impressed me less than his irrefutable, apodictic note. The new comrade did not discuss: he dictated opinions with scorn and with a certain anger] (1962, 69).

Moon's simplistic dogma stands in relief to the background and attitudes of the others. They were Republicans, Catholics, Romantics. Their sense of identity and understanding of what Ireland represents contained a richness and depth before which Moon's attitudes paled:

> Irlanda no sólo era para nosotros el porvenir utópico y el intolerable presente: era una amarga y cariñosa mitología, era las torres circulares y ciénagas rojas, era el repudio de Parnell y las enormes epopeyas que cantan el robo de toros que en otra encarnación fueron héroes y en otras peces y montañas. (1974, 492)

> [Ireland was for us not only the utopian future and the intolerable present; it was a bitter and cherished mythology; it was the circular towers and the red marshes, it was the repudiation of Parnell and the enormous epic poems which sang of the robbing of bulls which in another incarnation were heroes and in others fish and mountains.] (1962, 68)

These myths and legends provide an alternative vision of history to that of Moon's dogma. Borges extends and develops this tension further. The ranch in which the two hide out symbolizes the pluralistic labyrinthine complexity of the universe as well. It belongs to "General Berkeley," a not so subtle reference to the English philosopher, idealist, and skeptic who influenced Borges. It has an intertwining of corridors that mirror the universe. The museum and the enormous library on the ground floor contained "libros controversiales e incompatibles que de algún modo son la historia del siglo XIX (1974, 493). [Controversial and uncongenial books which are in some manner the history of the nineteenth century] (1962, 69). The reference has echoes of the story, "La biblioteca de Babel" (The Library of Babel), a story that depicts the pluralistic nature of our knowledge and the difficulty in defining certainty and truth. That conflict with dogmatic Marxism is underscored when the narrator relates that Moon's wound would not permit him to descend to the ground floor where the library is, that is, his dogmatic inflexibility excludes him from appreciating the complex diversity of the universe.

At the end, the surprise revelation that "el Inglés" is actually John Vincent Moon adds an extra ironic twist to the tension between

Marxism and nondogmatic visions. Not only Moon's cowardice, but also his lack of sensitivity toward diverse Irish culture, and his betrayal, discredit Communism. El Inglés's turnabout implies that he has rejected his former position as a Marxist and now sees the shortcomings of that stance.

Yet, Borges's stories take issue with more than just Marxism. "La biblioteca de Babel" (The Library of Babel) offers an example. The story portrays the universe as an intricate, indecipherable, but symmetric and periodic structure. The description carries with it certain political overtones. More than anything, the narrator expresses a skepticism about what can be known of this complex storehouse of books, and thus of knowledge, which offers nothing to the most diligent of searches. Illusion and repetition dominate the library. The infinite number of hexagons is duplicated by the mirrors in the hallways. Those who have sought vindication and personal meaning, almost without exception, have died without succeeding. These Vindications do exist. The narrator states that he has seen two of them referring to people in the future. The problem is that the possibility of finding one's own can be computed as virtually zero.

Those pursuing "el Hombre del Libro" (The Man of the Book), that is, the One who has access to the book that orders and organizes all the others, are unlikely to find him as well. Borges includes a reference to book burning and censorship, thus taking aim at those who believe in imposing their vision of the truth on others. Some, seeking to eliminate "useless" books, would leaf through one book and then destroy a whole shelf: "A su furor higiénico, ascético, se debe la insensata perdición de millones de libros" (1974, 469). [Their hygienic, ascetic furor caused the senseless perdition of millions of books] (1962, 56). In the universe of this story, a world in which absolutes such as meaning, truth, and certainty are beyond our reach and comprehension, any political system that pretends to represent those absolutes would probably confront a healthy skepticism from Borges. The Argentine author captures here the intellectual anarchy that he came to accept from his father.

Borges's general stance argues that all philosophical systems and ideologies are fictions that will be replaced by future constructs. They possess no universal truth-value. This central theme in his writings provides the foundation for the real/marvelous or magical realism. For Borges, the real/marvelous or magical realism highlights the role of the imagination and of man/woman as fiction-maker, but it is not simple escapism. On the contrary, it presents another vision, an alternative history, a different fiction or way of looking at the world. As such, politically, it offers openings for the marginalized and challenges the established authority's vision of history and reality.

In a selection from *Otras inquisiciones* (*Other Inquisitions*), entitled "Nuestro pobre individualismo" (Our Poor Individualism) he makes the connection between this anarchical, philosophical stance and a political position. He expresses political views that he later echoes in the prologue to *El informe de Brodie (Brodie's Report)*, although he connects the philosophical views of "La biblioteca de Babel" (The Library of Babel) to a political stance in a way here that he does not in the Prologue. In this text, he sets out to define the national character and political disposition of the Argentine. In contrast to the European or the American, the Argentine "no se identifica con el Estado" (1974, 658) [does not identify himself with the state] (1981, 167). He says that "el argentino es un individuo, no un ciudadano" (1974, 658) [the Argentine is an individual, not a citizen] (1962, 167). For him, the state is an abstraction, often corrupt and impersonal. He identifies with the underdog who may flout the law and challenge authority. His instincts affirm the sins and faults of all men:

> El mundo, para el europeo, es un cosmos, en el que cada cual íntimamente corresponde a la función que ejerce; para el argentino, es un caos. El europeo y el americano de Norte juzgan que ha de ser bueno un libro que ha merecido un premio cualquiera, el argentino admite la posibilidad de que no sea malo, a pesar del premio. En general, el argentino descree de las circunstancias. (1974, 659)

> [For the European the world is a cosmos where each person corresponds intimately to the function he performs; for the Argentine it is a chaos. The European and the North American believe that a book which has been awarded any sort of prize must be good; the Argentine acknowledges the possibility that it may not be bad, in spite of the prize. In general, the Argentine is a skeptic.] (1981, 168)

This essay, written in 1946, at the time Perón came to power and removed Borges from his position as librarian, serves as his response to monistic, authoritarian systems. At the end of this essay, he makes that link between the philosophical and the political:

> Se dirá que los rasgos que he señalado son meramente negativos o anárquicos; se añadirá que no son capaces de explicación política. Me atrevo

a sugerir lo contrario. El más urgente de los problemas de nuestra época (ya denunciado con profética lucidez por el casi olvidado Spencer) es la gradual intromisión del Estado en los actos del individuo; en la lucha con ese mal, cuyos nombres son comunismo y nazismo, el individualismo argentino, acaso inútil o prejudicial hasta ahora, encontrará justificación y deberes.

Sin esperanza y con nostalgia, pienso en la abstracta posibilidad de un partido que tuviera alguna afinidad con los argentinos; un partido que nos prometiera (digamos) un severo mínimo de gobierno. (1974, 659)

[Perhaps someone will say that the qualities I have mentioned are merely negative or anarchical ones, and will add that they are not capable of political application. I venture to suggest that the opposite is true. The most urgent problem of our time (already proclaimed with prophetical clarity by the almost forgotten Spencer) is the gradual interference of the state in the acts of the individual; in the struggle against this evil—called Communism and Fascism—Argentine individualism, which has perhaps been useless or even harmful up to now, would find justification and positive value.

Without hope and with nostalgia, I think of the abstract possibility of a political party that has some affinity with the Argentine character; a party that would promise us, say, a rigorous minimum of government.] (1981, 168)

Whether Borges's analyses of the Argentine character and its political attitude are accurate or not, he has defined his own political sensibilities here, sensibilities that would have ramifications beyond Argentina.

He links this individualistic nature of the Argentine to the gaucho past and expresses it in other writings. For instance, he defined the Argentine character similarly in "Historia del Tango" (History of the Tango) in *Evaristo Carriego*. He contends that the tango is linked to gaucho bawdry, and the desire to identify with a brave past, with honor and bravery. He says that the Argentines associate courage with the gaucho, not the soldier. The gaucho is a rebel, not in service of a cause. The Argentine is an individual, not a citizen, he contends here, and thus does not identify with the state. Consequently, the Argentine always has difficulty with a film that portrays a hero betraying a criminal friend to the police.

A number of his "realistic" fictions that deal with knife fights and gauchos capture this individualism and this attitude toward the law, authority figures, and police. "El indigno" (Unworthy) and "Historia de Rosendo Juárez" (The Story of Rosendo Juarez) from *El informe de Brodie* (*Brodie's Report*) (1970) illustrate this. In "El indigno" (Unworthy), Santiago Fischbein, a bookstore owner, relates an incident from his early years when he became indebted to a hoodlum, Francisco Ferrari. Fischbein betrays the gang leader Ferrari and his friends in a robbery. The police are brutal and kill Ferrari and his gang members unnecessarily. Distrust of the authority here is an underlying theme. The title for the story comes from the guilt that Fischbein continues to live with for betraying them.

Similarly, in "Historia de Rosendo Juárez" (The Story of Rosendo Juarez), the police are portrayed as corrupt. They release Juarez with the stipulation that he work with them to fix elections. In many of the other gaucho tales, the law is basically absent. Its absence comments on its lack of importance in defining order. In these and other stories, Borges's attitude toward the Argentine character comes into play through the depiction of characters.

In "El hombre en el umbral" (The Man on the Threshold), Borges writes a story that moves on metaphysical and political levels. While discussed earlier, revisiting it from a somewhat different perspective can further clarify Borges's political attitudes. The story about the disappearance of a stern, authoritarian British judge, David Alexander Glencairn, serving in India, comments on the nature of the universe and of justice, on the fate of colonial rule as well as on the fate of totalitarian regimes.

Borges hints at a symbolic and metaphysical dimension to the story when he refers to a proverb: "Un refrán dice que la India es más grande que el mundo; Glencairn, tal vez omnipotente en la ciudad que una firma al pie de un decreto le destinó, era una mera cifra en los engranajes de la administración del Imperio" (1974, 613). [There is a saying, you know—that India is larger than the world; Glencairn, who may have been all-powerful in the city to which he was fated by a signature at the end of some document, was a mere cipher in the coils and springs and working of the Empire] (1998, 270). The aged yet ageless quality of the man who tells the-story-within-the-story adds a timeless quality to the tale and gives it implications beyond the simple details of the plot. The house where the execution occurs creates the same effect. Its simplicity and yet complexity epitomize the labyrinthine complexity of the world. The tyrant in the story-within-the-story, and by extension, Glencairn were tried and judged like any other. What's important, he says, is knowing if it was built in heaven or hell. The labyrinthine sense of this search receives further development when Dewey enters the house. Inside, crowds of people flow past him. It amazes him that so many have been able to enter. He moves through several narrow patios until he finally reaches the last one, the center of the labyrinth or the universe, where he finds the madman with the bloodied sword.

Of course, the presence of the madman administering justice in the center of the labyrinthine universe raises important questions. Is that the nature of God? The old man goes to some length to explain the people's choice of judge. While it is believed that every generation contains four upright men who justify the universe before God, no one knows who those four are, not even those who are the selected. Therefore, all agreed on a madman "para que la sabiduría de Dios hablara por su boca y avergonzara las soberbias humanas" (1974, 615) [so that the wisdom of God might speak through his mouth and bring shame to human pride and overweening] (1998, 272). It is not that God is definitely a madman for Borges, but that God works even through the mad. Universal justice may appear arbitrary, but that is because of our own limitations in understanding the order of the universe.

I will not go into great detail in defining the anti-colonial commentary in the story, since Daniel Balderston has done that quite thoroughly already and since I referred to that earlier.[3] Suffice it to say that Borges uses the story to revisit Kipling and to suggest the shortcomings of trying to impose colonial rule and Western values on a foreign culture.

The general indictment of authoritarian rule relates to the criticism of colonialism but stands on its own, separate from it as well, and comments on totalitarian versus democratic rule. In telling his tale, Dewey names the missing judge, David Alexander Glencairn. He states that "los dos nombres convienen; porque fueron de reyes que gobernaron con un cetro de hierro" (1974, 612) [the two Christian names befit the man, for they are the names of kings who ruled with an iron scepter] (1998, 269). In elaborating on David Alexander Glencairn's totalitarian rule, Dewey states that Glencairn was greatly feared. The announcement of his arrival quieted the city. Dewey also relates that rigid censorship exists. The old man's perspective on Glencairn's rule differs from Dewey's, however. The English judge who stands at the center of the old man's story within the story, and serves as camouflage for Glencairn, obviously is corrupt:

no tardó en prevaricar y oprimir, en paliar delitos abominables y en vender decisiones . . . su afinidad con todos los malos jueces del mundo

era demasiado notoria, y al fin hubimos de admitir que era simplemente
un malvado. Llegó a ser un tirano. (1974, 614)

[no time did it take him to prevaricate and oppress, to find extenuation
for abominable crimes, and to sell his verdicts . . . his similarity to the
other evil judges of the world was too clear, and at last we had to admit
that he was simply an evil man. He soon became a tyrant.] (1998, 271)

Thus, Glencairn's iron-fisted, authoritarian rule stands juxtaposed
against the democratic tendencies of the people who act together to
kidnap and try him, and who choose one of the most feeble among
themselves, a madman, as arbiter and receptacle of the divine judgment. The story implies that tyrants who try to impose their dictatorial rule on the people will not succeed.

THE POSTMODERN AND POLITICS

This reading of Borges carries with it important implications for
understanding the political edge of the postmodern. Some have argued that the postmodern has no politics. In part, this argument derives from attempts by Jean François Lyotard and Umberto Eco,
among others, to define the postmodern as an ideal concept.[4] It also
derives from the parody that is a part of the postmodern and its tendency to appropriate and use existing stories and images ironically.
It also comes from some critics who have described the postmodern
as little more than pastiche. As suggested by my readings of the
above texts, a look at one who has provided a great deal of literary
and philosophical foundation for the postmodern discussion would
seem to argue that the postmodern is not apolitical.

The postmodern condition is a critical condition. It engages, employs, parodies, and undermines authorities. To the extent that it
espouses philosophical anarchy, that it has lost faith in the "grand
recits,"—Capitalism, Enlightenment Humanism, Marxism, Christianity—it serves a critical function and it tends to democratize. In
emphasizing ambiguity, in undermining the monisms of modernism, it argues for pluralism.

From this perspective, it is not surprising that much of the conception and thrust of postmodern writing and definition of postmodern culture has occurred in the New World in literary and
critical texts of the United States and of Latin America. Historically,

those regions have defined themselves and have been seen by the rest of the world as havens of political and cultural pluralism, although they have not always lived up to the highest standards of those visions.

As Borges suggests in texts in which he stresses self-referentiality, although the postmodern condition may be a critical condition, it is implicated in what it is criticizing. It professes a skepticism that it turns not only on its targets, but on itself. It is eminently self-critical and self-reflexive. It constantly challenges its own assumptions and bases and may resist drawing conclusions. As it is implicated in what it is criticizing, it is not revolutionary in its methods.

I have argued that the postmodern condition begins with the end of World War II and the ensuing intellectual crisis. If modernism must accept the blame for producing Hitler and Stalin, postmodernity must take responsibility for many of the political events that have occurred while it has dominated the cultural scene. Political movements linked to postmodern culture include the civil rights movement in the United States and the emphasis on ethnic identities as minority voices moved from the margins to the center, the "sexual revolution" that began in the 1960s, the anti-war and the activist feminist movements which also surged in the 1960s, the rise of the new conservatism in the United States as a backlash against the pluralism and secularism of postmodern culture, and the ecology movement.[5]

One disturbing result began with the Iranian revolution and the rise of the Ayatollah Khomeini. Both anticolonialism and the postmodern have figured in this rise of Islamic fundamentalism. As the death sentence on Salman Rushdie implied, the Khomeini revolution is a backlash against the pluralism, skepticism, and secularism of the postmodern and of the West. Both Iranian fundamentalism and that of Al Qaeda share that attitude, as the attacks on the World Trade Center and the Pentagon on September 11, 2001 prove. It was no accident that New York City suffered the brunt of the 9/11 attack. More than almost any city in the world, New York captures and symbolizes the rich diversity and pluralism of our planet. In many ways, this war seems to be a war between monism and pluralism. The monism they espouse believes in "Truth" with a capital T, and is premodern in its basic beliefs, but uses certain aspects of postmodern culture, such as loose networks, technology, and the internet to attack and attempt to destroy that culture.

There appear to be other international ramifications, both posi-

tive and negative. What has happened in Latin America is representative of a worldwide trend. In Latin American countries such as
Argentina, Chile, Brazil, Nicaragua, and Uruguay, dictatorships of
the right and of the left have fallen and have been replaced by more
or less pluralistic, democratic movements. Mexico's recent turn away
from authoritarian, single-party rule and toward pluralistic democracy is but another example. It seems that monistic, authoritarian,
totalitarian governments have relinquished power as their authority
and assumptions have lost support. Not the least of these was the
former Soviet Union, where Eastern Europe broke away and Communism lost its authority. Countries there are experimenting with
different degrees and forms of Western pluralistic democracy. Part
of the impetus for French poststructuralist writings was to find an
alternative to a failed Stalinist Marxism. Marcus W. Brauchli, in an
article entitled "More Nations Embrace Democracy—and Find It
Often Can Be Messy," printed in *The Wall Street Journal*, on June 25,
1996, asserts that according to Freedom House, a U.S. think tank,
in 1974, only thirty-nine countries, one in four of the independent
countries of the world, were democracies with freely elected governments. In 1996, more than a billion people in 117 independent
countries voted in open elections to choose their leaders.

On the one hand, there seems to be a movement toward forms of
"immanence" as Ihab Hassan refers to it. The unification of the
world through the mass media, the almost universal acceptance of
the issues of ecology, the economic integration through international markets and the free trade agreements, the internet, and
globalization offer examples.

On the other hand, there are tendencies toward division, separation, and nationalistic disintegration. The seemingly irresolvable
ethnic wars in the former Yugoslavia, in Somalia and Zaire, and in
other regions have postmodern overtones and highlight some of the
more troubling problems of this new pluralism with its rise in new
nationalism. These conflicts are movements away from the totalizing
(and sometimes totalitarian) tendencies of the past and toward ethnic division, separatism, and at times disintegration. The list goes
on. The nearly successful attempt of French Quebec to separate
from Canada is another example of the movement toward ethnic
diversity and, at times of division and separation.

In his presidential bid, Ross Perot's reference to that "giant suck-
ing sound" of jobs migrating to Mexico, represented certain fears of
the potential for backlash but also certain immanent tendencies of

the postmodern. Of course, many of these developments are still in the incipient stage. Only time will tell which infant movements and tendencies will survive and if so, in what form, and whether they will be more or less successful than modernism in creating humane and just societies. At any rate, an early postmodernist, Borges's writings have become partially implicated in these changes.

8

Borges, the Postmodern, and the Literature of the Americas: *Cien años de soledad* and *The Universal Baseball Association, Inc., J. Henry Waugh, Prop.*

WHEN I FIRST BEGAN THIS STUDY, I SOUGHT TO HIGHLIGHT BORGES'S presence in contemporary literature with a special emphasis on U.S. and Latin American literature. Borges has had a profound affect on the writings of authors on virtually every continent. It quickly became clear to me that to show how contemporary writers have created Borges as a precursor, I needed to write this book. It also became obvious that a thorough, effective, and specific discussion of Borges's impact on other writers lay beyond the scope of this book. It is a project in process, my next major one. However, it is possible and useful here to sketch out certain parameters of that influence.

Borges has impacted the post-World War II literature of the Americas in profound and dramatic ways both through his vision and through his symbols and techniques. Both north and south of the Rio Grande, the writings of authors such as Toni Morrison, John Barth, Robert Coover, William Kennedy, Julio Cortázar, Bioy Casares, Gabriel García Márquez, Isabel Allende, and Carlos Fuentes, to name a few, draw on the images of the labyrinth to highlight the inexplicable and pluralistic nature of our world and our limitations in understanding that world. They move away from literary realism and naturalism and employ fantasy or the real-marvelous or magical realism to underscore the blurring of the line between "reality" and dream, fiction, and the imagination. They incorporate myths, legends, and the fantastic into their stories to capture the sense of ontological doubt of our times, to emphasize that there are other ways of looking at the world. They emphasize the pluralistic and fictional nature of history and historical discourse. They give expression to voices that traditionally have been marginalized. They project a concept of the self that is divided, plural, fragmented, or a surface or façade where the self and other, the "I" and "you" vocalizations fold into each other. These techniques, methods, and visions derive in large part from Borges. I will discuss two works here, Gabriel García Márquez's *Cien años de soledad (One Hundred Years of Solitude)* and Robert Coover's *The Universal Baseball Association, Inc., J. Henry Waugh, Prop.*, to illustrate Borges's literary presence.

CIEN AÑOS DE SOLEDAD (ONE HUNDRED YEARS OF SOLITUDE), THE POSTMODERN, AND BORGES

Critics have called attention to numerous sources and influences for García Márquez's masterful novel, including Faulkner, Kafka, and others. In some ways it speaks to the poetic force of this work that it is indebted to everyone and no one. Borges has been mentioned as an influence, but there have been few detailed studies of that relationship. In his article, "Streams Out of Control: The Latin American Plot" (2002), Carlos Rincón asserts that the texts of two Latin American writers have determined and continue to determine the way Latin American fiction is viewed around the world, those of Borges and García Márquez. In this article, he selects García Márquez's *Cien años de soledad (One Hundred Years of Solitude)* for discussion because the novel pays tribute to "the Lord of the Labyrinth" (Rincón 2002, 158). James Higgins states that García Márquez draws heavily on literary sources for this novel, and that Borges appears to be the primary one. He points out that behind Borges lies the corpus of Western culture (Higgins 2002, 39). John Barth, in "The Literature of Replenishment," asserts that *Cien años de soledad (One Hundred Years of Solitude)* is the exemplary postmodernist novel (Barth 1980, 70).

Many of the symbols, characters, methods, literary innovations, strategies, themes, and ideas of the novel capture the shift of Western culture from modernism toward postmodern pluralism, and in doing so, show the mark of Borges. Like the writings of Borges, the novel first and foremost gives voice to the ontological uncertainty of our times (Higgins 2002, 37). The novel addresses the profound literary, philosophical, economic, and social implications of this postmodern debate for Western culture in general and for the peoples and countries of Latin America in particular. It calls attention to certain stories of Borges that I have discussed in this book that capture that uncertainty and emphasize those issues: "El Aleph" (The Aleph), "La casa de Asterión" (The House of Asterion), "La escritura del Dios" (The God's Script), "Deutsches Requiem," "El inmortal" (The Immortal), "La forma de la espada" (The Form of the Sword), "Las ruinas circulares" (The Circular Ruins), and "La biblioteca de Babel" (The Library of Babel).

García Márquez takes a lesson from Borges's admonition to the Argentine writers in "El escritor argentino y la tradición" (The Argentine Writer and Tradition) (1951). Working within Western tradition and with Western themes and myths in this work, he challenges its modernism. The Colombian novelist gives voice to a distinctive Latin American vision and at the same time underscores how the dynamics of modernism and monolithic views have marginalized the cultures and countries of the Americas. Whether it be the shrewish comic personality of Fernanda with her emphasis on royalty, class distinction, religiosity, and thus the Spanish conquest or the banana company, the Colombian author extensively laments the heritage and the past that has been lost with the imposition of foreign cultures.[1]

When *Cien años* first appeared, it garnered such international attention because it offered an alternative to the Eurocentric vision of reality. It accomplishes this, in large part, through the incorporation of the magical realism or the real-marvelous. While the real marvelous of García Márquez differs somewhat from the fantasy of Borges, they are both used to the same effect.[2] They are not simple escapism, but serve a critical function. Both not only create a space for utopian visions, but also argue for alternative visions of the world. Whether with the incredible Aleph, the stopping of time and a bullet in flight, a child with a pig's tail, a Priest levitating after drinking chocolate, or the portrayal of certain characters, both challenge not only the novel's conventional Eurocentric vision, but also the whole rationalistic tradition of the West. They argue for multiple ways of viewing our experiences. The Colombian and the Argentine both suggest that "reality" is myth and legend, that reality is a labyrinth, that reality is representation, that reality is circular, repetitive patterns, that reality is imagination and fiction. They assert that reality and history are written by the powerful, and that they can be rewritten.

Several of García Márquez's characters stretch the boundaries of traditional "reality" in this way. José Arcadio Buendía offers a prime example. Magical reason and scientific reason are juxtaposed in his consciousness (Jara Cuadra y Mejía 1972, 31–32). For him, a priest levitating while drinking chocolate is nothing out of the ordinary. Ice and other everyday occurrences can fascinate him because the experiences of the senses and the marvelous live side-by-side in his reality. His acceptance of the marvelous as everyday, and of the everyday as marvelous argues for another way of viewing the world, another perspective on life. As in the works of Borges, dreams and mirror images assume a certain privileged authority in this real-marvelous world, while subtly undermining modernism's faith in the senses and the reality of the senses. For instance, Macondo, the village around which the novel revolves, derives from José Arcadio Buendía's dream of "una ciudad ruidosa con casas de paredes de espejo" (García Márquez 1985, 81) [a noisy city with houses having mirror walls] (García Márquez 1991, 24).[3]

José Arcadio Buendía also proves to be a fascinating figure because at the same time that his real marvelous consciousness challenges modernity and the boundaries of realism, his relationship with Melquíades affirms them. Melquíades, as a missionary of progress with all his gadgets, brings with him certain modernistic attitudes, a faith in science, progress, and technology (Conniff 2002, 144–45). José Arcadio Buendía accepts those attitudes and welcomes his inventions. Melquíades's arrival undoes the socialist political experiment of the early part of the novel, helps usher in and garner acceptance of the banana company and other foreign influences, and ultimately contributes to the apocalyptic ending that suggests that science, technology, and modernity may not be the solution for Macondo's problems.

The two principal characters during the era of government, politics, and wars in the novel, the brothers, Colonel Aureliano and José Arcadio, also serve to critique the realism of modernity because of the way that myth and legend help form their identities. José Arcadio is an archetype of the adventurer, sexual hero, and sailor. Like Borges's sailor/narrator of "La lotería en Babilonia" (The Babylonian Lottery), he has traveled the world and experienced almost everything. García Márquez takes that model one step further. José Arcadio's extraordinary penis and his incredible adventures move him as a character into the realm of myths, legends, and epic, suggesting that these qualities play a role in defining the self. It parallels, in some ways, Borges's use of the images and legends of Martín Fierro and other gauchos in stories like "Biografía de Tadeo Isidoro Cruz (1829–74)" (A Biography of Tadeo Isidoro Cruz [1829–

1874]), or "El Sur" (The South) to define his characters, while suggesting at the same time that the self is a fiction. A mythical warrior and sexual hero, Colonel Aureliano is caught in the inescapable physical and psychological labyrinth of war and peace, pride and humility, like Borges's Minotaur on whom he seems partly modeled, and like Colombia, whose experiences he symbolizes. Much as Borges uses the solitary, lonely Minotaur, half-human half-monster who is caught in a labyrinth, who is proud and deceived, oppressor and oppressed, murderer and victim, to represent our existential dilemma, García Márquez uses the solitary, lonely Colonel Aureliano Buendía trapped in a labyrinth of ambushes, escapes, and uprisings to symbolize the political, social, and psychological tragedy and horror of his countrymen. Like the Minotaur, he becomes a monster of sorts, cold, dehumanized, and insensitive. He permits no one to approach him physically nor touch him emotionally as the chalk circle that he has drawn around himself implies. General Moncada asserts that he has become just like the military men against whom he is fighting and whom he hates. When at first he refuses to help Colonel Gerineldo Márquez, Úrsula tells him that it is the same as if he had been born with a pig's tail. Colonel Gerineldo Márquez noting the change in Colonel Aureliano warns him to watch out for his heart, because he is rotting alive.

As the narrator states, his inability to live with doubt and uncertainty further exacerbate his cold, encased solitude (García Márquez 1985, 212, 214 or García Márquez 1991, 169, 171). Only later in his life does he reach a modicum of accommodation with this solitude and thus the circular, labyrinthine, world that imprisons him, as his circular work of converting gold coins into goldfish suggests. Nevertheless, as Colonel Aureliano confronts his death, he is plagued by uncertainty and ambiguity once again. When his father faced his death, he found himself accompanied by Prudencio Aguilar and confronting a labyrinth of rooms and doors, a gallery of mirrors, suggesting the perplexing inexplicability and plurality of the world. The narrator tells us that he consoled himself with this dream, finding peace and comfort in this uncertainty. As Colonel Aureliano confronts death, Borgesian dreams and labyrinthine images come into play again. Like the Minotaur, he does not know whether he is awake or asleep. He dreams that he enters an empty house with white walls, and is the first human to enter it. In the dream, he dreams that he had dreamt the same dream the night before and many times in the last several years. However, it had been erased

from his memory upon awakening. One minute later, he is awak-
ened, and has the impression that he has slept briefly, and did not
have time to dream. These mirror and dream images emphasize that
the world is subjective and a fiction of our making, and that objective reality is beyond our grasp.

Colonel Aureliano's torment and emptiness from this labyrinthine world in which he lives are underscored in the contrast between his death and his father's. When José Arcadio Buendía
succumbs, he does so while tied to the family oak tree, that symbol
of the family, the community, and his past. Nature weeps for this
man who could juxtapose the magical and the realistic, unleashing
a rain of yellow flowers over the village. In contrast, Aureliano uri-
nates on that oak tree just before dying, and dies while trying to remember, without success, the circus of his youth. Rather than a rain
of flowers, vultures descend on his body.

The hand of Borges appears in several of the characters, episodes,
and incidents of the rest of the novel as well. Once again imitating
Borges's play on mirrors and his belief in the fluid indeterminacy of
the self, García Márquez comically presents the twins, José Arcadio
Segundo and Aureliano Segundo, as coordinating their appear-
ances and movements to appear like a trick of mirrors.

The history of the banana company, which figures centrally in the
novel, expresses a postmodern attitude toward history that shows the
mark of Borges. As Gene Bell-Villada (2002a) points out, the events
actually follow the historical record rather closely. José Arcadio Segundo lives through and tries to inform people of the banana company's and the government's massacre of the workers, the disposal
of their bodies, and the efforts to conceal what actually happened.
Like "Borges," the narrator of "La otra muerte" (The Other
Death), and Ryan, the great-grandson and chosen narrator of
"Tema del traidor y del héroe," José Arcadio Segundo realizes that
history and the past are remade in the retelling in the present. Like
Otto Dietrich zur Linde in "Deutsches Requiem," and the king of
"El espejo y la mascara" (The Mirror and the Mask), José Arcadio
Segundo discovers that the powerful write history, usually to their
liking. The manipulations of Mr. Jack Brown's attorneys also suggest
that the powerful write and/or control the law as well. As underscored in "El simulacro," "Tema del traidor y del héroe" (Theme
of the Traitor and the Hero), "Pierre Menard," and "La otra
muerte" (The Other Death), the massacre episode highlights that

the line between history and fiction often becomes indistinguishable.

The main themes and most prominent characters in the last section of the novel further develop these themes about the past and history and underscore Borges's presence as well. The two main characters during the last years of the family, Aureliano Babilonia and Amaranta Úrsula, are both severed from their ties to the past. Aureliano does not know who his parents are. His scholastic endeavors to reveal the meaning of the obscure parchments (and the universal history of Macondo) are spurred, in part, by his search for his own identity (Ludmer 1972, 181). He is much like the narrator in Borges's "La biblioteca de Babel" (The Library of Babel) who has spent his life searching for that book that will explain all other books and thus the nature of the library; that book that will allow him to arrive at the center of his labyrinthine world. As he deciphers the mysterious parchments at the end, Aureliano Babilonia discovers, much like Borges's wizard in "Las ruinas circulares" (The Circular Ruins) or Shakespeare in "Everything and Nothing" that he and his world are figments of a creator's dream. The loss of knowledge of the past that occurs in this section reflects modernism's tendency to subtly scorn and devalue the past by perceiving time and history as progressive, and considering the present superior to the past.

This emphasis on heritage, identity, and the need to recover and rewrite history is also underscored in other ways. Everyone with knowledge of the family heritage or of Macondo's founding, including the Buendía twins, Santo Sofía de la Piedad, Pilar Tenera, Úrsula, the four with whom Aureliano Babilonia establishes a bond of friendship and solidarity, has died or departed. As a woman of a "modern" spirit, Amaranta Úrsula, like Aureliano, has few roots in the past. She redecorates the house and throws away all the relics of the past. It is in this context of isolation, solitude, and estrangement from the past that Aureliano and Amaranta Úrsula fall in love and give birth to the child with the pig's tail.

One of the characters who contributes substantially to creating the comic and imaginary quality of this novel is Melquíades. Much like Borges's Homer from "El inmortal" (The Immortal) he has traveled the world and has experienced almost everything including reincarnation and eternal life. His character challenges the very nature of selfhood. Much as we discover that the unassuming character of "El inmortal" is Homer, so too we find that Melquíades is the author and the narrator of this novel. The technical achievement where the character within the story and the creator outside the story turn out to be the same person, suggests Borges's "La forma de la espada" (The Form of the Sword), where "he" becomes "I" as El Inglés and Moon turn out to be the same person. Both suggest a fluid, fictional, and indefinable self.

García Márquez's concept of time here has the marks of Borges as well. As suggested by the dual roles of Melquíades, two types of time govern this novel, the everyday and that of creation. The first is the conventional time in which events such as births and deaths, wars, and changes occur. A definite circularity or cyclical quality marks this time. The second, the time of creation, emphasizes the frozen moment in which past, present, and future coalesce, as the narrator states of Melquíades: "no había ordenado los hechos en el tiempo convencional de los hombres, sino que concentró un siglo de episodios cotidianos, de modo que todos coexistieron en un instante" (García Márquez 1985, 446). [(Melquíades) had not put events in the order of conventional time, but had concentrated a century of daily episodes in such a way that they coexisted in one instant] (García Márquez 1991, 421). Roberto González Echevarría points out in "Polemic: With Borges in Macondo" that García Márquez's style in the novel creates the illusion of eternity by simultaneity and order, and that the reference to ice in the beginning calls up the image of the Aleph in Borges' story (González Echevarría 1972, 59). Much as the creator/deity experience absolute time in which past, present, and future coalesce in "El Aleph" (The Aleph), or "La escritura del Dios" (The God's Script), or "El milagro secreto" (The Secret Miracle) or "Los teólogos" (The Theologians), (where one of the main characters is named Aureliano), so too does Melquíades. Much as the characters in "Las ruinas circulares" (The Circular Ruins), or "Los teólogos" (The Theologians), or "El inmortal" (The Immortal) or a number of the gaucho tales experience time as circular repetitions, so too do they abound for the Buendías. The repetitions of the characters' names and their psychological tendencies, the repetitious tendency toward incest, Colonel Aureliano turning gold coins into goldfish and selling them for gold coins all emphasize the circularity of time and all suggest a social and historical labyrinth from which the characters cannot escape.

Throughout the novel, García Márquez draws on the general vision, the specific stories, and strategies and methods of his Argentine predecessor to call into question our notions of certitude and ambiguity, myth, fiction and reality, the self and other, and objectivity and subjectivity. Similar to Borges, he affirms a Hispanic-American identity with a rich mythical and cultural heritage that the Eurocentric world has often ignored. Also like Borges, he challenges the boundaries of the established notions of "reality" and contends that "reality" is a fiction that we create and the "reality" of the novel is what the author makes believable. The work criticizes rather harshly the tin and plastic qualities of modernism and the modern world, underscoring its exploitation of nature, its decadence, emphasizing the tendency of industrialization to sever one from one's past, and subverting its faith in science, progress, and technology. On the one hand, the destruction at the end implies a sense of hopelessness and futility for the future.[4] However, this work subverts Western culture's division between the tragic and the comic and functions on both levels. Thus like Borges, it affirms that this was a work of the imagination, that man/woman are creators of fictions, and that literature is meant to be playful, entertaining, just plain fun.

WITH BORGES NORTH OF THE BORDER: *THE UNIVERSAL BASEBALL ASSOCIATION INC. J. HENRY WAUGH, PROP.*

Jorge Luis Borges's contribution to North American fiction has been mentioned with some frequency. The reasons behind the confluence of the Argentine's ideas and methods and the contemporary North American novel are diverse and complex. I have tried to suggest through the previous chapters that they derive from the confluence of shared aspects of the New World experience with the postmodern turn of the culture. At any rate, the centrality of the labyrinth, the sense of ontological doubt, the affirmation of a plurality of visions, the problematizing of the self, the dissolving of the divide between reason and fantasy, between dreaming and being awake, between play and anguish, and between the I and the not I all figure in the fiction of a number of U.S. writers, as they do in Borges's works. Like Borges, many of these writers avoid a radical relativism or a tilt toward nihilism. Borges's importance marks an interesting change in direction of literary influences and confluences in the American hemispheres. While they have moved largely from north to south previously, in the postmodern era they have flowed from south to north. Borges has definitely had an impact on Robert Coover's thinking and writing, among others. Ronald Christ in an article, "Forking Narratives" discusses Borges's experimentation with simultaneous alternatives, and mentions Borges's impact on Coover's collection of short stories, *Pricksongs and Descants.* He mentions Coover's stories "The Magic Poker," "The Babysitter," and "The Elevator" in particular (Christ 1979). Coover's novel, *The Universal Baseball Association, Inc., J. Henry Waugh, Proprietor,* offers a telling example of Borges's indisputable impact on the U.S. novel.

While one finds many intertextual suggestions of Borges's work in the Coover novel, four Borges short stories in particular stand out: "La lotería en Babilonia" (The Babylonian Lottery), "Las ruinas circulares" (The Circular Ruins), "Everything and Nothing," and "El Sur" (The South). While I have discussed "La lotería en Babilonia" (The Babylonian Lottery) in some detail in chapter 3 and "Everything and Nothing" in chapter 4, I will only briefly comment here on the details of those works. However, I will analyze in more detail here "Las ruinas circulares" (The Circular Ruins) and "El Sur" (The South), as my references to them have been brief in previous chapters.

The story "La lotería en Babilonia" (The Babylonian Lottery) is an allegorical representation of man's / woman's lack of certitude and of the seemingly haphazard, chaotic nature of the universe, or at least of our limits in understanding it. Much as Henry Waugh in Coover's novel throws a set of dice to decide the fates of his characters, the draw of the lottery becomes an intricate web of haphazard possibilities reaching into all spheres of a person's existence. To mask the role of chance, the Company begins to refer to magic and superstition to help explain the results. As I stated earlier, the narrator delineates the Godlike functions of the Company throughout the story, and highlights the metaphysical implications at the end, where he asserts that its functions are "comparable al de Dios" (comparable to God's) (see chapter 3, pages 56–58). In this allegorical story, Babylon represents the world and the individual lives within it, and the Company stands for the cosmic order. The story, like Coover's work, underscores that chance rather than reason and order often seem to govern our lives and determine our destinies.

"Las ruinas circulares" is another story that undercuts traditional realism. It emphasizes the dreamlike, illusory nature of existence and suggests Borges's affinity for idealism. A wizard disembarks from a canoe to visit the ancient ruins of a temple. His assignment is to dream into existence another human being. After first failing, the task is finally accomplished. With the help of the fire god, he instills the "son" with life and instructs him in the ways of the universe. Only the fire god and the wizard will know that he is not flesh and blood, however. Sometime later, the wizard achieves a realization much like that of the players in the last chapter of Coover's novel. The fire of death that surrounds and begins to consume the wizard does not burn him, but rather caresses and inundates him. With relief, humiliation and terror, he realizes, like the players in *The Universal Baseball Association,* that he too is only an apparition and that someone has dreamed him. The story calls attention to the idealistic aspects of Borges's vision that suggest that we exist because we are perceived by others. It emphasizes that reality is illusory. Like Coover's work, Borges's short story can also be read as a comment on the creative process. The wizard's efforts to dream a man amidst the circular ruins destroyed by fire suggest the artist's regression from rational consciousness to a prelogical, mythic state in an attempt to tap his maximum creative and poetic powers (McMurray 1980, 68). The grueling ordeal underscores the difficulties inherent in creativity. The final realization underscores that we all are fictions, that man creates myths and fictions, and that life and reality themselves are fictions.

As I discussed earlier, "Everything and Nothing" is another well-known short story of Borges that integrates the themes of idealism, the self as dream image of a creator, and the dream process as the raw material of poetic creation (see chapter 4, 83–84). Like the players of the UBA, Shakespeare discovers that God has dreamed the world much as he has dreamed the characters of his plays.

Another story that also emphasizes the dreamlike quality of existence and in which Borges incorporates myths and images of Argentine culture is "El Sur" (The South). Borges has referred to this piece, which unifies autobiographical, national, and universal motifs, as his best story (1974, 483). In facing death, Dahlmann chooses to identify with his maternal grandfather who is killed fighting Indians rather than his paternal grandfather, who was an Evangelical minister. Dahlmann picks up a copy of *Mil y una noches* (*The Arabian Nights*), and is hurrying up a dark staircase when he gashes his head on an open, freshly painted window. He wakes up the next morning feverish with lead poisoning and is rushed to the hospital.[5] On the edge of death and in great pain, he suddenly seems to recover and is released. He decides to recuperate in the family-owned ranch in the South. With his book *Mil y una noches* (*The Arabian Nights*), in hand, he rides the train through the vivid countryside relishing every minute. He is forced to disembark one stop early. While he is eating dinner and waiting for the carriage in a general store, three drunken ranch hands harass him. One of them ultimately challenges him to a knife fight. An old man who seems to be outside of time offers him a dagger. As Dahlmann picks up the dagger and they move out into the plains, he says to himself that if he could have chosen or dreamed his death, this is the one he would have selected.

This piece is about confronting death, about the line between the waking reality and the dream world and about the role and function of myth. The story relates Dahlmann's encounter with death. While we, as readers, cannot be certain whether Dahlmann did in fact die on the plains in a knife fight or in the hospital bed, that is, what is "reality" and what is fiction, the second half in which he travels to the South appears to be Dahlmann's fabrication, his dreamlike re-creation of his struggle with and acceptance of finality. A number of symmetries run through the two segments.[6] The hospital is located on "calle Ecuador," suggesting a line between two worlds. He takes the same carriage to the hospital that he takes to the train station. The injection with the needle and the operation parallel the puncture he will receive with the dagger. The brush on the head with the spitball suggests the initial accident. The employee in the hospital looks like the one in the general store. The book, *Mil y una noches (The Arabian Nights)*, appears in both segments. Thus, Dahlmann has drawn on the mythic raw material of the life of the gaucho to help him accept the inevitability of his death, much as Henry Waugh uses the mythic patterns of baseball for this same end. The book, *Mil y una noches (The Arabian Nights)*, emphasizes man's role as a creator of fictions and the world as a construct of fictions. Shahrazad, Dahlmann, and Henry Waugh are all characters within and creators of fictions.[7] The function of time in the story calls up the mythic qualities of the work. For Dahlmann, space is a metaphor for time, and the journey to the South is a journey into the ever-present, circular, mythic past. This sense of the frozen or repetitive moment is reflected by the cat and the gaucho who seem beyond time. The symmetries between the hospital and the dream-world trip to the South imply that the line between dream and "reality" often prove illusory and indistinguishable. In an essay "Cuando la ficción vive en la ficción" (When Fiction Lives in Fiction), published originally in *El hogar* (2 June 1939), Borges refers to Schopenhauer's metaphor for dreaming and wakefulness as pages of the same book. Schopenhauer asserts that to read them in order is to live, and to leaf through them at random is to dream. In "El Sur" (The South), the line between dreaming and waking blurs. Borges implies that we play roles and wear masks, that the self is determined by what we imagine it to be. Thus, Borges instills this story with qualities and mythic images of Argentine culture while subverting the line between objective and subjective reality. These are techniques and methods that Robert Coover, among other U.S. writers, has found quite attractive and useful.

Coover's *The Universal Baseball Association, Inc., J. Henry Waugh, Prop.* seems indebted to Borges. To begin with, it should be mentioned that Coover is fluent in Spanish (Gordon 1983, 13). Some of Coover's own words are useful in illustrating this confluence of visions. In explaining why John Barth and he have been saying similar things about contemporary literature, Coover asserted:

> I believe this can be traced to the general awareness by writers of both North and South America that we have come to the end of a tradition. I don't mean that we have come to the end of the novel or of fictional forms, but that our ways of looking at the world and of adjusting to it through fictions are changing. The New World is peculiarly alert to this. We are the outpost of Western culture and it is here that we sense collapse because the waves are beating on our rocks. (Gado 1973, 142)

The belief that the New World writers are on the cutting edge in a redefinition of reality is clear here. In regard to idealism and the illusory nature of existence, Coover explains:

> Those forms we associate with Platonism have a certain beauty, and now a potential for irony exists in them. But because we don't believe in a Godhead any more and the sense of purposeful unity has vanished, a true Platonist would say we are using these things sophistically. The abstractions are empty, aren't they? Even so, they are useful. It is easier for me to express the ironies of our condition by the manipulation of Platonic forms than by imitation of the Aristotelian. (Gado 1973, 143–44)

Along these same lines, he touches on Borges's notion of the world as a fiction when he states: "The world itself being a construct of fictions, I believe the fiction maker's function is to furnish better fictions with which we can reform our notions of things" (Gado 1973, 149–50). With these assertions, Coover aligns himself with Borges's thinking and vision. The novel itself is probably the most telling comment on the affinities of their visions.

The novel's main character, J. Henry Waugh, is a 56-year-old bachelor accountant who works for the firm of Dunkelmann, Zauber, and Zifferblatt. He has invented an elaborate baseball game that he plays during his off-hours with three dice and a series of charts, including an Extraordinary Occurrences Chart. Henry keeps intricate records of the action of the eight team league and its players, whom he has named. He keeps a chronicle of the personal lives and the thinking of the individual players and managers. After fifty-six seasons, the game has begun to lose some of its appeal for Henry. Then Damon Rutherford, a rookie, pitches a perfect game. Henry's interest in his creation soars as he identifies with Damon and is awed by the concept of perfection. After only one day's rest, Henry decides to pitch Damon against the rookie, Jock Casey. Henry is shattered with a sense of loss and is forced to confront the void when the throw of the dice determines that Damon is killed by Casey's bean ball. After acting out the funeral scene in which he has difficulty separating his imaginary world from his everyday world, Henry considers giving up the game. He decides to finish the season with the intent of destroying Casey and his team for what they have done. The dice, however, keep them winning. Henry finally resolves to intervene in the outcome of the dice by rolling 6-6-6, which on the Extraordinary Occurrences Chart means that Casey is killed by a line drive hit by Damon's catcher. This act of retribution saves the game for Henry. The whole affair has so engrossed and possessed him that he fails to report to work and eventually loses his job. In the eighth and final chapter of the book, Henry has disappeared as a character and the players ruminate on the nature of their existence, their God and their universe as they prepare to reenact the Damon Rutherford-Jock Casey duel.

Coover's novel displays striking similarities with Borges's writing and in particular with the four stories I have mentioned. His portrayal of a chaotic, haphazard universe, of the world as illusory and of man as a creator of fictions aligns him with the Argentine writer and is an example of how contemporary U. S. novelists have borrowed from Borges in redefining "reality" and their art. Like Babylonia and the lottery, the UBA is a metaphor for the world, and Henry playing his game captures the interaction of the world with the cosmic order of which Henry is the Godhead. The work addresses questions such as infinity, eternity, and First Cause. It depicts a chaotic universe whose purpose is no more coherent than the random throw of dice (Harris 1971, 133). The fates of the characters are determined by chance.

Coover employs Biblical symbols and myths to parody the sense of order and to underscore the haphazardness of existence. The allusions and references to the Jewish and Christian Bibles are extensive. J. Henry Waugh, the proprietor of the Association and main character of the novel, has the initials JHWH, which correspond to Yahweh or Jehovah and make him a Godlike figure, but without foresight. Coover's novel has eight chapters corresponding to the seven days of creation and the apocalypse. Coover employs multiple Christ figures that shift into anti-Christs, thus representing a shifting of meanings (Gordon 1983, 35). "Damon" (like daemon) seems to be the second divinity as he offers the Association rejuvenation and new hope. The reader realizes later that Jock Casey, whose initials are J.C., is the real Christ. Casey's death saves the UBA from destruction. It is ironic, however, that the reader tends to identify with Damon rather than Casey. There are a number of similar religious references. Henry's interference in the game to kill Casey parallels God interjecting his finger in man's affairs. The throw of the dice that kills Casey, the three sixes, is the number of the beast of revelation. Henry's friend, Lou Engel, has a name which is short for Lucifer the fallen angel. Lou brings in a pizza topped with a St. Andrew's cross of pepperoni. Lou's spilling of the beer over the game calls up the image of the flood. The Duel in the final chapter parallels the Christian sacraments as well as primitive initiation rites (Taylor 1972, 238). And no doubt the list goes on. The juxtaposition of these biblical myths, symbols, and stories with the image of Henry as Godhead parodies and undermines the biblical vision of order and of creation, and much like the story, "La lotería en Babilonia" (The Babylonian Lottery), emphasizes the random, chaotic nature of existence.[8]

A corollary to the concept of a random universe, in "El Sur" (The South) and "Las ruinas circulares" (The Circular Ruins) and in Coover's novel, is the notion that "reality" is idealistic and illusory and that man/woman is a creator of myths and fictions. In Coover's baseball book, that theme is expressed on several different levels. J. Henry Waugh is a man who creates fictions to help himself deal with reality. His games come to dominate all aspects of his life. Henry draws on the myths surrounding baseball. He composes ballads and uses his fictional personalities to relate to sex, aging, death, perfection, and virtually all aspects of life. The implication is that all systems, disciplines, and philosophies are constructs that assist man in dealing with reality, that absolutes are virtually nonexistent or not within our grasp, and as Henry realizes, that perfection is process, not stasis.

The last chapter brings many of these metafictional and idealistic themes into perspective. It is seen through the eyes of the players. Henry has disappeared. As Larry McCaffery points out, God has died, has disappeared or pantheistically is the Association (McCaffery 1982, 53). One player struggling with these teleological issues confirms that "God exists and he is a nut" (Coover 1968, 23). Another asserts that "Maybe this whole goddam Association has got some kind of screw loose" (227). Yet another suggests that the world is nothing but a series of forms or ideas when he quips: "We have no Mothers, Gringo. The ripening of their wombs is nothing more than a ceremonious parable. We are mere ideas, hatched whole and hapless, here to enact old rituals of resistance and rot" (230). These players, who have taken on a life of their own outside of their creator, are dream images, mirages, fictional creations of Henry's mind, much like the wizard and his son in "Las ruinas circulares" (The Circular Ruins) or like Shakespeare and his characters in "Everything and Nothing."

The motif of man/woman as a fiction maker also contains allusions for the role of the artist in Coover's work. Like Shakespeare or the wizard in Borges's tales, essentially J. Henry Waugh is an author who creates a mythical, fictional realm that subsumes him. Henry's battle between the world of his imagination and the outside world allegorically represents the artist's struggle with his material. And Coover's relationship to Henry parallels Henry's relationship to the UBA players (Anderson 1981, 62). Henry's decision to kill Casey and save the Association depicts Henry's and the artist's essential commitment to the craft. Thus, Coover's vision of the world as a collection of illusory fictions and his vision of man as a fiction-maker parallels Borges's conception in his short stories.

Coover's link to Borges extends beyond the general idea for the work and also includes some of the details of the plot and of character development. This is evident in the multiple purposes that Henry's game/creation serves for him. For one thing, it provides Henry with a sense of self-respect that he otherwise lacks. As he walks home with Hettie early in the novel, he feels proud and important when he can imply that he is the bookkeeper for the Association. This is not unlike the way Dahlmann achieves a sense of dignity through his fiction. The Association allows Henry to function socially with confidence, also. Identifying with the players he creates, such as Damon and Swanee Lee, permits him to perform sexually. It also permits him to deal with solitude. The three principal characters in the novel, Henry, Lou, and Hettie, are all trying to come to terms with loneliness and isolation, although they do so in different ways. Henry has the UBA, Lou eats and goes to movies, and Hettie uses sex and attendance at church to achieve a sense of community. Henry's method is certainly the most creative and perhaps the most effective.

Juan Dahlmann and J. Henry Waugh also express a similar searching, probing solitude that underscores the link between them and between the authors. It is important to note that the events that occur in the last part of "El Sur" (The South) and those that surround Damon Rutherford's death are creations of Juan Dahlmann's and J. Henry Waugh's imaginations. Both are solitary, single men more accustomed to thought and intellectual and imaginative exercises than to action. Dahlmann works in a library and Waugh is an accountant. Both struggle with the meaning of life and the void of death through their imaginative creations, and both choose to identify with men of action and with cultural and mythic projections of such men in order to come to terms with death. They are embodiments of a similar, solitary intellectual figure who confronts these metaphysical issues with his imagination and yet is uncomfortable with the fact that he is not a man of action.

Coover's use of the myths and images surrounding baseball also is worthy of note. He draws on the distinctive myths of the national pastime to help project and define his culture and himself as a writer, much as Borges does with the myths of the gauchos. The game speaks to and engrosses Henry for much the same reason that it captivates the reader. The game is a part of the mythic life of the United States, and the images of it that Coover captures have implications for community and isolation, conquest and defeat, love and sex, art and song, order and chaos, justice and injustice, and life and death.

The Association also provides Henry with a means of escaping from a boring, personal reality. Henry's day-to-day existence in the world of Dunkelmann, Zauber, and Zifferblatt is drab and uneventful. For years, Henry has been secretly inventing games to avoid the tediousness of the workplace. Henry's fictions, like Dahlmann's, are a way of escaping from that world.

Furthermore, the game provides Henry with a way of both comprehending and ignoring the terrorizing features and nebulous gray areas of the greater world. He wants to believe that the kinds of statistics and measurements he is compiling are what history is all about. As Henry glares at a newspaper one morning, he notes that the paper spoke of bombs, births, weddings, wars, social events, infiltrations, and other such things. He then states to Lou: "History. Amazing, how we love it. And did you ever stop to think that without numbers or measurements, there probably wouldn't be any history?" (Coover 1968, 39) Henry echoes a similar notion later on when he dismisses a suggestion for a bloodless space race as a substitute for war:

> People needed casualty lists, territory footage won and lost, bounded sets with strategies and payoff functions, supply and communication routes disrupted or restored, tonnage totals, and deaths, downed planes, and prisoners socked away like a hoard of calculable runs scored. (Coover 1968, 131)

This attitude toward history as reflecting man's need for statistics helps give his own creation legitimacy as it implies that his play of the imagination is an expression of the same need as the events in the newspaper. It thus tends to blur the distinction between fiction and reality and permits him to escape from facing the absurdity of those events and of life.

Yet, perhaps the most important function of the game is the way it offers Henry, as it does Juan Dahlmann, a means of confronting and reaching an accommodation with death. When Damon pitches the perfect game, Henry senses the possibility of immortality through perfection. However, as Lois Gordon states, Damon's death drives home the fact that perfection is process, that process occurs through time and that time is the undoing of all men (Gordon 1983, 45). In the aftermath of Damon's death, Henry seems to come to terms with his own mortality. He relates a part of the events surrounding the funeral from the perspective of Rag Rooney, who himself is afraid of death. The funeral episode ends with Henry lost in the labyrinth of the blackened stadium and finally having the lights come on as he stumbles into the center of the stadium.

The actual accommodation with death occurs in the final chapter, however, where Paul Trench is a focus of attention. Juan Dahlmann accepts the reality and the imminence of death when he picks up the knife and agrees to the duel. Henry, through Paul, seems to arrive at a similar sense of inner peace. Paul is a participant in the Damonsday duel to the death between the representative of Damon Rutherford and that of Jock Casey. Paul, as the outstanding rookie catcher, must play out the role of Royce Ingram, Damon's catcher who, in revenge, kills Casey with a line drive. After wrestling with questions relating to life, death, and the meaning of his existence, Paul realizes that "it doesn't even matter that he's going to die, all that counts is that he is here and here's The Man and here's the boys and there's the crowd, the sun, the noise" (Coover 1968, 242). Paul, and by implication Henry, affirm life and the moment and accept death with those comments. While Henry's mental state at this point is unknown, he seems to have used his fiction to work through the difficulties that Damon's death and death in general created for him.

Jorge Luis Borges has been a central figure in defining the vision and the symbols of postmodernity. That vision and those symbols and metaphors have left an imprint on Robert Coover's *The Universal Baseball Association, Inc., J. Henry Waugh, Prop*. Borges's mark is evident in the way in which the mythic raw material of his culture is used, in the portrayal of man as a fiction-maker, in the depiction of the cosmos as unknowable, and seemingly random and chaotic, in the description of reality as an illusion, and in the creation and projection of major characters who use their fictions to confront the absurdities of life and the void of death.

Both García Márquez in *Cien años de soledad (One Hundred Years of Solitude)*, and Coover in *The Universal Baseball Association, Inc., J. Henry Waugh, Prop*. seem to avoid a radical relativism. At any rate, both works tilt toward a vision of the world and universe as labyrinthine macrocosms and microcosms. Rather than being definitely chaotic visions, they create worlds that symbolically may have an order, but that we are limited in understanding. They both create mysterious Godlike figures, Melquíades and Henry, who function as creators for other characters. These are but examples of how the postmodern turn, as Borges has helped represent and express it, has redefined the twentieth century fiction of the New World.

9
Borges in His Own Words and Some Implications for the Postmodern Debate

THROUGHOUT THIS BOOK, I HAVE ARGUED THAT JORGE LUIS BORGES defined a pluralistic stance in his writings that avoids a radical relativism, that is, a pluralism with limits that is very much at the forefront of the current debate on postmodernity. Because of his role as a precursor of postmodern culture, and one who thus challenged the foundations of monistic modernism, many critics have tended to associate postmodernity and Borges with subversion of the established order, with anarchy, with chaos, and with nihilism. However, Borges's position is usually quite different. Borges does define values and does not deny necessarily the existence of absolutes and of a God. Rather, he forces us to admit the limitations of our reason and our knowledge in actually knowing and confirming our narratives of meaning. His writings argue for another perspective, another vision, another philosophy, another system, another discovery, another history, another text, another world, another fiction that will supplant our former one, the one of which we were so certain.

This tendency to challenge and negate the One, has led some to ignore that he does affirm the Many, while carefully avoiding nihilism, absolute or radical relativism, or a monism of negation. He subtly and extensively employs the symbol of the labyrinth to describe our limitations and shortcomings. He suggests that this symbol may offer hope, as it suggests a structure and a plan to the universe, but one that is beyond our reach. He lays out a pluralism, but a pluralism that does not radically overturn Western philosophy and culture. He challenges the self-righteous certainty of religious doctrine, but basically steps back from an atheistic stance. In fact, he draws heavily upon religious visions and a quest for spirituality in his prose, stories, and poems. Some postmodern critics have ignored, overlooked, or have been unable to strike that balance in defining their own positions.

166

Toward the end of his life, Borges participated in a number of conversations, dialogues, and interviews that provide further insight into his thinking and offer guidelines for approaching certain postmodern issues. With regard to religious issues that have broad implications for his views, he repeatedly asserts that he is an agnostic, at least intellectually. However, he explains and qualifies that stance on a number of different instances and seems to distinguish between what we can understand rationally and a certain emotional response. In a series of interviews with Richard Burgin, he admits that he enjoys reading theology but considers it all imaginative fiction. He says that he gets a similar pleasure from reading detective novels or science fiction. He then states: "Of course, you may believe in God, I daresay there is a God, but I don't believe in Him because of those arguments. I should say that I believe in God in spite of theology" (Borges 1969, 140). He admits constantly looking for the symmetries, the mirrors, the labyrinths in life, and states: "But perhaps coincidences are given to us that would involve the idea of a secret plan, no? Coincidences are given to us so that we may feel there is a pattern—that there is a pattern in life, that things mean something" (Borges 1969, 110). He then cites a coincidence from his own life (110–11). In most of his comments, he dismisses the idea of a personal God and of personal immortality. In discussing the origin of physical pain and suffering, he draws on the Gnostics and expresses an affinity with the notion of a clumsy God who does not do its job very well.

His poem "El Golem" (The Golem) captures this sense of a somewhat inept God. Rabbi Judá León of Prague discovers the letters of God's name and thus the key to creation and creates a humanoid, the Golem. The Golem is marked by its limitations: it does not master language; it can do little more than sweep the synagogue; and, it considers Rabbi León a god and worships him as the Rabbi does God. The closing stanza draws out the parallels between the Rabbi and the Golem and between God and the Rabbi: "En la hora de angustia y de luz vaga, / En su Golem los ojos detenía. / ¿Quién nos dirá las cosas que sentía / Dios, al mirar a su rabino en Praga?" (1974, 887) [In the hour of anguish and of hazy light, / His eyes rested on his Golem. / Who might tell us the things God / was feeling while gazing on his Rabbi in Prague?] (translation mine) The poem emphasizes the Golem's and our limitations in understanding our creator. It suggests that God perhaps erred in making us. It emphasizes the mirrorlike nature of reality and hints at an idealistic series of microcosmos and macrocosmos.

As Borges suggests in some of his stories and essays, Buddhism, idealism, pantheism, and the Kabbalah also have influenced his metaphysical thinking and have offered a model for dealing with right and wrong behavior. When the interviewer, Osvaldo Ferrari, states that he seems to recognize the existence of a transcendence without calling it "God," Borges accepts that and again calls attention to our limitations in knowing or understanding such a transcendence. He believes that:

[E]s más seguro no llamarlo Dios; si lo llamamos Dios, ya se piensa en un individuo, y ese individuo es misteriosamente tres, según doctrina—para mi inconcebible—de la Trinidad. En cambio, si usamos otras palabras—quizá menos precisas, o menos vívidas—podríamos acercarnos más a la verdad; si es que ese acercamiento a la verdad es posible, cosa que también ignoramos. (Borges 1985, 145–46)

[And, I believe that it is safer not to call it God; if we call it God, one starts to think of an individual, and that individual is mysteriously three, according to the doctrine, for me inconceivable, of the Trinity. On the other hand, if we use other words—perhaps less precise or less vivid—we could come closer to the truth; if it is possible to approach the truth, something that we also ignore.] (translation mine)

For Borges, the limitations of our knowledge do not impede our ability to make judgments about right and wrong. When asked if he believes in God, he responded: "Si Dios significa algo en nosotros que quiere el bien sí; ahora, si se piensa en un ser individual, no, no creo. Pero creo en un propósito ético, no sé si del universo, pero sí de cada uno de nosotros" (Borges 1985, 143). [If God means something in us that wants the good, yes; now, if one is thinking of an individual being, no, I don't believe in him. But I believe in an ethical purpose, I am not sure about the universe, but yes, for each one of us].

This ethical sense of right and wrong is an instinctive quality, he believes. Religion justifies itself through its ethical orientation. He states:

Y, al cabo del día, sin duda habremos tomado muchas decisiones éticas; y habremos tenido que elegir—simplificando el tema—entre el bien y el mal. Y, cuando hemos elegido el bien, sabemos que hemos elegido el bien; cuando elegimos el mal, lo sabemos, también. (Borges 1985, 266)

[And, at the end of the day, without a doubt, we will have made many ethical decisions; and we will have had to choose — I am simplifying the question—between good and evil. And when we have chosen the good, we know that we have chosen the good; when we choose evil, we know it also.] (translation mine)

He goes on to say that the important thing is to judge each act by itself rather than its consequences since the consequences of all acts are infinite and branch into the future. In the course of time, the consequences all even out. So judging an act by its consequences actually is immoral. Then, Borges takes the argument one step further, challenging the prevalent attitude that people who act righteously are fools and people who act evilly are intelligent. He states that those doing evil do not imagine the effect that their actions can produce in the consciousness of others, and he asserts that there is more innocence in wickedness and more intelligence in goodness (Borges 1985, 269).

A number of years earlier, in the poem "Una oración" (A Prayer), in *Elogio de la sombra* (*In Praise of Darkness*) (1969), Borges expressed a very similar ethical sense in some of its closing lines when he stated: "Desconocemos los designios del universo, pero sabemos que razonar con lucidez y obrar con justicia es ayudar a esos designios, que no nos serán revelados" (1974, 1014). [We do not know the designs of the universe, but we do know that to think lucidly and to act justly is to aid those designs, which will not be revealed to us.] (translation mine)

The Argentine writer's thinking on ethics has implications for his belief in progress and time, as well. His ideas differ somewhat from the modernist conception of progress. In the modernist conception, the present stands superior to the past and opens into a future that will always be better. It is based, in part, on the Judeo-Christian temporal notion of a beginning and an end of time and a spiritual eternity removed from time. Simultaneously, this attitude is coupled with a conflicting, critical mode that views the present as decadent, corrupt, and superficial, and foresees a utopian fulfillment occurring in the future within history. In one of the dialogues with Osvaldo Ferrari, Borges discusses his anarchistic view of the disappearance of the state. He suggests that it will not happen within his lifetime, but perhaps at some future point. He states that he agrees with the statement "I believe dogmatically in progress." He asserts that hope is necessary, and that we must believe in progress, even if it does not exist. He then discusses Goethe's beautiful metaphor for the concept. For Goethe, progress is not a straight line, but a spiral that circles back and returns. He contends that if we do not believe in progress, we deny all possibility of action (Borges 1985, 82). Progress, for Borges, is not connected with a faith in reason, nor a faith in science, nor in the direction of universal history. Rather, it is a belief or fiction that we affirm, but cannot confirm, in order to make our lives and the world more meaningful and palatable.

Borges goes on to connect this concept of progress with his notion of free will (Borges 1985, 82–83). He states that, if you were to tell him that all his past actions had been determined, that would not be of great import. However, if you were to tell him that he cannot act freely, he would despair. He sees a parallel between progress vis-à-vis history and between free will vis-à-vis the individual. The fact that hypocrisy exists suggests progress as well, he contends. If there is hypocrisy, that means that there is a consciousness of evil. Those who act evilly know that they are acting evilly, and that is progress, he argues.

PLURALISM, MORALITY, VALUES, AND THE POSTMODERN

As is clear from his writings and from these comments, Borges has found his own way to "get there:" to make his way through the labyrinth, to create a sense of order, of purpose, of meaning. The ultimate skeptic, he realizes all along that the paths he maps out are provisional. While his reliance on idealism, pantheism, the Kabbalah, and Buddhism may offer him some directions, they are, by no means, a universal highway on which everyone can travel comfortably. However, if postmodernism involves a tilt toward cultural and philosophical pluralism, in a general sense Borges's perspective can provide certain guideposts for addressing a number of questions and issues that arise from such a pluralism.

The issues themselves are far-reaching and complex. If our traditional notions of truth, justice, right and wrong no longer have the transcendent validity that was assumed for them, how do we make judgments about such concepts? In a relativistic world, how do we say that the death sentence against Salman Rushdie was wrong?

What do we say to someone who denies that the Holocaust ever occurred, if there is no objective history? Or to someone who insists
that the September 11th terrorist attacks were planned and carried
out by the C. I. A.? How do we affirm any morality? How do we distinguish between Roosevelt and Hitler? How do we distinguish between
astronomy and astrology, between alchemy and chemistry? How do
we confirm our knowledge and decide what merits inclusion in our
canons, and what does not?

A postmodernity that follows the thinking of Borges, that affirms
a pluralism but not chaos, offers some answers to those questions.
The Holocaust provides an interesting example, because it has
broad implications for truth, morality, history, and absurdity, among
other things. With regard to history, what do you tell a Holocaust
denier?

That question asks, in effect, what are the limits of pluralism, and
how do we understand history? Borges's writings offer some answers,
as a number of his works concern just that. On the one hand, stories
such as "Deutsches Requiem," "El espejo y la mascara" (The Mirror
and the Mask), and "Pierre Menard autor del *Quijote*" (Pierre Menard, Author of the *Quixote*) contend that the victorious write history
to their liking, and that the present cannot objectively recreate the
past. They suggest that there are innumerable historical perspectives. Yet as I explained throughout, while Borges subverts the
One, his repeated use of the labyrinth emphasizes that not all perspectives are equal, that truth and an ordered universe may exist,
although from our limited perspective we will never understand
them in their totality. Nonetheless, he repeatedly urges an attempt
at positive knowledge. For instance, in the story, La otra muerte"
(The Other Death), the narrator, "Borges," attempts to resolve conflicting interpretations and even suggests some miraculous solutions
to resolve the conflicts. The point he makes subtly is that we need to
attempt to arrive at some positive knowledge or truths, even if they
may be provisional. Similarly, the narrator of "La biblioteca de
Babel" (The Library of Babel) never gives up his search for the ultimate meaning of the Library, although he realizes he will probably
never discover it.

Following the lead of Borges, it seems to me that you tell a Holocaust denier that the Holocaust was an incomprehensible event that
no one will ever understand in its totality. We will never understand
fully why it happened, how it could have happened, what actually
happened in all their gory details, who showed courage and who did

not. The victims, the eyewitnesses, the poets, the artists, the novelists, the photographers, the sociologists, the psychologists, the historians, the biologists, the film directors, the philosophers, the economists, and the political scientists will all give us different and sometimes conflicting accounts and responses to those questions. Those who lived through it will grasp its horror and comprehend its commentary on humanity and our times in a different way than those of us who were born in the generation after it occurred. As Borges's story "Pierre Menard autor del *Quijote*" (Pierre Menard, Author of the *Quixote*) suggests, those who live three hundred years from now also will understand and explain it in a different way.

While we will never come to a total consensus about the Holocaust, we have methods that we as a society use to confirm our sense of what is "real." That is, we have abundant representations: eyewitness reports, photographs, confessions, films, written statements, etc. Any doubter need only consult the bulk of this evidence to realize that something of the magnitude that is usually referred to did occur. If this is a world where total consensus and objectivity are impossible, one must be vigilant that the case be presented over and over again, to make sure that the children and that future generations have an understanding and a grasp of the dimensions of what happened, so as not to repeat it in other places in different ways. We would use similar methods in confirming other past knowledge and historical events.

No doubt, historians, novelists, poets, critics, film directors, and others will continue to argue over how we understand the past and express historical discourse. However, a principal issue around which a flurry of debate seems to be coalescing is how we make sense of the world, that is, our consciousness. The issue has begun to draw fairly clear lines of distinction between monism and pluralism, between the modern and the postmodern, and to outline what may prove to be a battlefield for future discourse relating to postmodernity. There has been a profuse number of studies on the subject in recent years. Neuroscientists, philosophers, physicists, psychologists, and others have entered the fray. If some of the principal combatants agree on anything, it is that the work is at a very incipient stage. Philosopher David Chalmers says that the situation parallels "physics 500 years before Newton" (James Gordon 1997, B7).

Paul Churchland's book, *The Engine of Reason, the Seat of the Soul (1997)*, lays out a number of the issues. In his book, Churchland argues that cognitive neuroscience will one day explain "consciousness" by detailing how the brain works biologically and materially, that is, by showing how the neurons and the chemical reactions function in our brains. He suggests that the brain organizes and understands by means of vector coding. He defines consciousness in terms of seven functions:

1. Consciousness involves short-term memory . . .
2. Consciousness is independent of sensory inputs . . .
3. Consciousness displays steerable attention . . .
4. Consciousness has the capacity for alternative interpretations of complex or ambiguous data . . .
5. Consciousness disappears in deep sleep . . .
6. Consciousness reappears in dreaming, at least in muted or disjointed form . . .
7. Consciousness harbors the contents of the several basic sensory modalities within a single unified experience.
(Churchland 1997, 213–14)

Churchland also suggests that it is very likely that we will create machines that duplicate consciousness.

The issue has broad implications for the nature of the self and the nature of reality and of being, issues that Borges certainly has weighed in on. Those seeking to define consciousness are not unlike those seeking the Man of the Book in "La Biblioteca de Babel" (The Library of Babel), that compendium that will explain all other books. In contrast to the discussion of the Holocaust, the issue here is not the limits of pluralism, but rather the limits of monism. The key lies in Churchland's definition of "consciousness." If it is defined within the parameters of scientific research and discourse, then yes, science may eventually explain it and recreate it. However, if it is defined in terms that preclude a purely biological, materialistic definition, for instance as the quality that distinguishes woman/man from animals, then it very likely will not.

A story Borges published late in his life, "La rosa de Paracelso" (The Rose of Paracelsus) from *La memoria de Shakespeare* (*Shakespeare's Memory*) (1983), subtly challenges the privileging of scientific reason and the scientific method as a singular truth and suggests a place for the fantastic mode and other realities. In the tale, Paracelso prays to his God to send him a disciple. The disciple arrives at his door and offers Paracelso his possessions and his many gold coins for his help. Paracelso rejects them. The disciple then requests a proof of his power. He asks Paracelso to burn and resurrect the rose that he is carrying in his other hand. Paracelso is indignant that he must prove himself, insisting that belief, not proof, is required. As the disciple insists, he burns the rose and then is unable to recreate it. When the disciple leaves, Paracelso brings the rose back from the ashes.

The money and the proof that the disciple demand symbolize this materialistic / scientific approach to "reality." Paracelso and Borges imply that there are other realities, other ways of understanding the world, and, in order to experience them, one must not limit oneself to the proofs of the senses. Along these same lines, the story implies that there are things that we cannot and will not understand.

Robert Wright, in a review of Churchland's book, makes a similar argument. He says that a claim to explain consciousness can explain two things. It can explain all our subjective experiences, such as a sense of taste, in terms of biological functions. Or it can answer the question, Why does consciousness exist? Why did evolution invent it? Wright does not take issue with the contention that science may eventually explain materially the function of the brain. However, he asserts that science will never successfully deal with questions like: "What is consciousness?"; "Why is it like something to be a person, but not like something to be a Chevrolet?"; and "Why are we conscious?" Science must, by necessity, either redefine it, skirt it, or ignore it. The questions, by their nature, move us into the realm of metaphysics, and deal with issues such as meaning and purpose (Wright 1995, 16–17). Wright is saying, as Borges probably would, that there will always be competing explanations, competing truths about the nature of being, and that a monistic, materialistic perspective will never provide all the answers. To claim that it will, to set itself up as the privileged knowledge in that debate, it must ignore or redefine some of the central questions.

In defining a pluralism that strikes a balance between monism and chaos, and in defining the value and knowledge of artistic and literary discourse, Nelson Goodman offers some insight in approaching issues like this. Goodman argues that the pluralist is not antiscientific but rather accepts science at full value. He contends that the pluralist's chief adversary is the "monopolistic materialist or physicalist who maintains that one system, physics, is preeminent and all-inclusive, such that every other version must eventually be reduced to it or rejected as false or meaningless" (Goodman 1978, 4). The pluralist's acceptance of other versions of knowledge, and her/his implicit challenge to science as privileged knowledge do not imply a relaxation of rigor. Rather, it recognizes standards that are different but equally exacting for evaluating, for instance, artistic and literary expressions (Goodman 1978, 5). In other words, it views artistic expressions as expressions of human consciousness that science cannot adequately reduce and explain.

With regard to questions of morality, what is right and what is wrong, what is the "best" and what is the "worst" of human nature, the monists have as much to explain as the pluralists. The leaders of the Spanish Inquisition were certain that they knew what Truth, Morality, and Justice were. Those products of modernist culture, Stalin and Hitler, were no doubt following the monistic inner logic of Marxism and Fascism when they committed their horrendous crimes that were probably an important part of the demise of modernism. The Ayatollahs had no doubt about Truth, Objectivity, and Morality when they issued their death warrants against writers such as Salman Rushdie, nor did the Al Qaeda members who planned the attack on the World Trade Center. Pat Robertson certainly believes he has a window on the Truth and Objectivity when he tells his followers that the United States is a Christian country and Freedom of Religion is not guaranteed in the Constitution.

Those who affirm a radical relativism and assert that there are no values and that all judgments about justice, morality, truth, and literature are totally arbitrary offer chaos rather than alternatives. Their absolute relativism is monistic in its totality and does not really affirm pluralism or a diversity. They challenge not only monism, but any sort of consensus or community of values. Their threat to what Matei Calinescu calls a "dialogic pluralism" is as real as that of certain monists (Calinescu 1991).

The questions, however, remain. How do we define right and wrong, moral and ethical behavior, if concepts such as truth, history, justice, and God are so elusive? Virtually any singular "Truth" that everybody in the world could agree on is either so general, or so reduced, basic, or bizarre as to be almost meaningless. Nelson Goodman appears to strike a balance similar to Borges. He asserts in *Ways of Worldmaking*, "Most of us learned long ago such fundamental principles as that truths never really conflict, that all true versions are true in the only actual world, and that apparent disagreements among truths amount merely to differences in the frameworks or conventions adopted" (Goodman 1978, 110). Our world is multiple, diverse, and plural, but that does not preclude hierarchies and limits. Goodman asserts:

> Willingness to accept countless alternative true or right world versions
> does not mean that everything goes, that tall stories are as good as short
> ones, that truths are no longer distinguished from falsehoods, but only
> that truth must be otherwise conceived than as correspondence with a
> ready-made world. Though we make worlds by making versions, we no
> more make a world by putting symbols together than a carpenter makes
> a chair by putting pieces of wood together at random. The multiple
> worlds I countenance are just the actual worlds made by and answering
> to true or right versions. (Goodman 1978, 94)

This pluralism does not preclude some agreement on goals, methods, and values. We unify these diverse worlds by creating a world that encompasses them (Goodman 1978, 5).

Whether discussing international politics or the academic canon, the uneasy balance between the One and the Many that Borges strikes offers some assistance. In terms of international politics, we have not yet achieved a balance between this diversity and the respect for individual freedom and dignity that would prevent occurrences such as death warrants on Salman Rushdie, or atrocities in ethnic wars, or the mutilation of young girls in certain cultures to preserve their virginity and/or deny them sexual pleasure. The United Nations is an attempt to create a rule of law that would strike such a balance and prevent such abuse, but with limited success to date. Every pluralistic democracy tries to do likewise, but on a smaller scale. We declare certain "unalienable rights" based on "universal" values, although those values are not yet totally universal in acceptance and practice. As a culture, we may declare that these freedoms and dignities derive from the Natural Law and/or Divine Providence. Proof of that origin, of course, is another matter. We must realize that it is not only others that fall short of these values. U.S. society has fallen short in implementing principles such as equal opportunity for all or in accepting certain economic principles such as freedom from hunger, the right to meaningful work that offers a living wage, or ready access to medical care—concepts that other cultures have embraced or have more successfully implemented.

The postmodern does not eliminate value and knowledge; rather, it asserts that it does not derive from a provable, transcendent source. Within our individual worlds we create contexts for value, for judging, based on rightness and consistency (Calinescu 1991). Within our academic and literary disciplines we have standards and criteria that are generally agreed upon, that we use to define whether a given study is rigorous and acceptable as an addition to the knowledge of the discipline. It is presented publicly and subject to refutation or disproof. If it withstands that test, it becomes part of the canon of knowledge until it is revised, rejected, or replaced. This pluralistic dialogue legitimates and validates it. It is based on an acceptance of freedom of thought and expression such as those for which John Stuart Mill argued. No doubt Borges knew his writings well. Mill writes:

> The beliefs which we have most warrant for have no safeguard to rest on but a standing invitation to the whole world to prove them unfounded. If the challenge is not accepted, or is accepted and the attempt fails, we are far enough from certainty still, but we have done the best that the existing state of human reason admits of: we have neglected nothing that could give the truth a chance of reaching us; if the lists are kept open, we may hope that, if there is a better truth, it will be found when the human mind is capable of receiving it; and in the meantime we may rely on having attained such approach to truth as is possible in our own day. This is the amount of certainty attainable by a fallible being, and this the sole way of attaining it. (Mill 1956, 26)

However, this pluralism can be subverted by totalities, fanatics, and monistic and totalitarian ideas that claim to have a corner on the Truth.

In many ways, literature and aesthetics have created a mode of pluralism that works quite effectively. We accept without question literary differences between the poetry of the mystic poet San Juan de la Cruz and the Marxist poet César Vallejo or between the writings of James Joyce and those of Homer, and yet find merit in both. They have worth and value in their literary, historical, geographical, and philosophical contexts, and we grant them that.

As we reconsider the "canon," it is important that we continue to make critical and aesthetic judgments. Certainly, we want to avoid the rigidity and exclusiveness of the past. We want a fluidity that admits communities that have been marginalized previously. Yet, even within communities, not all male European writers are equal. Not all Hispanic male poets of the last forty years are equal. Not all Hispanic female novelists of the last forty years are equal. Not all writers of color are equal. Some critics prefer not to make such judgments. Yet, we cannot avoid them if we work in the academy. When we select a theme for a course, when we choose writers to include in the course, when we write books, articles, and conference papers, we make aesthetic judgments. Perhaps the important things are that we be self-conscious of our aesthetics and forthright about them, that we realize their relative and pluralistic nature, and that they be open to question and challenge.

Similarly, within our social, legal, and religious systems, we create hierarchies of value, of rightness. We define acceptable norms of behavior, which we call laws, morality, and truths, to regulate our lives. We may disagree about some of the finer points. We are reared in, we establish, and we identify with communities that determine and reflect our attitudes toward some of those issues. We should and we will continue to do so. We need to strive to outlaw and eliminate political torture, murder, oppression, and similar crimes, and to obtain more "universal" respect in word and in deed, for rule of law, for human rights such as freedom of expression, equality under the law, for assuring that basic human needs, such as nourishment, work, and medical care, are satisfied.

Yes, understanding and attaining ultimate beauty, truth, justice, and morality may be beyond our reach. Yes, we may be part of a labyrinthine universe that we will never totally fathom. However, that does not preclude establishing boundaries and markers so that we can find our way around part of it and move toward those ends. Yes, we might be able to move from one part of it to another, again using boundaries and markers that we define with our mind and our imagination. That labyrinth does not mean that all our pursuits end in obstructions and dead ends. If we follow the signs and use our faculties and our imaginations to mark, to highlight, and to trace the paths, yes, we might be able to get there from here. That is important, and at times worth celebrating. However, we must always be mindful that, if we do get "there," we have not ultimately reached the center, and almost certainly have not exited from the larger labyrinth. We must be mindful also, that others may get there as well, but via different paths and by a different means.

Notes

Chapter 1. Introduction

1. Modernity has been marked by a utopian faith in the future and in "progress" into the future. The future offers change. The future is always becoming. The future will always be better. In its conflicted way, aesthetic modernism accepts this faith in progress, science, history, and the future, but at the same time undermines it with a vision of the present as empty, superficial, and decadent. See: Matei Calinescu, 1987a, and Octavio Paz, 1981, 1974.

2. I situate the beginning of postmodernism right after the end of World War II. Some critics contend that it starts in the 1960s or even the 1970s, but World War II is a more appropriate transition marker. The actions of Hitler and Stalin, the Holocaust, the failures of capitalism to adequately foresee and deal with the Great Depression, the destruction of Europe, and the development of the atomic bomb, create a serious crisis in Western thought, challenge the notion of inevitable progress and a utopian future, and for practical purposes, mark the failure and the end of aesthetic modernism. While the foundations for the postmodern precede the outbreak of the war, and while the transitions to postmodern culture and thought are not immediate, the war provides the best marker for this change.

Chapter 2. A Latin American Postmodernism?

1. Paz objects to the use of the term postmodernism, (and modernism, as well). He sees it as demeaning to Latin American literature. Latin American critics first coined those terms to speak about poetic movements within Latin American literature. They were later applied to all of Western literature and culture, but with different meanings. Instead he uses "la vanguardia," the vanguard, in much of his discussion. Paz is correct, I believe. I hope that future literary historians will rectify this insensitivity to Latin American poetry.

2. Gene Bell-Villada, 1999, *Borges and his Fiction: A Guide to His Mind and Art,* University of Texas Press, offers a thorough defense of Borges as an Argentine and Latin American writer. See pages 7–12, and especially 286–96.

Chapter 3. Pluralism, Meaning, Postmodernity, and Borges

1. Hans Bertens' article (1993), "The Postmodern Weltanschauung and its Relation to Modernism: An Introductory Survey," *A Postmodern Reader,* 25–70, develops

this dichotomy in regard to literature in particular. Pauline Marie Rosenau, (1992), *Postmodernism and the Social Sciences: Insights, Inroads, and Intrusions* (Princeton: Princeton University Press), sees this tension as being quite central to the social sciences. It is one of the primary theses of her work.

2. "Mapping the Postmodern" in *New German Critique* 33 (fall 1984); Huyssen, *After the Great Divide,* Indiana University Press, 1987; Joseph Natoli and Linda Hutcheon, editors, *A Postmodern Reader* (Albany: State University Press of New York, 1993); Linda J. Nicholson, ed., *Feminism/Postmodernism* (New York: Routledge, 1990), 234–77.

Chapter 4. Borges, the Self, and the Postmodern

1. That "Greek" very well may have been Heraclitus, who states: "Nothing endures but change" (*On the Universe*). However, it also may have been Shelley, who writes in *Mutability* (1816) I, st.4: "Man's yesterday may ne'er be like his morrow; / Nought may endure but Mutability."

Chapter 5. Women, Feminism, Postmodernity, and Borges

1. In subverting the concepts of civilization and barbarity, this story also challenges the privileging of European values as superior and more "civilized." Those attitudes played an important role in the conquest of the Americas, and in attitudes toward Latin America, which Borges attempts to redefine. See chapter 2.

Chapter 6. Borges, Universal History, and Historical Representation

1. See Santiago Colás's discussion of Jameson's treatment of the Third World in his work, "The Third World in Jameson's Postmodernism or the Cultural Logic of Late Capitalism," *Social Text* (1992) 10:2–3 (31/32), 858–70.

2. See Hutcheon, *The Politics of Postmodernism,* 1989, 47–61 and 62–92 for a detailed discussion.

3. Balderston (1993) has a very interesting and thorough discussion of how history and fiction intersect in this story. See *Out of Context,* 115–31.

4. The textuality of the universe, of history, of knowledge and of truth derives, in part, from Borges's reading of the Kabbalah as well. (See: Alazraki 1988a, and Aizenberg 1984.

5. See McMurray 1980, 77–97, and Aizenberg (1990); Borges Lecture, "Baruch Spinoza."

6. See Alazraki, 1988a.

7. Borges himself suggests as much. See his talk, "The Kabbalah," in Alazraki 1988a, 54–61.

Chapter 7. Borges, Politics, and the Postmodern

1. Emir Rodríguez Monegal mentions how Borges's writings became embroiled in a debate about the political and cultural role of the writer. Borges and his work came under critical attack. Rodríguez Monegal, (1978), mentions among others, an article in *Sur* (June–July 1948) by H. A. Murena; Adolf Prieto, "Borges and the New Generation 1954;" a new journal, *Ciudad* (No. 2–3, 1955), dedicated to Borges; Jorge Abelardo Ramos, *Crisis and the Resurrection of Argentine Literature*, 1954, where he accuses Borges of being a representative of the ranch owner's oligarchy and accuses him of writing an alienated, gratuitous, aristocratic literature. See *Jorge Luis Borges: A Literary Biography*, 423–24.

Daniel Balderston, (1993), in an interesting work, *Out of Context*, goes to some length to outline historical reference, which has some implications for political views.

2. The central issue of this story, I believe, is not Borges's political stance, but rather, his concept of the self. I elaborate on that in chapter 4, on the self.

3. See Balderston (1993), 98–114. Balderston's methods of reading Borges are particularly effective with this story.

4. See Matei Calinescu's article on the theatrical fallacies of the postmodern (1987b).

5. See my article on the postmodern, the real marvelous, and a changing attitude toward the natural world, relating to the ecology movement: "Nature, Postmodernity, and the Real Marvelous: Faulkner, Quiroga, Mallea, Rulfo, Carpentier" (fall 1995/spring 1996), 67–82.

Chapter 8. Borges, the Postmodern, and the Literature of the Americas

1. García Marquez uses the character of Fernanda to masterfully and comically criticize the conquest. Her shrewish personality makes her one of the more contemptible, yet comic characters in the novel. She comes from the Colombian highlands, considers herself royalty, and in many ways represents the heritage of the Spanish conquest and its imposition on Macondo and Latin America. She speaks a corrupted Spanish that is a throwback to Peninsular Spanish. Her surnames Argote and Carpio, suggest that she has descended from two of Spain's most famous Golden Age authors, Luis de Góngora y Argote and Lope de Vega Carpio. Like the landlocked Spanish galleon overgrown with vegetation, her religiosity, aristocratic pretensions, and emphasis on class distinctions all refer back to the Spanish cultural heritage and suggest an outmoded mental framework that has prevented Latin America from achieving its full potential in the modern world. See Griffin 2002, 59 and Higgins 2002, 41.

2. In using the real marvelous, García Márquez develops a tension between the oral and written history, by interpreting and presenting events as perceived by the local people to create and represent a third world experience. Rather than relying on the documentary approach of realistic or naturalistic fiction that is Eurocentric

in origin, he gives expression to local voices living in isolation from the modern world. See Higgins 2002, 37–39.

3. All page references to *Cien años de soledad* are to: Gabriel García Márquez, *Cien años de soledad* (Madrid: Espasa-Calpe, S.A., 1985). All page references to the translation are to: Gabriel García Márquez, *One Hundred Years of Solitude,* Trans. Gregory Rabassa (New York: Harper Perennial, 1991).

4. As James Higgins (2002) points out, for García Márquez, perhaps there is hope through the demise of the Buendía's class and a socialist revolution. See pages 45–46.

5. Borges suffered a similar accident while working as a librarian.

6. For an extended discussion of these symmetries, see Zunilda Gertel, "'El Sur' de Borges: Búsqueda de identidad en el laberinto," *Nueva Narrativa Hispanoamericana,* 1.2 (1971) 35–55.

7. Gertel also has a useful analysis of the role of *The Arabian Nights* in the story.

8. Max Schulz, quoting Milton in part, in *Black Humor Fiction of the Sixties,* writes that the novel: "parodies the Old and New Testament accounts of man, as well as such post Christian theological controversies as 'Of Providence, Foreknowledge, Will and Fate/Fixt Fates, Free Will, Foreknowledge Absolute' of transubstantiation and the reality of the communion host, evolutionary doctrine and the perfectibility of man, existential skepticism and the notion that God is dead" (1973, 85).

A Selected Bibliography

Primary Works

Borges, Jorge Luis. 1962, 1964. *Labyrinths: Selected Stories and Other Writings.* Edited by Donald A. Yates and James Irby. New York: New Directions.

———. 1969. *Conversations with Jorge Luis Borges.* Edited by Richard Burgin. New York: Holt, Rinehart and Winston.

———. 1974. *Obras Completas 1923–1972.* Buenos Aires: Emecé Editores.

———. 1979a. *Borges: memoria de un gesto. Interviews.* Edited by Jairo Osorio and Carlos Bueno. Medellín, Colombia: Ediciones Hombre Nuevo.

———. 1979b. *Borges, oral.* Buenos Aires: Emecé Editores/Editorial de Belgrano.

———. 1981. *Borges A Reader: A Selection From the Writings of Jorge Luis Borges.* Edited by Rodríguez Monegal, Emir and Alastair Reid. New York: E. P. Dutton.

———. 1982a. *Borges at Eighty: Conversations.* Edited by Willis Barnstone. Bloomington: Indiana University Press.

———. 1982b. *Seven Conversations with Jorge Luis Borges.* Edited by Fernando Sorrentino. Translated by Clark M. Zlotchew. Troy, N. Y.: The Whitston Publishing Co.

———. 1984a. *Conversaciones con Borges.* Edited by Roberto Alifano. Buenos Aires: Editorial Atlántida, S.A.

———. 1984b. *Twenty-Four Conversations with Borges, Including a Selection of Poems— Interviews by Roberto Alifano, 1981–83.* Edited by Roberto Alifano. Housatonic, Mass.: Lascaux Publishers.

———. 1985. *Borges en diálogo: Conversaciones de Jorge Luis Borges con Osvaldo Ferrari.* Edited by Osvaldo Ferrari. Buenos Aires: Grijalbo S.A.

———. 1988. "The Kabbalah." In Jaime Alazraki, *Borges and the Kabbalah and Other Essays on His Fiction and Poetry.* Cambridge, Mass.: Cambridge University Press. 54–61.

———. 1989a. *Obras Completas 1975–85.* Buenos Aires: Emecé Editores.

———. 1989b. *Las obsesiones de Borges.* Interview. Edited by Dante Escóbar Plata. Buenos Aires: Editorial Distal.

———. 1990. "Baruch Spinoza." *Borges and His Successors: The Borgesian Impact on Literature and the Arts.* Edited by Edna Aizenberg. Columbia: University of Missouri Press.

———. 1996. *Obras completas IV 1975–88.* Buenos Aires: Emecé Editores.

———. 1998. *Collected Fictions.* Translated by Andrew Hurley. New York, Penguin Books.

———. 1999a. *Selected Non-Fictions*. Edited by Eliot Weinberger. New York: Penguin Books.

———. 1999b. *Selected Poems*. Edited by Alexander Coleman. New York: Penguin Books.

Borges, Jorge Luis and Osvaldo Ferrari. 1986a. *Diálogos últimos*. Edited by Osvaldo Ferrari. Buenos Aires: Editorial Sudamericana.

Borges, Jorge Luis and Osvaldo Ferrari. 1986b. *Libro de diálogos*. Interviews. Edited by Osvaldo Ferrari. Buenos Aires: Editorial Sudamericana.

Borges, Jorge Luis and Ernesto Sabato. 1976. *Diálogos*. Edited by Orlando Barone. Buenos Aires: Emecé.

Coover, Robert. 1968. *The Universal Baseball Association, Inc., J. Henry Waugh, Prop.* New York: The New American Library.

García Márquez, Gabriel. 1985. *Cien años de soledad*. Madrid: Espasa-Calpe, S.A.

———. 1991. *One Hundred Years of Solitude*. Translated by Gregory Rabassa. New York: Harper Perennial.

SECONDARY WORKS

Aizenberg, Edna. 1983. "A Kabbalistic Heroine in Borges's Fiction." *Studies in American Jewish Literature* 3: 223–35.

———. 1984. *The Aleph Weaver: Biblical, Kabbalistic and Judaic Elements in Borges*. Potomac, Md.: Scripta Humanistica.

———. 1986. *El tejedor del Aleph: Biblia, kábala y judaísmo en Borges*. Madrid: Altalena Editores.

———. 1990. *Borges and His Successors: The Borgesian Impact on Literature and the Arts*. Columbia: University of Missouri Press.

———. 1992. "Borges, Postcolonial Precursor." *World Literature Today* 66, no. 1: 21–26.

Alazraki, Jaime. 1977a. "Borges o el difícil oficio de la intimidad: reflexiones sobre su poesía más reciente." *Revista Iberoamericana* 43.100–101: 449–63.

———. 1977b. *Versiones, inversiones, reversiones: el espejo como modelo estructural en los cuentos de Borges*. Madrid: Editorial Grados.

———. 1988a. *Borges and the Kabbalah and Other Essays on His Fiction and Poetry*. Cambridge, Mass.: Cambridge University Press.

———. 1988b. "Borges: entre la modernidad y la postmodernidad." *Revista Hispánica Moderna* 41, no. 2: 175–79.

Almond, Ian. 1988. "Tlön, Pilgrimages and Postmodern Banality." *Bulletin of Hispanic Studies*. 75, no. 2 (April): 229–35.

Alonso, Carlos. 1990. *The Spanish American Regional Novel: Modernity and Autochthony*. Cambridge, Mass.: Cambridge University Press.

———. 1994. "The Mourning After: García Márquez, Fuentes and the Meaning of Postmodernity in Spanish America." *MLN* 109, no. 2: 252–67.

Altamiranda, Daniel. 1994. "Jorge Luis Borges." In *Latin American Writers on Gay and Lesbian Themes: A Bio-critical Sourcebook.* Edited by David William Foster. Westport, Conn: Greenwood Press.

Alvarez, Nicolás. 1983–84. "La realidad trascendida: Dualismo y rectangularidad en Emma Zunz." *Explicación de textos literarios.* 12, no. 1: 27–36.

Anderson, Richard. 1981. *Robert Coover.* Boston: Twayne.

Ayala, Francisco. 1973. "Comentarios textuales a 'El Aleph' de Borges." *Explicación de textos literarios* 2: 3–5.

Balderston, Daniel. 1993. *Out of Context: Historical Reference and the Representation of Reality in Borges.* Durham, N.C.: Duke University Press.

———. 1995. "The 'Fecal Dialectic': Homosexual Panic and the Origin of Writing in Borges." In *¿Entiendes?: Queer Readings, Hispanic Writings.* Edited by Emilie L. Bergmann and Paul Julian Smith. Durham, N.C.: Duke University Press.

Barrenechea, Ana María. 1965. *Borges: The Labyrinth Maker.* Translated and edited by Robert Lima. New York: New York University Press.

———. 1984. *La expresión de la irrealidad en la obra de Borges.* Buenos Aires: Bibliotecas Universitarias Centro Editor de América Latina.

Barth, John. 1967. "The Literature of Exhaustion." *The Atlantic Monthly* (August): 29–34.

———. 1980. "The Literature of Replenishment." *The Atlantic Monthly* (January): 65–71.

Baudrillard, Jean. 1983. "The Ecstasy of Communication." In *The Anti Aesthetic: Essays on Postmodern Culture.* Edited by Hal Foster. Port Townsend, Wash.: Bay Press.

Bell, Daniel. 1973. *The Coming of Post Industrial Society.* New York: Basic Books.

Bell, Steven M., Albert H. LeMay, and Leonard Orr, eds. 1993. *Critical Theory, Cultural Politics and Latin American Narrative.* South Bend, Ind.: Notre Dame University Press.

Bell-Villada, Gene H. 1999. *Borges and His Fiction: A Guide to His Mind and Art. Rev. Edition.* Austin: University of Texas Press.

———. 2002a. "Banana Strike and Military Massacre: *One Hundred Years of Solitude* and What Happened in 1928." In *Gabriel García Márquez's* One Hundred Years of Solitude: *A Casebook.* Edited by Gene H. Bell-Villada. New York: Oxford University Press.

———, ed. 2002b. *Gabriel García Márquez's* One Hundred Years of Solitude: *A Casebook.* New York: Oxford University Press.

Benhabib, Seyla. 1995. "Feminism and Postmodernism: An Uneasy Alliance." In *Feminist Contentions: A Philosophical Exchange.* Benhabib, Seyla, Judith Butler, Drucilla Cornell and Nancy Fraser. New York: Routledge.

Benhabib, Seyla, Judith Butler, Drucilla Cornell, and Nancy Fraser. 1995. *Feminist Contentions: A Philosophical Exchange.* New York: Routledge.

Benítez Rojo, Antonio. 1996. *Repeating Island: The Caribbean and the Postmodern Perspective.* Translated by James Maraniss. Durham, N.C.: Duke University Press.

———. 1998. *La isla que se repite.* Barcelona: Casiopea.

Bertens, Hans. 1986. "The Postmodern Weltanschaung and its Relation to Modernism: An Introductory Survey." In *Approaching Postmodernism.* Edited by Douwe Fokkema and Hans Bertens. Amsterdam: John Benjamins Co. Reprinted in *A*

Postmodern Reader. Edited by Joseph Natoli and Linda Hutcheon. Albany, N.Y.: State University of New York Press, 1993.

————. 1987. "Postmodern Characterization and the Intrusion of Language." In *Exploring Postmodernism: Selected Papers Presented at a Workshop at the XIth International Comparative Literature Congress 20–24 August 1985.* Amsterdam: John Benjamins Publishing Co. 139–59.

Beverly, John, and José Oviedo, eds. 1993. *The Postmodern Debate in Latin America,* Special Issue, *boundary 2* 20, no. 3. Durham, N.C.: Duke University Press.

Bloom, Harold, ed. 1986. *Jorge Luis Borges.* New York: Chelsea House Publishers.

Bluher, Karl Alfred, and Alfonso de Toro, eds. 1992. *Jorge Luis Borges: Variaciones interpretativas sobre sus procedimientos literarios y bases epistemológicas.* Frankfurt: Vervuert.

Booth, Wayne. 1992. *Critical Understanding: The Powers and Limits of Pluralism.* Chicago: The University of Chicago Press.

Borinsky, Alicia. 1986. "Repetitions, Museums, Libraries." In *Jorge Luis Borges.* Edited by Harold Bloom. New York: Chelsea House Publishers.

Brodski, Bella. 1990. "Borges and the Idea of Woman." *Modern Fiction Studies* 36, no. 2: 149–66.

Butler, Christopher. 1980. *After the Wake: An Essay on the Contemporary Avant Garde.* Oxford: Clarendon Press.

Butler, Judith. 1990. "Gender Trouble, Feminist Theory, and Psychoanalytic Discourse." In *Feminism/Postmodernism.* Edited by Linda J. Nicholson. New York: Routledge.

————. 1993. *Bodies That Matter: On the Discursive Limits of "Sex."* New York: Routledge.

————. 1995. "Contingent Foundations: Feminism and the Question of 'Postmodernism.'" In *Feminist Contentions: A Philosophical Exchange.* New York: Routledge.

Byrne, K. B. Conal. 1999. "Inventing the New World: Finding the Mythology of Jorge Luis Borges." *Hispanófila* 126 (May): 67–83.

Calinescu, Matei. 1987a. *Five Faces of Modernity: Modernism, Avant Garde, Decadence, Kitsch, Postmodernism.* 2nd ed. Durham, N.C.: Duke University Press.

————. 1987b. "Introductory Remarks: Postmodernism, the Mimetic and Theatrical Fallacies." In *Exploring Postmodernism.* Edited by Matei Calinescu and Douwe Fokkema. Amsterdam: John Benjamins Publishing Co.

————. 1991. "From the One to the Many: Pluralism in Today's Thought." In *Zeitgeist in Babel: The Postmodern Controversy.* Edited by Ingeborg Hoesterey. Bloomington and Indianapolis: Indiana University Press.

Calinescu, Matei, and Douwe Fokkema, eds. 1987. *Exploring Postmodernism: Selected Papers Presented at a Workshop on Postmodernism at the XIth International Comparative Literature Congress, Paris, 20–24 August 1985.* Amsterdam: John Benjamins Publishing Co.

Caramello, Charles. 1991. "Performing Self as Performance: James Joyce and the Postmodern Turn." *Southern Humanities Review* 15, no. 4: 301–5.

Carlos, Alberto J. 1966. "Dante y 'El Aleph' de Borges." *Duquesne Hispanic Review* 5: 35–50.

Carpentier, Alejo. 1969. *El reino de este mundo*. Montevideo: Arca.

Chamberlain, Daniel. 1997. "Latin American Narrative: Perspectives and the Postmodern Context." In *Latin American Postmodernisms*. Edited by Richard A. Young. Amsterdam: Rodopi.

Chanady, Amaryll, ed. 1994. Introduction to *Latin American Identity and Constructions of Difference*. Minneapolis: University of Minnesota Press.

Christ, Ronald. 1967. "Jorge Luis Borges: An Interview." *Paris Review* 40 (winter–spring): 116–63.

———. 1969. *The Narrow Act: Borges' Art of Illusion*. New York: New York University Press.

———. 1979. "Forking Narratives." *Latin American Literary Review* 7, no. 4 (spring–summer): 52–61.

———. 1986. "The Immortal." In *Jorge Luis Borges*. Edited by Harold Bloom. New York: Chelsea House Publishers. Originally published in Ronald Christ, *The Narrow Act: Borges' Act of Illusion*. New York: New York University Press, 1969.

Churchland, Paul M. 1995. *The Engine of Reason, the Seat of the Soul: A Philosophical Journey Into the Brain*. London: MIT Press.

Cohen, Ralph, ed. 1989. *The Future of Literary Theory*. New York: Routledge.

Colás, Santiago. 1992. "The Third World in Jameson's Postmodernism or the Cultural Logic of Late Capitalism." *Social Text* 10: 858–70.

———. 1994. *Postmodernity in Latin America: The Argentine Paradigm*. Durham, N.C.: Duke University Press.

Collin, Françoise. 1990. "The Third Tiger, or From Blanchot to Borges." In *Borges and his Successors: The Borgesian Impact on Literature and the Arts*. Edited by Edna Aizenberg. Columbia: University of Missouri Press.

Concha, Jaime. 1983. "El Aleph: Borges y la historia." *Revista Iberoamericana* 49, nos. 123–24 (April–September): 471–85.

Conniff, Brian. 2002. "The Dark Side of Magical Realism: Science, Oppression, and Apocalypse in *One Hundred Years of Solitude*." In *Gabriel García Márquez's* One Hundred Years of Solitude: *A Casebook*. Edited by Gene H. Bell-Villada. New York: Oxford University Press.

Currie, Peter. 1987. "The Eccentric Self: Anti-Characterization and the Problem of the Subject in American Postmodern Fiction." In *Contemporary American Fiction*. Edited by Malcolm Bradbury and Sigmund Ro. London: Edward Arnold Ltd.

Dauster, Frank. 1962. "Notes on Borges' Labyrinths." *Hispanic Review*, 30: 142–48.

de Man, Paul. 1986. "A Modern Master." In *Jorge Luis Borges*. Edited by Harold Bloom. New York: Chelsea House Publishers. First printed in *New York Review of Books* 5 Nov. 1964.

Dembo, L. S. 1970. "Interview with Jorge Luis Borges." *Wisconsin Studies in Contemporary Literature* 11: 315–23.

D'haen, Theo, and Hans Bertens, eds. 1988. *Postmodern Fiction in Europe and the Americas*. Amsterdam: Rodopi; Antwerpen: SL

Di Stefano, Christine. 1990. "Dilemmas of Difference: Feminism, Modernity, and Postmodernism." In *Feminism/Postmodernism*. Edited by Linda J. Nicholson. New York: Routledge.

Dorfman, Ariel. 1981. *Some Write to the Future: Essays on Contemporary Latin American Fiction.* Durham, N.C.: Duke University Press.

Dussel, Enrique. 1993. "Eurocentrism and Modernity (Introduction to the Frankfurt Lectures)." In *The Postmodern Debate in Latin America.* Edited by John Beverly and José Oviedo. Special Issue, *boundary 2* 20, no. 3: 65–76.

Earnshaw, Steven, ed. 1997. *Just Postmodernism.* Amsterdam: Rodopi.

Eco, Umberto. 1984. Postscript to *The Name of the Rose.* New York: Harcourt Brace Jovanovich.

Eco, Umberto, and Stefano Rosso. 1991. "A Correspondence on Postmodernism." In *Zeitgeist in Babel: The Postmodern Controversy.* Edited by Ingeborg Hoesterey. Bloomington and Indianapolis: Indiana University Press.

Escalante, Evodio. 1988. "Jorge Luis Borges, ¿iniciador de la postmodernidad?" *Casa del Tiempo* Vol. 8, 80 (noviembre–diciembre): 18–20.

Fernandez-Ferrer, Antonio. 1992. "'El Aleph' de *El Aleph.*" *Cuadernos Hispanoamericanos: Revista Mensual de Cultura Hispánica* 505–507 (July–September): 481–93.

Flax, Jane. 1990. "Postmodernism and Gender Relations in Feminist Theory." In *Feminism/Postmodernism.* Edited by Linda J. Nicholson. New York: Routledge.

Fokkema, Douwe. 1984. *Literary History, Modernism and Postmodernism: The Harvard Univ. Erasmus Lectures, Spring 1983.* Amsterdam: John Benjamins Publishing Company.

Fokkema, Douwe, and Hans Bertens, eds. 1986. *Approaching Postmodernism: Utrech Publication in General and Comparative Literature, Vol. 21.* Amsterdam: John Benjamins Publishing Company.

Foster, David William. 1997. *Sexual Textualities: Essays on Queer/ing Latin American Writing.* Austin: University of Texas Press.

Foster, Hal, ed. 1983. *The Anti Aesthetic: Essays on Postmodern Culture.* Port Townsend, Wash.: Bay Press.

Fraser, Nancy. 1995. "False Antithesis: A Response to Seyla Benhabib and Judith Butler." In *Feminist Contentions: A Philosophical Exchange.* New York: Routledge.

Fraser, Nancy, and Linda J. Nicholson. 1990. "Social Criticism Without Philosophy: An Encounter between Feminism and Postmodernism." In *Feminism/Postmodernism.* Edited by Linda J. Nicholson. New York: Routledge.

Frisch, Mark. 1989. "Self-Definition and Redefinition in the New World: Coover's Universal Baseball Association and Borges." *Confluencia: Revista Hispánica de Cultura y Literatura* 4, no. 2: 13–20.

———. 1990. "Borges and Nabokov's Lolita: Reality as Fictional Dream Image." *Cincinnati Romance Review* 9: 98–108.

———. 1995–1996. "Nature, Postmodernity and the Real Marvelous: Faulkner, Quiroga, Mallea, Rulfo, Carpentier." *The Faulkner Journal.* 11, nos. 1 and 2 (fall 1995/spring 1996): 67–82.

Fullbrook, Kate. 1997. "The Godfather: Borges and the Ethics of The Labyrinth." In *Just Postmodernism.* Edited by Steven Earnshaw. Amsterdam: Rodopi.

Gado, Frank. 1973. "Robert Coover." In *First Person: Conversations on Writers and Writing.* Schenectady, N.Y.: Union College Press.

Garzilli, Enrico. 1972. *Circles Without Center: Paths to the Discovery and Creation of Self in Modern Literature.* Cambridge: Harvard University Press.

Gertel, Zunilda. 1971. "'El sur' de Borges; Busqueda de identidad en el laberinto." *Nueva Narrativa Hispanoamericana* 1, no. 2: 35–55.

Goić, Cedomil. 1972. *Historia de la novela hispanoamericana.* Valparaíso: Edited by Universitarias de Valparaíso.

Gómez de la Serna, Ramón. 1964. "Borges en Paris." *Alcor* 33.

González Echevarría, Roberto. 1972. "Polemic: With Borges in Macondo." *Diacritics* 2, no. 1: 57–60.

Goodman, Nelson. 1978. *Ways of Worldmaking.* Indianapolis, Ind.: Hackett.

Gordon, James. 1997. "Consciousness Studies: From Stream to Flood." *New York Times* 29 April 1997: B7+.

Gordon, Lois. 1983. *Robert Coover: The Universal Fictionmaking Process.* Carbondale and Evansville: Southern Illinois University Press.

Greenberg, Clement. 1991. "The Notion of Postmodernism." In *Zeitgeist in Babel: The Postmodern Controversy.* Edited by Ingeborg Hoesterey. Bloomington and Indianapolis: Indiana University Press.

Griffin, Clive. 2002. "The Humor of *One Hundred Years of Solitude.*" In *Gabriel García Márquez's* One Hundred Years of Solitude: A Casebook. Edited by Gene H. Bell-Villada. New York: Oxford University Press.

Grossman, Rudolph. 1980. "Konventionelle und magische Zeit in dem Roman *Cien años de soledad* des Kolumbianers Gabriel García Márquez." *Romanica Europae et Americana: Festschrift für Harri Meier.* Edited by Hans Dieter, Artur Grieve, and Dieter Woll. Bonn: Bouvier.

Gugelberger, Georg M., ed. 1996. *The Real Thing: Testimonial Discourse and Latin America.* Durham, N.C.: Duke University Press.

Guibert, Rita. 1973. *Seven Voices: Seven Latin American Writers Talk to Rita Guibert.* Translated by Frances Partridge. New York: Alfred A. Knopf.

Habermas, Jürgen. 1993. "Modernity vs. Postmodernity." Translated by Seyla Benhabib. In *A Postmodern Reader.* Edited by Joseph Natoli and Linda Hutcheon. Albany, N.Y.: State University of New York Press. First printed in *New German Critique* 22 (winter 1981) 3–14.

Hall, J. B. 1982. "Deception or Self-Deception? The Essential Ambiguity of Borges' 'Emma Zunz.'" *Forum for Modern Language Studies* 18: 258–65.

Harris, Charles B. 1971. *Contemporary American Novelists of the Absurd.* New Haven: College and University Press.

Hassan, Ihab. 1987a. "Pluralism in Postmodern Perspective." In *The Postmodern Turn: Essays in Postmodern Theory and Culture.* Columbus: Ohio State University Press. First printed in *Critical Inquiry,* 12, (spring 1986), 503–20.

———. 1987b. *The Postmodern Turn: Essays in Postmodern Theory and Culture.* Columbus: Ohio State University Press.

———. 1988. "Quest for the Subject: The Self in Literature." *Contemporary Literature* 29: 420–37.

———. 1990. "Ideology, Theory, and the Self." In *Criticism in the Twilight Zone: Post-*

modern Perspectives on Literature and Politics. Edited by Danuta Zadworna Fjellestad and Lennart Bjork. Stockholm: Almqvist and Wiksell International.

Hassan, Ihab, and Sally Hassan. 1983. *Innovation/Renovation: New Perspectives on the Humanities.* Madison: University of Wisconsin Press.

Higgins, James. 2002. "Gabriel García Márquez: *Cien años de soledad.*" In *Gabriel García Márquez's* One Hundred Years of Solitude: *A Casebook.* Edited by Gene H. Bell-Villada. New York: Oxford University Press.

Hoesterey, Ingeborg. 1991. "Postmodernism as Discursive Event." Introduction. In *Zeitgeist in Babel: The Postmodern Controversy.* Edited by Ingeborg Hoesterey. Bloomington and Indianapolis: Indiana University Press.

Holland, Norman. 1983. "Postmodern Psychoanalysis." In *Innovation / Renovation: New Perspectives on the Humanities.* Editors Ihab Hassan and Sally Hassan. Madison: University of Wisconsin Press.

———. 1985. *The I.* New Haven: Yale University Press.

Hughes, Psiche. 1979. "Love in the Abstract: The Role of Women in Borges' Literary World." *Chasqui* 8, no. 3 (May): 34–43.

Hutcheon, Linda. 1988. *A Poetics of Postmodernism: History, Theory, Fiction.* New York: Routledge.

———. 1989. *The Politics of Postmodernism.* New York: Routledge.

———. 1993. "Beginning to Theorize Postmodernism." In *A Postmodern Reader.* Edited by Joseph Natoli and Linda Hutcheon. Albany, N.Y.: State University Press of New York.

Huyssen, Andreas. 1984. "Mapping the Postmodern." *New German Critique* 33 (fall): 5–52.

Jacobs, Naomi. 1990. *The Character of Truth: Historical Figures in Contemporary Fiction.* Carbondale and Edwardsville: Southern Illinois University Press.

Jameson, Fredric. 1986. "On Magic Realism in Film." *Critical Inquiry* 12, no. 2: 301–25.

———. 1991. *Postmodernism, or, The Cultural Logic of Late Capitalism.* Durham, N.C.: Duke University Press.

Jara Cuadra, René y Jaime Mejia. 1972. "Las claves del mito en Gabriel García Márquez." In *La novela hispanoamericana: descubrimiento e invención de América.* Edited by Ricardo Vergara. Valparaíso: Ediciones Universidad de Valparaíso.

Kason, Nancy M. 1994. *Borges y la posmodernidad: un juego con espejos desplazantes.* México, D.F.: Universidad Nacional Autónoma de México.

———. 1996. "Del margen al centro: La voz femenina en la cuentística de Borges." *Alba de América: Revista Literaria* 14, nos. 26–27: 353–61.

Kason Poulson, Nancy. 1997. "Borges y el palimpsesto posmoderno: 'El otro' y 'Veinticinco agosto, 1983.'" *Cuadernos americanos* 64 (julio–agosto): 204–12.

Keiser, Graciela. 1995. "Modernism/Postmodernism in 'The Library Of Babel': Jorge Luis Borges's Fiction as Borderland." *Hispanofila* 115 (September): 39–48.

Koslowski, Peter. 1991. "The (De) Constructive Sites of the Postmodern." Translated by John H. Smith. In *Zeitgeist in Babel: The Postmodern Controversy.* Edited by Ingeborg Hoesterey. Bloomington and Indianapolis: Indiana University Press.

Kushigian, Julia. 1989. "La economía de las palabras: Disipador del miedo inefable en Borges y Silvina Bullrich." *Inti: Revista de literatura hispánica.* 29–30: 207–14.

Lévy, Salomón. 1976. "El Aleph, símbolo cabalístico y sus implicaciones en la obra de Jorge Luis Borges." *Hispanic Review* 44, no. 2: 143–61.

Lindstrom, Naomi. 1990. *Jorge Luis Borges: A Study of the Short Fiction.* Boston: Twayne Publishing.

Ludmer, Josefina. 1972. *Cien años de soledad: una interpretación.* Buenos Aires: Editorial Tiempo Contemporáneo.

Lyotard, Jean François. 1984. *The Postmodern Condition: A Report on Knowledge.* Translated by Geoff Bennington and Brian Massuni. Minneapolis: University of Minnesota Press.

Magnarelli, Sharon. 1983. "Literature and Desire: Women in the Fiction of Jorge Luis Borges." *Revista/Review Interamericana* 13, nos. 1–4: 138–49.

McBride, Mary. 1977. "Jorge Luis Borges, Existentialist: 'El Aleph' and the Relativity of Human Perception." *Studies in Short Fiction* 14: 401–3.

McCaffery, Larry. 1982. *The Metafictional Muse: The Works of Robert Coover, Donald Barthelme and William H. Gass.* Pittsburgh: University of Pittsburgh Press.

———— ed. 1986. *Postmodern Fiction: A Bio-Bibliographical Guide.* New York: Greenwood.

McMurray, George R. 1977. *Gabriel García Márquez.* New York: Frederick Ungar Publishing Company.

————. 1980. *Jorge Luis Borges.* New York: Frederick Ungar Publishing Company.

————. 1985. "'The Aleph' and *One Hundred Years of Solitude*: Two Microscopic Worlds." *Latin American Literary Review* 13, no. 25 (January–June): 55–64.

Mill, John Stuart. 1956. *On Liberty.* New York: Bobbs-Merrill Company.

Moon, Harold K. 1989. "Wordsworth the Guide: Borges's 'Emma Zunz' and Similitude in Dissimilitude." *Hispanofila* 32, no. 2, 95: 65–71.

Müller, Gerd F. 1974. "*Hundert Jahre Einsamkeit* und der Mythus Der ewigen Wiederkehr." *Orbis Litterarum: International Review of Literary Studies* 29: 268–82.

Natoli, Joseph, and Linda Hutcheon, eds. 1993. *A Postmodern Reader.* Albany, N.Y.: State University Press of New York.

Nicholson, Linda J., ed. 1990. *Feminism/Postmodernism.* New York: Routledge.

Ortega, Julio. 1984. *Poetics of Change.* Translated by Galen D. Greaser. Austin: University of Texas Press.

————. 1988. "Postmodernism in Latin America." In *Postmodern Fiction in Europe and the Americas.* Editors Theo D'haen and Hans Bertens. Amsterdam: Rodopi.

————. 1994. *Arte de innovar.* México, D.F.: Ediciones del Equilibrista.

————. 1997. *El principio radical de lo nuevo: postmodernidad, identidad, y novela en América Latina.* México, D.F.: Fondo de Cultura Económica.

Paz, Octavio. 1967. *El laberinto de la soledad.* México: Fondo de Cultura Económica.

————. 1974. *Children of the Mire; Modern Poetry from Romanticism to the Avant-garde.* Translated by Rachel Phillips. Cambridge: Harvard University Press.

————. 1981. *Los hijos del limo: Del romanticismo a la vanguardia.* Barcelona: Seix Barral, S.A.

———. 1985. *The Labyrinth of Solitude and Other Writings.* Translated by Lysander Kemp, Yara Milos, and Rachel Phillip Belash. New York: Grove Press.

———. 1987. "El romanticismo y la poesía contemporania." *Vuelta* 11 (127) (junio): 20–27.

Perez, Alberto C. 1971. *Realidad y suprarealidad en los cuentos fantásticos de Jorge Luis Borges.* Miami: Ediciones Universal.

Perez-Gallego, Candido. 1967. "El descubrimiento de la realidad en 'El Aleph' de Jorge Luis Borges." *Cuadernos Hispanoamericanos* 72: 186–93.

Phillips, Allen W. 1963. "'El Sur' de Borges." *Revista Hispánica Moderna* 29: 140–47.

Piola, María Eugenia. 1999. "Utopia y posmodernidad en América Latina: ser o no ser . . .". *Cuadernos americanos* 13, no. 3 (75): 102–22.

Radhakrishnan, R. 1983. "The Post-Modern Event and the End of Logocentricism." *boundary 2* 12: 33–60.

Rincón, Carlos. 1993. "The Peripheral Center of Postmodernism: On Borges, García Márquez and Alterity." *The Postmodern Debate in Latin America: A Special Issue of boundary 2.* Edited by John Beverly and José Oviedo. 20, no. 3 (fall): 162–79.

———. 1995. "Posmodernismo, poscolonialismo y los nexos cartagráficos del realismo mágico." *Neue Romania* 16: 193–210.

———. 2002. "Streams Out of Control: The Latin American Plot." In *Gabriel García Márquez's* One Hundred Years of Solitude: *A Casebook.* Edited by Gene H. Bell-Villada. New York: Oxford University Press.

Rodríguez Monegal, Emir. 1978. *Borges: A Literary Biography.* New York: E. P. Dutton.

———. 1987. *Borges: Una biografía literaria.* Translated by Homero Alsina Thevenet. México, D.F.: Fondo de Cultura Económica.

Rosenau, Pauline Marie. 1992. *Postmodernism and the Social Sciences: Insights, Inroads, and Intrusions.* Princeton: Princeton University Press.

Schulz, Max F. 1973. *Black Humor Fiction of the Sixties: A Pluralistic Definition of Man and his World.* Athens: Ohio University Press.

Sebreli, Juan José. 1992. *El asedio a la modernidad: crítica del relativismo cultural.* Barcelona: Editorial Ariel, S.A.

Shaw, Donald L. 1976. *Borges, Ficciones.* London: Grant and Cutler: Tamesis.

———. 1994. "Which Was the First Novel of the Boom?" *Modern Language Review.* 89, no. 2: 360–71.

Silverman, Kaja. 1988. "Splits: Changing the Fantasmatic Scene." *Revista de Estudios Hispánicos.* 22 no. 3 (October): 65–86.

Sims, Robert L. 1998. "The Question of History and the Postmodern Debate in Latin America." *Comparatist: Journal of the Southern Comparative Literature Association.* May 22, 1998: 145–67.

Stavans, Ilan. 1986. "Emma Zunz: The Jewish Theodicy of Jorge Luis Borges." *Modern Fiction Studies* 32: 469–75.

Stevens, Robert, and G. Roland Vela. 1980. "Jungle Gothic: Science, Myth and Reality in *One Hundred Years of Solitude.*" *Modern Fiction Studies* 26: 262–66.

Stimpson, Catherine R. 1989. "Wolf's Room, Our Project: The Building of Feminist

Criticism." In *The Future of Literary Theory*. Edited by Ralph Cohen. New York: Routledge.

Straub, Kristina. 1991. "Feminist Politics and Postmodernist Style." In *Image and Ideology in Modern/Postmodern Discourse*. Edited by David B. Downing. Albany: State University of New York Press.

Taylor, Mark. 1972. "Baseball as Myth." *Commonweal*, 12 May: 237–39.

Thiem, Jon. 1988. "Borges, Dante, and the Poetics of Total Vision." *Comparative Literature* 40, no. 2: 97–121.

Toro, Alfonso de. 1991."Postmodernidad y Latinoamérica (con modelo para la narrativa postmoderna)" *Revista Iberoamericana* 57, nos. 155–56: 441–67.

———. 1992. "El productor 'rizomórfico' y el lector como 'detective literario': La aventura de los signos o la postmodernidad del discurso borgesiano (Intertextualidad-palimpsesto desconstrucción-rizoma)." In *Jorge Luis Borges: Variaciones sobre sus procedimientos literarios y bases epistemológicas*. Frankfurt: Verbuert.

———. 1997. "The Epistemological Foundations of the Contemporary Condition: Latin America in Dialogue with Postmodernity and Postcoloniality." In *Latin American Postmodernisms*. Edited by Richard A. Young. Amsterdam: Rodopi.

Vargas Llosa, Mario. 1971. *García Márquez: historia de un deicidio*. Barcelona: Barral Editores.

Weissert, Thomas P. 1991. "Representation and Bifurcation: Borges's Garden of Chaos Dynamics." In *Chaos and Order: Complex Dynamics in Literature and Science*. Edited by Katherine N. Hayles. Chicago: University of Chicago Press.

White, Hayden. 1973. *Metahistory: The Historical Imagination in Nineteenth Century Europe*. Baltimore: The Johns Hopkins University Press.

———. 1976. "Fictions of Factual Representation." In *The Literature of Fact*. Edited by Agnus Fletcher. New York: Columbia University Press.

———. 1978a. "The Historical Text as Literary Artifact." In *The Writing of History: Literary Form and Historical Understanding*. Edited by Robert H. Canary and Henry Kozicki. Madison: University of Wisconsin Press.

———. 1978b. *Tropics of Discourse: Essays in Cultural Criticism*. Baltimore: The Johns Hopkins University Press.

———. 1984. "The Question of Narrative in Contemporary Historical Theory." *History and Theory* 23, no. 1: 1–33.

———. 1986. "Historical Pluralism." *Critical Inquiry*. 23, no. 3: 480–93.

———. 1987. *The Content of the Form: Narrative Discourse and Historical Representation*. Baltimore: The Johns Hopkins University Press.

Wilde, Alan. 1981. *Horizons of Assent: Modernism, Postmodernism and the Ironic Imagination*. Baltimore: The Johns Hopkins University Press.

Williams, Raymond Leslie. 1995. *The Postmodern Novel in Latin America: Politics, Culture and the Crisis of Truth*. New York: St. Martin's Press.

Wright, Robert. 1995. "It's All in Our Heads." Review of *The Engine of Reason, the Seat of the Soul: A Philosophical Journey Into the Brain*. *The New York Times Book Review*. 9 July: 1, 16–17.

Yates, Donald A. 1988. "Jorge Luis Borges and the Revision of Reality: The Biographer's Perspective." *Revista de Estudios Hispánicos*. 22 (October): 57–63.

Young, Richard, ed. 1997. *Latin American Postmodernisms.* Amsterdam: Rodopi.

Young, Robert M. 1989. "Postmodernism and the Subject: Pessimism of the Will." *Discours Social—Social Discourse: Analyse du Discours et Sociocritique des Textes Discourse Analysis and Text Sociocriticism.* 2: 69–82.

Yúdice, George. 1992. "Postmodernity and Transnational Capitalism in Latin America." In *On Edge: The Crisis of Contemporary Latin American Culture.* Edited by George Yúdice, Jean Franco, and Juan Flores. Minneapolis: University of Minnesota Press.

Zavala, Iris. 1988. "On the (Mis-)Uses of the Postmodern: Hispanic Postmodernism Revisited." In *Postmodern Fiction in Europe and the Americas.* Edited by Theo D'haen and Hans Bertens. Amsterdam: Rodopi.

Index